OUTDOOR COOKING

Editorial Director   Arthur Hettich
Special Books Editor   Marie T. Walsh
Art Director   Joseph Taveroni
Managing Editor   Susan Kiely Tierney
Art Associate   Walter Schwartz
Associate Editor   Ceri E. Hadda
Assistant Editor   Raeanne B. Hytone
Photographer   Gordon E. Smith
Production Manager   Kathy Maurer Reilly

Created by Family Circle Magazine and published 1978 by Arno Press Inc., a subsidiary of The New York Times Company. Copyright © 1978 by The Family Circle, Inc. All rights reserved. Protected under Berne and other international copyright conventions. Title and Trademark FAMILY CIRCLE registered U.S. Patent and Trademark Office, Canada, Great Britain, Australia, New Zealand, Japan and other countries. Marca Registrada. This volume may not be reproduced in whole or in part in any form without written permission from the publisher. Printed in U.S.A. Library of Congress Catalog Card Number 78-56339. ISBN 0-405-10073-6.

Most of the material in this volume first appeared in "Best-Ever Barbecues"
published by Family Circle Great Ideas.

A New York Times Company Publication.

contents

All recipes tested by Family Circle Great Ideas.

great idea?

Are backyard barbecues really America's contribution to the world of cuisine? Great Ideas says "yes" and to prove the point we traveled west to California, truly the home of this form of outdoor eating, to find out what's new and exciting in barbecues and to photograph this entire issue.

January, 1978 was not exactly a sunny month in California, but Mother Nature smiled on our crew and allowed the rain clouds to leave, just long enough to let us show you some of the beauties that make California the golden state.

What's new in barbecues? Kettle-grilling is more and more popular, since it gives the outdoor chef the opportunity to cook show-stopping roasts, such as Crown Roast of Lamb and California Pork Loin with a minimum amount of work. Then too, casseroles, such as Arroz Con Mariscos and Pollo alla Simi can cook to perfection in this grill.

Charcoal Water Smokers are an ancient cooking method updated for the use of the patio chef. Chips of hickory or handfuls of herbs mingle with coals and water to make extra-moist and flavorful roasts and birds, such as Smoked Turkey Orientale.

The Imperial Valley in Southern California is the heart of salad country. Imperial Salad Bowl, our version of a chef's salad, illustrates the bounty of its luscious greens and vegetables. Fresh vegetables are really appreciated on the West Coast; see the kabobs on page 71, with the array of tiny patty pan squash, little white turnips and baby artichokes, along with the more traditional kabob vegetables.

From San Diego to San Francisco, desserts and beverages feature the fruits of the West and the Islands and we include papaya, kiwi and casaba melon, along with the more traditional varieties such as strawberries, peaches and watermelon.

Here is our plan for your wonderful summer of barbecues, for 2 or 100, for brunch, lunch or dinner, all designed to make eating in the outdoors great fun.

ALL-AMERICAN CLASSICS
Ground beef and hot dogs are everybody's favorite. Do try these special recipes.

LOUISIANA FRANKS

Coffee-flavored tomato sauce bastes bacon-wrapped hot dogs.

Grill for 20 minutes.
Makes 4 servings.

- 1 can (3 ounces) tomato sauce
- 1 tablespoon instant coffee powder
- 1 tablespoon sugar
- 1 package (1 pound) frankfurters
- 8 green onions, trimmed
- 8 slices bacon

1. Build a hot fire, or set gas or electric grill to high, following manufacturer's directions.
2. Mix tomato sauce, instant coffee and sugar in a small bowl.
3. Split frankfurters lengthwise; brush inside with part of the sauce mixture, then place a green onion in each. Wrap with a bacon slice; fasten with wooden food picks.
4. Grill, 6 inches from heat, turning and brushing often with more sauce, 20 minutes, or until bacon is crisp. Serve in toasted frankfurter rolls with RAINBOW SALAD (recipe, page 94).

BACON BURGERS

You love eating potato chips with burgers, now try them inside the burgers.

Grill for 8 to 16 minutes.
Makes 8 servings.

- 8 slices bacon
- 2 pounds ground beef
- 1 small onion, grated
- 1 cup crushed potato chips
- 1 egg
- ¼ cup catsup
- 2 tablespoons Worcestershire sauce
  Dash bottled red pepper seasoning
- ½ teaspoon salt
- ¼ teaspoon pepper
- 1 can (11 ounces) mushroom gravy
- ¼ cup dry red wine

1. Build a medium fire, or set gas or electric grill to medium, following manufacturer's directions.
2. Cook bacon in a large metal skillet with flameproof handle on grill, 4 inches from heat, just until fat starts to cook out; remove and drain on paper towels.
3. Mix ground beef lightly with onion, potato chips, egg, catsup, Worcestershire sauce, red pepper seasoning, salt and pepper in a medium-size bowl until well blended; shape into 8 patties about 1-inch thick. Wrap bacon slice around each; fasten with moistened wooden food picks. (Dampening picks first keeps them

from charring.) Chill until ready to grill.
4. Grill, 4 inches from heat, 4 to 8 minutes on each side, or until beef is done as you like.
5. While burgers grill, combine mushroom gravy and red wine in a small metal saucepan with flameproof handle; heat to boiling. Spoon over burgers; serve with French bread.

BERLIN FRANKS

Curry powder and tomato sauce give an authentic flavor to these skillet wurst.

Grill for 15 minutes.
Makes 6 servings.

- 2 packages (1 pound each) frankfurters
- 2 tablespoons vegetable oil
- 1 large onion, chopped (1 cup)
- 2 to 4 teaspoons curry powder
- 1 tablespoon paprika
- 1 can (15 ounces) tomato sauce

1. Build a medium fire, or set electric or gas grill to medium, following manufacturer's directions.
2. Cut frankfurters into 2-inch diagonal pieces.
3. Heat oil in a large metal skillet with flameproof handle on grill, 6 inches from heat; sauté onion in pan until soft. Add frankfurter pieces and sauté 3 minutes.
4. Add curry powder and paprika and sauté 2 minutes; stir in tomato sauce. Simmer 10 minutes, or until bubbly-hot.

SANTA FE CHEESEBURGERS

Chili powder and garlic season these barbecue specials.

Grill for 40 minutes.
Makes 6 servings.

- 1 pound ground beef
- ½ cup finely chopped celery
- 1 medium-size onion, finely chopped (½ cup)
- 1 to 3 teaspoons chili powder
- 1 teaspon salt
- ⅛ teaspoon pepper
- ⅛ teaspoon garlic powder
- 1 can (6 ounces) tomato paste
- ¼ cup water
- ¼ cup (½ stick) butter or margarine, softened
- 12 slices white bread
- 1 package (8 ounces) sliced process American cheese

1. Build a medium fire, or set gas or electric grill to medium, following manufacturer's directions.
2. Combine ground beef, celery, on-

ion, chili powder, salt, pepper and garlic powder in a medium-size bowl, mixing just until well blended; shape into a large patty in a large metal skillet with flameproof handle.
3. Grill, 4 inches from heat, 5 minutes on each side; break up into small chunks; stir in tomato paste and water; simmer 15 minutes.
4. Spread butter or margarine on bread; turn 6 slices buttered-side down; divide beef mixture into 6 portions and spread to sides of each of the 6 slices; top with cheese slices; top with remaining buttered bread.
5. Grill, 4 inches from heat, 3 minutes on each side, or until toasted and cheese melts.

THE GIANT HAMBURGER

So big, you can serve a whole gang, with lots of fun for everyone.

Grill for 24 to 30 minutes.
Makes 6 servings.

- ⅔ cup dry red wine
- ⅔ cup prepared mustard
- ⅔ cup catsup
- ⅓ cup firmly packed light brown sugar
- ¼ teaspoon bottled red pepper seasoning
- 2 pounds ground beef
- 1 tablespoon grated onion
- 1½ teaspoons salt
- 1 large tomato, chopped
- 1 small cucumber, pared and chopped
- 1 small green pepper, halved, seeded and chopped

1. Combine wine, mustard, catsup, brown sugar and red pepper seasoning in a medium-size saucepan; bring to boiling; lower heat; simmer 30 minutes.
2. Build a medium fire, or set gas or electric grill to medium, following manufacturer's directions.
3. Combine ground beef, grated onion and salt in a large bowl; mix lightly, just until blended. Shape into a 1½-inch-thick patty; brush generously with sauce. Place patty in a wire-hinged grill rack.
4. Grill, 4 inches from heat, 12 to 15 minutes; turn wire rack and baste patty with sauce. Cook 12 to 15 minutes longer, or until beef is done as you like.
5. Remove patty to heated serving platter and top with chopped tomato, cucumber and green pepper. Serve with baked potatoes and roasted corn.
COOK'S TIP: You can also split and heat a loaf of Italian bread; brush with sauce and top with burger.

4

PINEAPPLE FRANKS

Barbecue for the kids? Here's the perfect choice—sweet and sour hot dogs.

Grill for 20 minutes.
Makes 8 servings.

- 1 **large onion, chopped (1 cup)**
- 3 **tablespoons vegetable oil**
- 2 **tablespoons cornstarch**
- 1 **to 2 tablespoons curry powder**
- ½ **teaspoon ground allspice**
- 1 **teaspoon salt**
- 1 **can (about 1 pound, 5 ounces) crushed pineapple in heavy syrup**
- 2 **tablespoons cider vinegar**
- 2 **packages (1 pound each) frankfurters, cut diagonally into 1-inch pieces**

1. Build a medium fire, or set gas or electric grill to medium, following manufacturer's directions.
2. Sauté onion in oil until soft in a large metal <u>skillet</u> with flameproof handle on grill, 6 inches from heat.
3. Mix cornstarch, curry powder, all-spice and salt in a cup; stir into onion mixture; cook, stirring constantly, just until bubbly.
4. Stir in pineapple and syrup and vinegar; cook, stirring constantly, until sauce mixture thickens and boils 3 minutes.
5. Place frankfurter pieces in sauce; heat to boiling; cover. Simmer 15 minutes, or until heated through.

FRANKFURTER WRAP-UPS

Cheese-flavored pastry bakes along with juicy franks—delicious!

Grill for 20 minutes.
Makes 4 servings.

- 1 **cup all purpose flour**
- 1½ **teaspoons baking powder**
- ½ **teaspoon salt**
- 2 **tablespoons vegetable shortening**
- ½ **cup shredded Cheddar cheese**
- ½ **cup milk**
  Few drops bottled red pepper seasoning
- 1 **package (1 pound) frankfurters**

1. Combine flour, baking powder and salt in a medium-size bowl; cut in shortening with a pastry blender; stir in cheese with a fork.
2. Add milk and red pepper seasoning; stir with fork to make a soft dough; turn out onto a lightly floured pastry cloth or board; knead gently for 30 seconds.
3. Roll out dough to a 15-inch round; cut into eighths; place frankfurters, one at a time, at wide end of each pastry wedge and roll up until completely covered with pastry. Insert a skewer at one end of each frankfurter.
4. Build a medium fire, or set electric or gas grill to medium, following

manufacturer's directions.
5. Grill, 4 inches from heat, turning often, 20 minutes, or until pastry is golden and frankfurters are juicy.

LAMB GRILL

Ground lamb takes the place of traditional ground beef in this meal-on-a-roll.

Grill for 15 minutes.
Makes 4 servings.

- 1½ **pounds ground lamb**
  OR: 1½ pounds ground meatloaf mixture
- 1½ **cups soft bread crumbs (3 slices)**
- ⅓ **cup finely chopped green onion**
- ¼ **cup lemon juice**
- 1½ **teaspoons salt**
- 1 **teaspoon paprika**
- ¼ **teaspoon pepper**
- 1 **large tomato**
- 1 **large green pepper**
- 6 **Kaiser or crusty rolls**

1. Build a medium fire, or set gas or electric grill to medium, following manufacturer's directions.
2. Combine ground lamb or meatloaf mixture, bread crumbs, onion, lemon juice, salt, paprika and pepper in a large bowl; mix lightly, just until blended. Shape into 4 patties the shape of rolls.
3. Grill, 4 inches from heat, 8 minutes; turn with pancake turner; cook 7 minutes longer, or until burgers are done as you like.
4. Core tomato and cut into 6 slices; halve, seed and cut green pepper into strips; split rolls.
5. Place burgers on rolls and top with a tomato slice and green pepper strips.

HOT DOG BURGERS

Wrap a burger around a frank and grill to perfection.

Grill for 15 minutes.
Makes 8 servings.

- 1 **package (1 pound) frankfurters**
- 1 **package (8 ounces) sliced process American cheese**
- 1 **pound ground beef**
- 1 **teaspoon salt**
- ¼ **teaspoon seasoned pepper**
  Spicy Barbecue Sauce (recipe, page 97)

1. Slit each frankfurter lengthwise. Cut cheese (no need to separate slices) into 8 even-width strips; stuff one into each frankfurter.
2. Season ground beef with salt and pepper; divide into 8 even mounds. Place each between two squares wax paper; press into ¼-inch-thick patties. Wrap each patty around the middle of a stuffed frankfurter, using wax paper as a rolling guide. (Ends of frankfurters will be uncovered.) Refrigerate until ready to grill.

3. Build a medium fire, or set gas or electric grill to medium, following manufacturer's directions.
4. Grill, 6 inches from heat, turning often and basting with SPICY BARBE-CUE SAUCE, 15 minutes, or until beef is done as you like.

PICKLED BEEFBURGERS

Sweet pickle relish and mustard are grilled right into these thick burgers.

Grill for 12 to 20 minutes.
Makes 8 servings.

- 3 **pounds ground beef**
- 1 **medium-size onion, finely chopped (½ cup)**
- ⅓ **cup sweet pickle relish**
- ⅓ **cup catsup**
- 1 **tablespoon prepared mustard**
- 2 **teaspoons seasoned salt**
- ¼ **teaspoon seasoned pepper**

1. Combine ground beef, onion, pickle relish, catsup, mustard, salt and pepper in a large bowl; mix lightly, just to blend. Shape mixture into eight 1-inch-thick patties. Chill while preparing grill.
2. Build a medium-hot fire, or set electric or gas grill to medium-high, following manufacturer's directions.
3. Grill, 3 inches from heat, 6 minutes for rare, 8 minutes for medium and 10 minutes for well done; turn with a pancake turner. Grill on other side, 6 minutes for rare, 8 minutes for medium and 10 minutes for well done. Serve on toasted sesame seed rolls.

PIZZA BURGERS

All the best flavors of a pizza make a delicious hamburger.

Grill for 8 to 16 minutes.
Makes 6 servings.

- 2 **pounds ground beef**
- ½ **cup bottled Italian salad dressing**
- 1 **package (8 ounces) sliced mozzarella cheese, cut in triangles**

1. Shape ground beef into 6 patties about ¾-inch thick; place in a shallow glass casserole. Pour salad dressing over; turn patties to coat well with dressing; cover dish with plastic wrap. Chill, turning several times, at least one hour to season.
2. Build a medium fire, or set gas or electric grill to medium, following manufacturer's directions.
3. Grill, 4 inches from heat, basting with remaining dressing, 4 to 8 minutes on each side, or until beef is done as you like.
4. Top each patty with 2 or 3 cheese triangles; continue grilling 1 to 2 minutes longer, or just until cheese melts. Serve on slices of Italian bread.

ROASTS & FINGER FOODS

A treasury of mouth-watering nibbles to eat with your hands—from glazed riblets to tangy chicken wings. Plus hearty roasts prepared from the less expensive cuts of meat.

SUCCULENT Balboa Beef Roast—chuck or shoulder roast marinated in an herbed soy sauce mixture and spun on a rotisserie.

THE CROWNING TOUCH
Tender and succulent Crown Roast of Lamb, with a wild and whole-grain rice stuffing, raises any barbecue to an elegant, gourmet level. Garnish of lemon leaves, pineapple slices and whole apricots suggests the tropical lushness of Southern California. And such spectacular results are easy to achieve, following our recipe for kettle-grilling on page 12.

BALBOA BEEF ROAST

Boneless chuck or shoulder roast becomes party fare when marinated in our special sauce mixture, then grilled to a turn on the rotisserie. Shown on a hill near San Diego, on our cover and page 6.

Rotis 1 hour, 30 minutes to 2 hours, 30 minutes.
Makes 12 servings.

1   beef chuck cross rib roast or eye round roast (about 6 pounds)
    Special Marinade (recipe, page 115)
    Grilled Onions & Mushrooms (recipe, page 117)
    Baked Potatoes (recipe, page 119)
    Grilled Corn (recipe, page 120)

1. Place beef in a large plastic bag; add SPECIAL MARINADE; seal bag; turn meat over several times and place in a shallow utility dish. Refrigerate overnight, turning several times. Remove meat from refrigerator at least 1 hour before starting to rotis.
2. Build a hot fire in grill with rotisserie with drip pan, following directions on page 45, or set gas or electric grill to high, following manufacturer's directions.
3. Insert spit through center of meat, lengthwise, and test for balance by rotating spit in hands. Fasten meat with holding forks, so it won't slip while roasting. Insert a meat thermometer in thickest part of meat.
4. Place rotisserie rod into position.
5. Rotis, basting every 30 minutes with marinade, 1 hour, 30 minutes for rare, 2 hours for medium and 2 hours, 30 minutes for well done, or until beef is done as you like it. Remove rod and allow to "rest" 20 minutes on carving board, lightly covered with aluminum foil. Serve with GRILLED ONIONS & MUSHROOMS, BAKED POTATOES and GRILLED CORN.

Suggested Variations: For *SMOKED BEEF ROAST,* prepare your charcoal water smoker, following manufacturer's directions. Place marinated beef on cooking grill. Cover smoker and cook 4 hours for rare, 5 hours for medium and 6 hours for well done, or until a meat thermometer registers beef as you like it.

Nibble on luscious finger foods while the bigger roasts and steaks finish grilling. Tangy plum glaze enhances Santa Rosa Riblets, a treat for lamb lovers. Cranberry-orange relish gives Sea Rose Chicken Wings a rosy coating. Pork spareribs, always a favorite, team beautifully with Lemon-Pineapple Glaze in Santa Cruz Ribs. Recipes begin on page 11.

SANTA CRUZ RIBS

Spareribs never tasted better! Grill first as a whole rack for ease in turning, then cut and brush with glaze for the last few minutes of cooking. Seen in finger-food photograph on page 10.

Grill for 1 hour, 30 minutes.
Makes 8 appetizer servings.

1   side fresh spareribs (about 3 pounds)
1   lemon
1   teaspoon salt
¼   teaspoon pepper
    Lemon-Pineapple Glaze (recipe, page 114)

1. Trim excess fat from spareribs; halve lemon and rub on both sides of meat; season with salt and pepper. Allow to stand at room temperature while heating grill.
2. Build a medium fire, or set gas or electric grill to medium, following manufacturer's directions.
3. Grill, 10 inches from heat, turning several times, 1 hour, 15 minutes. Remove spareribs to a carving board. Cut into individual serving-size pieces; brush generously with LEMON-PINEAPPLE GLAZE.
4. Grill, turning and basting several times, 15 minutes or until richly glazed. Serve with bottled teriyaki barbecue marinade for dipping and plenty of paper napkins.

GRILLED LAMB SHANKS

Give an Italian touch to your next barbecue—serve meaty lamb shanks glazed with herbed tomato sauce.

Grill for 20 minutes.
Makes 4 servings.

4   lamb shanks
1   teaspoon leaf rosemary, crumbled
2   teaspoons salt
1   small onion, chopped (¼ cup)
4   cups water
½   cup bottled barbecue sauce
½   cup catsup
1   teaspoon mixed Italian herbs, crumbled

1. Place lamb shanks, rosemary, salt, onion and water in a large saucepan. Bring to boiling; simmer 1 hour, or until shanks are tender when pierced with a two-tined fork; drain. (If cooked ahead, chill, then remove from refrigerator about 30 minutes before grilling.)
2. Build a medium fire, or set electric or gas grill to medium, following manufacturer's directions.
3. Combine barbecue sauce, catsup and Italian herbs in a small bowl; brush generously over shanks.
4. Grill, 6 inches from heat, turning and basting shanks, 20 minutes, or until richly glazed.

PENNSYLVANIA BARBECUE

Choose this pot of bubbling beef in its sweet-sour sauce to greet a hungry gang.

Grill for 1 hour.
Makes 8 servings.

2   pounds ground beef
2   large onions, chopped (2 cups)
2   large green peppers, halved, seeded and chopped
1   can (15 ounces) tomato sauce
¼   cup firmly packed brown sugar
1   tablespoon Worcestershire sauce
2   teaspoons salt
¼   teaspoon pepper

1. Build a medium fire, or set electric or gas grill to medium, following manufacturer's directions.
2. Shape ground beef into a large patty in a large heavy metal kettle.
3. Brown beef in kettle on grill, 4 inches from heat, 5 minutes; cut into quarters; turn with a pancake turner; brown on second side 5 minutes; remove from kettle and break into tiny pieces.
4. Sauté onions and green peppers in pan drippings until soft; stir in tomato sauce, brown sugar, Worcestershire sauce, salt and pepper until well blended; return ground beef to kettle.
5. Cook, 6 inches from grill, stirring often, 30 minutes or until hot.

TEXAS SHORT RIBS

Chili gives a Texan taste to meaty beef ribs.

Grill for 2 hours.
Makes 4 servings.

3   to 4 pounds beef short ribs
2   teaspoons salt
¼   teaspoon pepper
1   can (8 ounces) tomato sauce
¼   cup catsup
⅓   cup firmly packed brown sugar
¼   cup cider vinegar
2   tablespoons prepared mustard
1   medium-size onion, chopped (½ cup)
1   clove garlic, minced
1   tablespoon chili powder

1. Build a low fire around a disposable foil pan, following directions on page 45, or set gas or electric grill to slow, following manufacturer's directions.
2. Grill ribs, 6 inches from heat, turning occasionally, 1 hour, 30 minutes, or until ribs are tender. Season with salt and pepper.
3. Combine tomato sauce, catsup, brown sugar, vinegar, mustard, onion, garlic and chili powder in a small metal saucepan with a flameproof handle; simmer on grill 5 minutes.
4. Brush ribs generously with sauce. Grill, brushing with sauce and turning occasionally, 30 minutes, or until richly glazed. Serve with baked potatoes.

SEA ROSE CHICKEN WINGS

While chicken wings are not technically ribs, the thicker joints of chicken wings make delicious finger food. Shown in a garden, on page 10.

Grill for 30 minutes.
Makes 8 appetizer servings.

- **16 chicken wings**
- **¼ cup vegetable oil**
- **¼ cup lemon juice**
- **1 teaspoon seasoned salt**
- **¼ teaspoon seasoned pepper**
- **½ cup cranberry - orange relish**
- **¼ cup light corn syrup**

1. Cut chicken wings into individual joints, reserving tips for soup kettle; place remaining joints in a large glass utility dish.
2. Combine oil, lemon juice, seasoned salt and pepper in a 1-cup measure; pour over chicken pieces. Allow to marinate while heating grill.
3. Build a medium fire, or set gas or electric grill to medium, following manufacturer's directions.
4. Grill, 6 inches from heat, turning several times, 20 minutes. Stir cranberry-orange relish and corn syrup into remaining marinade; brush generously over chicken pieces.
5. Grill, basting several times, 10 minutes, or until richly glazed. Serve with mango chutney or bottled barbecue sauce for dipping.

CROWN ROAST OF LAMB

Spectacular to serve, unforgettable to eat —moist, succulent lamb grills to absolute perfection with a wild and white rice stuffing. Shown against the Pacific Ocean in La Jolla, California, on page 8.

Grill for 1 hour, 30 minutes to 2 hours, 30 minutes
Makes 8 servings.

- **1 crown roast of lamb (about 5 pounds)**
  OR: 2 whole racks of lamb ribs (about 2½ pounds each)
- **8 slices bacon**
- **1 whole leek**
  OR: 1 bunch green onions
- **2 packages (5½ ounces each) long grain and wild rice mix**
- **4 cups boiling water**
  Salt and papper
- **½ cup apricot-pineapple jam**

1. Order a crown roast from butcher a few days ahead of time, or buy racks of lamb ribs and make crown yourself, following directions on page 32.
2. Build a medium fire around a foil drip pan, following directions on page 45, in a kettle grill, or set gas or electric grill to medium, following manufacturer's directions.
3. Fry bacon until limp in a large heavy metal skillet; remove with tongs and roll up slices with two forks.

Reserve as garnish for platter.
4. Trim and wash leek well; cut into slices, or trim and slice green onions; sauté until soft in bacon drippings.
5. Stir in rice from mix and toss to coat well with drippings; add boiling water and both seasoning packets from rice mixes; bring to boiling; lower heat; cover pan. Simmer 5 minutes, or until rice is tender and liquid is absorbed.
6. Season lamb with salt and pepper; fill crown with rice stuffing; cover stuffing and tips of ribs with a layer of aluminum foil.
7. Grill, 6 inches from heat, 1 hour, 30 minutes for rare, 2 hours for medium, and 2 hours 30 minutes for well done, or until lamb is done as you like. During last 15 minutes of grilling, brush roast with heated apricot-pineapple jam. Allow roast to "rest" 20 minutes after removing from grill. Arrange roast on a heated platter and garnish with lemon leaves, halved pineapple slices, whole apricots and reserved bacon rolls. Carve between ribs and serve with rice stuffing and a dry white California wine.

POLLO ALLA SIMI

Chicken and wine just seem meant for each other when simmered together with a basket full of vegetables in our memorable patio casserole. Photographed in Simi Winery and shown on page 16.

Grill for 2 hours, 30 minutes.
Makes 8 servings.

- **1 roasting chicken, cut up (about 6 pounds)**
- **⅓ cup all purpose flour**
- **2 teaspoons salt**
- **¼ teaspoon freshly ground pepper**
- **¼ cup olive or vegetable oil**
- **1 large onion, chopped**
- **2 cloves garlic, minced**
- **1 pound fresh mushrooms**
  OR: 2 cans (6 ounces each) whole mushrooms
- **2 cups white wine**
- **1 can condensed chicken broth**
- **2 teaspoons mixed Italian herbs, crumbled**
- **1 pound carrots, pared and thinly sliced**
- **1 bunch leeks, trimmed, quartered and thoroughly washed**
- **1 can (10 ounces) artichoke hearts, drained**
- **½ cup pitted ripe olives**

1. Build a medium fire in a covered grill, or set electric or gas grill to medium, following manufacturer's directions.
2. Shake chicken pieces, part at a time, in flour, salt and pepper in a plastic bag to coat evenly.
3. Heat oil in a large heavy skillet; brown chicken, part at a time, in oil; remove with slotted spoon and reserve.

4. Sauté onion and garlic in oil until soft; add mushrooms and sauté 3 minutes; remove with slotted spoon and reserve; shake any remaining flour from plastic bag into pan and stir to blend well.
5. Stir in wine, chicken broth and Italian herbs; bring to bubbling; lower heat; simmer 3 minutes.
6. Layer browned chicken pieces, carrots, leeks, onion-mushroom mixture, artichoke hearts and ripe olives in a 12-cup flameproof casserole; pour sauce over; cover casserole.
7. Simmer on grill, 10 inches from heat in covered grill, 2 hours, 30 minutes, or until chicken and vegetables are tender. Serve with an orange and purple onion salad, bread sticks and a California Pinot Noir wine.

MARYLAND GLAZED HAM

Pockets of chopped greens in a meaty ham make good eating, Southern-style.

Rotis for 2 hours.
Makes 12 servings.

- **1 boned rolled ready-to-eat ham (about 6 pounds)**
- **1 cup chopped escarole**
- **1 cup chopped parsley**
- **¼ cup finely cut chives**
- **½ cup honey**
- **½ cup cranberry-orange relish**
- **1 teaspoon pumpkin pie spice**

1. Build a medium fire in grill with rotisserie, positioning coals around drip pan, following directions on page 45, or set electric or gas grill to medium, following manufacturer's directions.
2. Stand ham upright on a wooden board. Cut off end clip, if any, but leave wrapping on while preparing meat. To make cavities for stuffing, work rotisserie spit through ham in 4 places, then enlarge each hole with a wooden-spoon handle.
3. Mix escarole, parsley and chives in a medium-size bowl; stuff about ½ cup of the greens mixture into each hole, packing it in firmly with wooden-spoon handle. Peel wrapping from ham.
4. Insert spit through center of ham, lengthwise, and test for balance by rotating spit on hands. Fasten ham with holding forks. Place rotisserie rod into position.
5. Rotis, checking several times while turning, 1 hour, 30 minutes.
6. Combine honey, cranberry-orange relish and pumpkin pie spice in a small saucepan with a flameproof handle; heat over grill until bubbly.
7. Brush ham generously with glaze. Rotis, brushing several times, 30 minutes, or until richly glazed. Remove to serving platter and serve with baked sweet potatoes.

CALIFORNIA PORK LOIN

Tangy orange juice flavors the stuffing and glazes the pork in this show-stopping dish. Shown in sunny California on page 14.

Grill for 3 hours, 30 minutes.
Makes 6 servings.

- 1 twelve-chop pork loin, center cut
- 1 bunch green onions
- ½ cup (1 stick) butter or margarine
- ¾ cup water
- 1 can (6 ounces) frozen concentrate for orange juice, thawed
- 1 package (8 ounces) ready-mix bread stuffing
- ½ cup honey
- 2 tablespoons bottled steak sauce

1. Build a medium fire in a kettle grill or set gas or electric grill to medium, following directions for arranging coals around foil pan on page 45.
2. Trim excess fat from roast; make slits between chops, about 2 inches deep, with a sharp knife.
3. Trim green onions; reserve several for garnish; slice remaining ones. Sauté sliced green onions in butter or margarine in a large saucepan; add water and ¼ cup of the thawed concentrate for orange juice; bring to boiling. Remove saucepan. Stir in stuffing mix until well blended. Pack stuffing into pockets in pork roast.
4. Grill, 8 inches from heat, 3 hours, or until a meat thermometer inserted in a thick, meaty portion registers 160°.
5. Combine remaining concentrate for orange juice, honey and steak sauce in a small metal saucepan with a flameproof handle; heat over grill until bubbly. Brush roast and stuffing with mixture.
6. Grill, basting several times, 30 minutes longer, or until meat is well glazed and meat thermometer registers 170°. Place on heated serving platter and allow to "rest" 20 minutes. Garnish platter with reserved green onions and orange slices. Serve with tall glasses of apple cider and BAKED POTATOES (recipe, page 119).

SPARERIBS BOMBAY

Curry powder and a rich fruit glaze make them finger-lickin' good.

Grill for 1 hour, 30 minutes.
Makes 4 servings.

- 4 pounds fresh spareribs
- 1 can (12 ounces) beer or ginger ale
- 1 large onion, chopped (1 cup)
- ¼ cup peanut or vegetable oil
- 1 tablespoon curry powder
- 1 jar (5 ounces) baby-pack applesauce
- 2 tablespoons lemon juice
- 2 teaspoons salt

1. Cut spareribs into 2- or 3-rib pieces.
2. Build a medium fire, or set electric or gas grill to medium, following manufacturer's directions.
3. Grill ribs, 6 inches from heat, basting with beer or ginger ale and turning several times, 1 hour.
4. Sauté onion in oil in a small metal saucepan with flameproof handle on grill. Add curry powder and cook 2 minutes; stir in applesauce, lemon juice and salt. Heat until bubbly. Brush ribs generously with curry sauce.
5. Grill, turning and brushing often with remaining curry sauce, 30 minutes, or until meat is tender and richly browned. Serve with cucumber slices in yogurt and pita bread.

SAGE MEATLOAF

You can grill two of these loaves at a time, then chill one to make delicious cold sandwiches if it isn't eaten first.

Grill for 1 hour, 30 minutes.
Makes 6 servings.

- 2 pounds meatloaf mixture OR: 2 pounds ground beef
- 2 eggs
- 1 cup quick-cooking oats
- 1 medium-size onion, grated
- 1 cup canned applesauce
- 2 teaspoons salt
- ¼ teaspoon pepper
- 1 teaspoon leaf sage, crumbled
- 1 tablespoon bottled steak sauce

1. Build a low fire in a covered grill, or set gas or electric grill to slow, following manufacturer's directions.
2. Combine meatloaf mixture or ground beef with eggs, oats, onion, applesauce, salt, pepper and sage in a medium-size bowl; mix lightly, just until blended.
3. Pack firmly into a 9x5x3-inch loaf pan; unmold into a shallow metal casserole. Score top in crisscross pattern; brush with steak sauce.
4. Grill with cover on grill, 6 inches from heat, 1 hour, 30 minutes, or until loaf is well glazed. Serve with baked potatoes and corn on the cob.

BEEF TACOS

America's favorite fast food, Mexican style, makes a show-stopping choice for a first course at your next party.

Grill for 30 minutes.
Makes 12 tacos.

- 2 pounds ground beef
- 1 package (1¾ ounces) taco seasoning mix
- 1 cup tomato juice
- 12 taco shells
  Shredded iceberg lettuce
  Diced ripe tomato
  Shredded Cheddar cheese

1. Build a medium fire, or set electric or gas grill to medium, following manufacturer's directions.
2. Shape ground beef into a large patty in a large metal skillet with a flameproof handle.
3. Brown beef in skillet on grill, 4 inches from heat, 5 minutes; cut into quarters; turn with a pancake turner; brown on second side 5 minutes; break into tiny pieces.
4. Stir in taco seasoning mix and tomato juice until well blended. Push pan to side of grill and simmer 15 minutes, stirring several times.
5. Place a second metal skillet with a flameproof handle on grill and heat; wipe pan with a paper towel coated with vegetable oil. Cook taco shells in skillet, one minute on each side; shape into a "U" with tongs and keep warm at side of grill.
6. Spoon beef mixture into taco shells, dividing evenly; spoon shredded lettuce, diced tomato and shredded cheese on top.

CONTINENTAL MEATLOAF

French bread and grated vegetables give special flavor to a meatloaf.

Grill for 1 hour, 15 minutes.
Makes 6 servings.

- 1½ cups cubed French bread
- 1 cup milk
- 2 pounds ground beef
- ½ cup finely chopped celery
- ½ cup grated carrot
- 1 small onion, grated
- 1 egg
- 1 tablespoon prepared horseradish
- 2 teaspoons salt
- ¼ teaspoon pepper
  Molasses Barbecue Sauce (recipe, page 115)

1. Build a low fire in a kettle grill, or set gas or electric grill to slow, following manufacturer's directions.
2. Combine bread cubes and milk in a large bowl; let stand 5 minutes, or until milk is absorbed.
3. Add ground beef, celery, carrot, onion, egg, horseradish, salt and pepper, mixing lightly, just until blended. Shape into a large patty in a large metal skillet with a flameproof handle. Make deep cuts in top, making 6 even portions.
4. Grill, 6 inches from heat with cover on grill, 1 hour; brush generously with MOLASSES BARBECUE SAUCE. Grill 15 minutes longer, or until well glazed. Serve with toasted French bread and buttered green beans.

COOK'S TIP: Meatloaves are especially flavorful when cooked in a kettle-grill. You can bake potatoes or acorn squash along with the meatloaf for a delicious meal.

ZIPPY LAMB RIBLETS

Chili sauce combined with steak sauce makes a simple, yet zesty, glaze.

Grill for 1 hour.
Makes 4 servings.

- **4 pounds breast of lamb**
- **1 bottle (8 ounces) oil-and-vinegar salad dressing**
- **1 cup bottled chili sauce**
- **¼ cup bottled steak sauce**

1. Trim any excess fat from lamb. Cut lamb into 1- or 2-rib pieces; place in a shallow glass utility dish.
2. Mix salad dressing and chili and steak sauces in a small bowl; pour over ribs; turn pieces to coat well; cover dish with plastic wrap. Refrigerate, turning several times, 2 hours to season.
3. Build a medium fire, or set electric or gas grill to medium, following manufacturer's directions.
4. Grill, 6 inches from heat, turning and basting several times, 1 hour, or until ribs are richly glazed. Serve with baked beans and sourdough bread.

SANTA ROSA RIBLETS

Lamb riblets with a rich plum glaze make delectable finger-lickin' food. (Photographed in Pacific Beach, on page 10.)

Grill for 1 hour.
Makes 8 appetizer servings.

- **4 pounds lamb riblets**
- **1 clove garlic**
- **1 teaspoon salt**
- **¼ teaspoon freshly ground pepper**
- **1 teaspoon leaf rosemary, crumbled Plum Chutney Glaze (recipe, page 114)**

1. Trim excess fat from riblets; peel and halve garlic; rub over surface of meat; season with salt, pepper and rosemary. Allow to stand at room temperature while heating grill.
2. Build a medium fire, or set gas or electric grill to medium, following manufacturer's directions.
3. Grill, 6 inches from heat, turning several times, 50 minutes. Remove lamb to a carving board. Cut into individual riblets; brush generously with PLUM CHUTNEY GLAZE.
4. Grill, turning and basting several times, 10 minutes, or until richly glazed. Serve with scented moist towels for easy clean-up.

California Pork Loin features a tangy, orange-flavored stuffing and mouth-watering glaze. Barbecue grilling is a great way to cook larger cuts of meat, and the best way to serve a hungry crowd. Recipe is on page 13.

MEXICAN ROLLUPS

Soft tortillas are rolled with a cumin-flavored meat sauce.

Grill for 30 minutes.
Makes 6 servings.

- **2 pounds meatloaf mixture (ground beef, pork and veal) OR: 2 pounds ground beef**
- **1 large onion, chopped (1 cup)**
- **2 to 4 teaspoons chili powder**
- **2 tablespoons all purpose flour**
- **1 can (8 ounces) tomatoes**
- **½ cup water**
- **2 teaspoons salt**
- **1 teaspoon ground cumin**
- **1 can (11 ounces) tortillas**
- **¼ cup (½ stick) butter or margarine Crisp shredded lettuce Diced green pepper Grated Cheddar cheese**

1. Build a medium fire, or set electric or gas grill to medium, following manufacturer's directions.
2. Shape meatloaf mixture or ground beef into a large patty in a large metal skillet with flameproof handle. Brown 5 minutes on each side, then break up into chunks and push to one side. Stir in onion and chili powder; cook 5 minutes longer.
3. Sprinkle flour over meat mixture, then stir in tomatoes, water, salt and cumin. Heat to boiling; simmer, stirring several times, 15 minutes, or until very thick.
4. Sauté tortillas, a few at a time, adding butter or margarine as needed, in a second metal skillet over grill 1 minute, or just until soft; remove and keep warm.
5. Spoon meat mixture onto each tortilla; sprinkle with shredded lettuce, green pepper and grated cheese; roll up to eat; serve with limeade and avocado salad.

PICCOLO PIZZAS

Perfect appetizer for a patio party.

Grill for 45 minutes.
Makes 48 appetizers.

- **3 pounds ground beef**
- **2 cloves garlic**
- **1 teaspoon salt**
- **2 cans (3 or 4 ounces each) chopped mushrooms**
- **2 teaspoons leaf oregano, crumbled**
- **3 cans condensed tomato soup**
- **¼ pound salami, diced**
- **24 slices white bread**
- **2 cups grated Cheddar cheese (8 ounces)**
- **2 cups grated mozzarella cheese (8 ounces)**

1. Build a medium fire in a covered grill, or set electric or gas grill to medium, following manufacturer's directions.

2. Shape ground beef lightly into two large patties. Brown, one at a time, in a metal Dutch oven on grill, 4 inches from heat, 5 minutes on each side; break up into small chunks.
3. Mash garlic with salt; stir into Dutch oven with mushrooms and their liquid, oregano and tomato soup; cover. Simmer, stirring often, 20 minutes, or until thick; stir in salami.
4. Toast bread lightly on grill; arrange in a single layer on large cookie sheets or in large metal baking pans.
5. Mix Cheddar and mozzarella cheeses. Spoon hot meat mixture onto each slice of toast; sprinkle with cheeses.
6. Grill, one pan at a time, in covered grill, 5 minutes, or until cheese melts; cut into triangles with sharp knife.
COOK'S TIP: Use this appetizer recipe as a basic recipe, change the meat to bulk or sweet Italian sausage and substitute 2 jars (1 pound each) spaghetti sauce for the tomato soup.

BEEF ROAST ITALIANO

Here is a flavorful recipe for the kettle-type grill. Don't have a top for your's? A double layer of heavy-duty aluminum foil can cover roast—not as well, but it works.

Grill for 1 hour, 15 to 45 minutes.
Makes 8 servings.

- **1 boneless cross rib roast (about 4 pounds)**
- **1 cup dry white wine**
- **¼ cup olive or vegetable oil**
- **1 medium-size onion, chopped (½ cup)**
- **1 clove garlic, minced**
- **¼ cup chopped parsley**
- **¼ teaspoon ground allspice**
- **¼ teaspoon ground nutmeg**
- **2 teaspoons salt**
- **¼ teaspoon freshly ground pepper**

1. Trim excess fat from roast; place roast in a large plastic bag in a large, shallow pan.
2. Add wine, oil, onion, garlic, parsley, allspice and nutmeg to plastic bag; seal bag securely; turn roast in bag to coat evenly. Allow to stand at room temperature 2 hours, or marinate overnight in refrigerator and allow meat to stand at room temperature for 1 hour before grilling.
3. Build a fire for kettle-roasting around aluminum foil pan, following directions on page 45, or set gas or electric grill to low, following manufacturer's directions.
4. Remove beef from marinade, reserving marinade; and season with salt and pepper.
5. Roast in covered grill, basting often with marinade, 1 hour, 15 minutes for rare, 1 hour, 30 minutes for medium and 1 hour, 45 minutes for well done.

(Recipes continued on page 102.)

VINTAGE CASSEROLE
In Pollo Alla Simi, roast chicken simmers on the grill to juicy perfection with leeks, carrots and artichoke hearts in a wine-rich sauce. Recipe, page 12.

PHOTOGRAPHED AT VACATION VILLAGE, SAN DIEGO, CALIFORNIA

18

Hamburgers and hot dogs are naturals for the grill. Their super versatility makes them perfect on a toasted bun or in a main-dish casserole. Served simply or given the "works," they're everybody's favorite barbecue food. In this chapter are recipes for a delectable line-up of hamburgers, hot dogs and sausages, plus all the fixings.

Kids of all ages will want seconds of our Crown Roast of Hot Dogs with a bread and corn stuffing. Meatloaf Wellington features a mashed-potato topping. Recipes, page 20.

HAMBURGERS HOT DOGS

CROWN ROAST OF HOT DOGS

Treat the birthday boy or girl to a crown made up of favorite foods—franks and stuffing. Photographed in sunny San Diego and shown on page 18.

Grill for 40 minutes.
Makes 8 to 10 servings.

    2 packages (1 pound each)
         frankfurters
    ½ cup (1 stick) butter or margarine
    1 large onion, chopped (1 cup)
    1 loaf (1 pound) sliced white bread,
         cut into small cubes
    2 teaspoons salt
    1 teaspoon leaf basil, crumbled
    ½ cup hot chicken broth
    1 can (12 or 16 ounces) whole kernel
         corn
    2 pimientos, diced
    ¾ cup light corn syrup
    3 tablespoons prepared yellow
         mustard
         Carrot Pennies (recipe, page 116)

1. Build a medium fire in a covered grill, or set gas or electric grill to medium, following manufacturer's directions.
2. Thread a trussing or crewel needle with cotton twine, not thread. Insert needle through center of frankfurters to make a long chain of hot dogs; knot twine at ends to make a circle; place on a circle of aluminum foil cut to fit "crown" on a metal pizza pan.
3. Melt butter or margarine in a large saucepan; sauté onion in butter until soft; stir in bread cubes, salt and basil until evenly coated with onion-butter mixture; pour in chicken broth and toss with a fork until blended. Add corn and liquid and pimientos; toss.
4. Pile stuffing inside hot dog "crown"; brush frankfurters generously with a mixture of corn syrup and mustard.
5. Grill, 5 inches from heat, with grill covered, basting several times with mustard mixture, 40 minutes, or until hot dogs are glazed and stuffing is piping hot. Slide onto serving platter with a pancake turner. Surround with CARROT PENNIES.

ITALIAN SAUSAGE DOGS

Grill for 25 minutes.
Makes 8 servings.

    2 pounds Italian sweet or hot
         sausage
         Tomato-Beer Baste (recipe,
         page 114)
         Morganville Sauce (recipe,
         page 114)
    2 packages (8 buns each) hot dog
         buns, toasted

1. Build a medium fire, arranging coals around a drip pan, following directions on page 45, or arrange briquets of electric or gas grill around drip pan and set grill on medium.

2. Prick sausages all over with a two-tined fork.
3. Grill, 6 inches from heat and directly over drip pan, turning often, 15 minutes. Baste with TOMATO-BEER BASTE or MORGANVILLE SAUCE. Grill 10 minutes longer, or until well glazed.

Suggested Variations:

NEW YORK DOGS: Sauté 1 medium-size zucchini, diced, in 2 tablespoons olive or vegetable oil until soft in a medium-size saucepan over low heat; add 1 can (8 ounces) tomatoes and ½ teaspoon leaf basil, crumbled; simmer 5 minutes. Top grilled Italian sausages in toasted hot dog buns with mixture.

MASSACHUSETTS DOGS: Fill toasted hot dog buns with roasted red and green pepper strips and sprinkle with grated Parmesan cheese; top with grilled Italian sausages.

OHIO DOGS: Place grilled Italian sausages in toasted buns and top with Provolone cheese; grill until cheese melts; top with chopped ripe olives.

DELAWARE DOGS: Place grilled Italian sausages on toasted buns and top with marinated artichoke hearts and capers.

MEATLOAF WELLINGTON

Kids of all ages will love this new twist to their old meat and potatoes favorite. Shown at Mission Bay in photo on page 18.

Grill for 1 hour, 30 minutes.
Makes 8 servings.

    2 pounds ground beef
    2 cups soft white bread crumbs
         (2 slices)
    2 eggs
    ¼ cup chopped parsley
    2 teaspoons salt
    ¼ teaspoon pepper
         Instant mashed potatoes,
         prepared for 8 servings
    1 egg yolk
    1 tablespoon water
         Cheery Cherry Tomatoes (recipe,
         page 116)

1. Build a medium fire in a covered grill, or set electric or gas grill to medium, following manufacturer's directions.
2. Combine ground beef, bread crumbs, eggs, parsley, salt and pepper in a large bowl; mix lightly, just until blended.
3. Shape meat mixture into an 8-inch-long meatloaf on a metal pizza pan.
4. Grill, 6 inches from heat in covered grill, 1 hour; remove meatloaf on tray.
5. Spread ½ cup of prepared instant mashed potatoes into a ½-inch-thick layer on a piece of wax paper; allow to chill in refrigerator.
6. Wipe all meat juices from pizza pan with paper towels; spread remain-

ing instant mashed potatoes over meatloaf to coat evenly and smoothly. Beat egg yolk and water in a cup; brush over potatoes to make surface very smooth.
7. Cut chilled mashed potatoes into stars with a small cutter or tip of paring knife. Place on meatloaf and brush with remaining egg mixture.
8. Grill in covered grill 30 minutes longer, or until potatoes are golden. Loosen meatloaf around bottom with pancake turner and slide onto serving platter. Surround with CHEERY CHERRY TOMATOES.

TURKEY FRANKFURTERS

Grill for 10 minutes.
Makes 8 servings.

    2 packages (1 pound each) turkey
         frankfurters
         Chutney Barbecue Glaze (recipe,
         page 115)
         Molasses Barbecue Sauce (recipe,
         page 114)
    2 packages (8 buns each) hot dog
         buns, toasted

1. Build a hot fire, or set gas or electric grill to high, following manufacturer's directions.
2. Score turkey frankfurters with cuts about ¾-inch deep. Brush with CHUTNEY BARBECUE GLAZE or MOLASSES BARBECUE SAUCE.
3. Grill, 6 inches from heat, turning and brushing once or twice with more sauce, 10 minutes, or until richly glazed.

Suggested Variations:

MINNESOTA DOGS: Crisscross the scoring on turkey dogs and place 2 on each toasted bun; spread hot dog relish around.

KENTUCKY DOGS: Top grilled turkey dogs in toasted buns with cranberry relish and diced green pepper.

MARYLAND DOGS: Combine shredded lettuce and bottled coleslaw dressing; line toasted hamburger buns with lettuce; place grilled turkey dogs over and top with chopped pecans or walnuts.

CONNECTICUT DOGS: Place grilled turkey dogs in toasted buns and top with cubes of cranberry jelly and sliced sweet pickle.

VIRGINIA DOGS: Brush grilled turkey dogs in toasted buns with apricot preserves; top with chopped pecans.

COLORADO DOGS: Top grilled turkey dogs in toasted buns with sautéed onion slices and mushrooms flavored with basil.

NEVADA DOGS: Top grilled turkey dogs in toasted buns with diced avocado and ripe olives; garnish with lemon wedges.

AVERY ISLAND BURGERS

Louisiana barbecue cooks wouldn't think of grilling without a bottle of red pepper seasoning on hand.

Grill for 8 to 16 minutes.
Makes 8 servings.

- 3 pounds ground beef
- 1 cup tomato juice
- 1 tablespoon salt
- ¼ teaspoon bottled red pepper seasoning
  Brown Sugar Glaze (recipe, page 97)

1. Build a medium fire, or set gas or electric grill to medium, following manufacturer's directions.
2. Combine ground beef, tomato juice, salt and red pepper seasoning in a large bowl; mix lightly, just until blended. Shape into 8 patties.
3. Grill, 4 inches from heat, 4 to 8 minutes; turn with a pancake turner; brush with BROWN SUGAR GLAZE; cook 4 to 8 minutes longer, or until done as you like. Serve on toasted hamburger rolls with thick tomato slices.

CEREAL BURGERS

Whole wheat flakes give crunch as well as flavor to these tall cheeseburgers.

Grill for 8 to 16 minutes.
Makes 6 servings.

- 2 pounds ground beef
- ½ cup wheat flakes cereal
- ½ cup chopped walnuts
- ½ teaspoon seasoned salt
- ½ cup beef broth
- 6 slices sharp Cheddar cheese

1. Mix ground beef lightly with cereal, walnuts, seasoned salt and beef broth in a medium-size bowl; shape into 6 patties about 1-inch thick.
2. Build a medium fire, or set electric or gas grill to medium, following manufacturer's directions.
3. Grill, 4 inches from heat, 4 to 8 minutes on each side, or until beef is done as you like. Top with Cheddar cheese slices and grill, just until cheese melts. Serve on toasted rye bread with spinach salad, if you wish.

SKILLET FRANKFURTERS

Here's the perfect way to keep hot dogs moist and juicy over the grill.

Grill for 15 minutes.
Makes 8 servings.

- 1 bottle (15 ounces) chili sauce
- 2 large green peppers, halved, seeded and chopped
- 1 large onion, chopped (1 cup)
- ⅔ cup sweet pickle relish
- ½ cup cider vinegar
- ¼ cup firmly packed brown sugar

- 1 tablespoon prepared mustard
- ¼ teaspoon bottled red pepper seasoning
- 2 packages (1 pound each) frankfurters

1. Build a hot fire, or set electric or gas grill to high, following manufacturer's directions.
2. Combine chili sauce, green peppers, onion, relish, vinegar, brown sugar, mustard and red pepper seasoning in a large metal skillet with flameproof handle.
3. Cook sauce on grill, 6 inches from heat, until bubbly; add frankfurters; simmer 15 minutes. Serve on toasted frankfurter rolls.

OLIVE-CHILI FRANKS

Chili sauce and chopped olives make a zesty filling for hot dogs.

Grill for 10 minutes.
Makes 8 servings.

- 2 packages (1 pound each) frankfurters
- ¾ cup chili sauce
- 1 envelope (2 to a package) toasted onion dip mix
- ½ cup chopped pimiento-stuffed olives

1. Build a medium fire, or set gas or electric grill to medium, following manufacturer's directions.
2. Slit each frankfurter lengthwise about three-quarters of the way through; open each out flat.
3. Blend chili sauce, onion dip mix and olives in a small bowl; spoon over center of each frankfurter.
4. Grill, 6 inches from heat, 10 minutes, or until puffed. Serve with potato chips and CARROT SLAW (recipe, page 92).

CARAWAY BURGERS

Rye bread and caraway cheese give a Scandinavian touch to burgers.

Grill for 10 to 16 minutes.
Makes 4 servings.

- 1½ pounds ground beef
- 1 egg
- ½ cup soft bread crumbs (1 slice)
- 2 tablespoons milk
- 1 teaspoon salt
- ¼ teaspoon ground nutmeg
- ⅛ teaspoon pepper
- 2 slices caraway cheese, halved
- 4 slices rye bread

1. Build a medium fire, or set electric or gas grill to medium, following manufacturer's directions.
2. Combine ground beef with egg, bread crumbs, milk, salt, nutmeg and pepper in a medium-size bowl; mix lightly, just until blended. Shape into 4 patties, about 1-inch thick.
3. Grill, 4 inches from heat, 5 to 8

minutes on each side, or until meat is done as you like. Lay cheese slices on top of patties. (Heat from meat will melt cheese slightly.)
4. Serve on rye bread with pickled beets, if you wish.

HAMBURGER FOLDOVERS

A cheese filling turns this into a ground beef "turnover".

Grill for 8 to 16 minutes.
Makes 6 servings.

- 2 pounds ground beef
- 1½ teaspoons salt
- ¼ teaspoon pepper
- 1 cup shredded Cheddar cheese (4 ounces)
- ¼ cup bottled steak sauce
- 2 medium-size tomatoes, sliced
- 1 large onion, sliced and separated into rings

1. Build a medium fire, or set electric or gas grill to medium, following manufacturer's directions.
2. Mix ground beef lightly with salt and pepper; divide into 6 portions.
3. Pat each into a 6-inch round on a piece of wax paper or foil; spoon about 2 tablespoons cheese in center. Fold round in half, using paper or foil to lift meat; press edges together to seal. Brush patties with steak sauce.
4. Grill, 4 inches from heat, 4 to 8 minutes on each side, or until beef is done as you like. Serve on toasted hamburger rolls with tomato slices on onion rings.

WEST COAST BURGERS

Onions, cheese and tomatoes top flavorful beef patties.

Grill for 8 to 16 minutes.
Makes 6 servings.

- 2 pounds ground beef
- 1 tablespoon bottled steak sauce
- 1 teaspoon salt
- ¼ teaspoon pepper
- 6 thick slices mild onion
  Vegetable oil
- 6 slices tomato
- ¼ cup crumbled blue cheese

1. Mix ground beef lightly with steak sauce, salt and pepper in a medium-size bowl; shape into 6 patties about 1-inch thick.
2. Build a medium fire, or set gas or electric grill to medium, following manufacturer's directions.
3. Grill, 4 inches from heat, 4 to 8 minutes per side, or until beef is done as you like.
4. Brush onion slices with oil; grill 3 minutes on each side. Place an onion slice on each burger, then add a tomato slice and top with cheese. Grill, just until cheese melts. Serve on toasted club rolls with dilled cucumber slices.

WISCONSIN DOG

ILLINOIS BURGER

NEW MEXICO BURGER

MONTANA DOG

HAWAIIAN DOG

COLORADO BURGER

KANSAS BURGER

NEW YORK DOG

CALIFORNIA DOG

IDAHO BURGER

PENNSYLVANIA BURGER

ARIZONA DOG

THE WINNERS' CIRCLE
Paired with a zesty topping or filling, the everyday burger or frank is raised from the ordinary to the sublime! Uncle Sam, Jr. is facing the delightful dilemma of choosing a winning hamburger and hot dog from among the 100 we've created and named in honor of the states. Better not wait for his decision....we have a feeling he'll be back for seconds! You'll find the recipes for these star-spangled creations on the following pages.

HAMBURGERS & HOT DOGS

23

MILE HIGH BURGERS

They're big enough to be a meal on a bun, but be sure to have enough for seconds. Shown around Uncle Sam on page 22.

Grill for 10 to 20 minutes.
Makes 4 servings.

2 pounds ground beef
2 teaspoons seasoned salt
2 teaspoons seasoned pepper
2 tablespoons grated onion

1. Build a medium fire, or set gas or electric grill to medium, following manufacturer's directions.
2. Mix ground beef lightly with salt, pepper and grated onion in a medium-size bowl. Shape into 4 thick patties.
3. Grill, 4 inches from heat, 5 to 10 minutes per side, or until beef is done as you like it. Serve on toasted hamburger bun with one of the suggested toppings below.

Suggested Toppings:
COLORADO BURGER: Top burgers with sliced cherry tomatoes, sprinkle with mixed Italian herbs and top with Provolone cheese. Continue to grill until cheese melts.

IDAHO BURGER: Top with grilled green pepper rings and spoon 3-bean salad from jar into center.

MAINE BURGERS: Top with grilled red onion slices and GREEN PEPPER JAM (recipe, page 29).

KANSAS BURGERS: Wrap 2 slices cooked bacon around each burger and tuck a green pepper ring on top.

NEW YORK BURGERS: Melt a thick slice sharp Cheddar cheese on each burger and top with sautéed onion slices.

NEW MEXICO BURGERS: Spoon bottled hot chili sauce on burgers and garnish with a pickled yellow pepper and ripe olives.

PENNSYLVANIA BURGERS: Brush grilled burgers with soy sauce and top with sautéed mushroom slices and diced pimiento.

ILLINOIS BURGERS: Line toasted hamburger bun with lettuce; add a tomato slice, then grilled burger and top with a sauce made of equal parts mayonnaise or salad dressing and chili sauce; top with a sweet pickle slice.

OKLAHOMA BURGERS: Top burgers with sharp mustard; spread with smoky cheese and grill just until cheese melts.

VIRGINIA BURGERS: Top with grilled ham slices and Swiss cheese; grill just until cheese melts.

CALIFORNIA BURGERS: Top with thin avocado slices and spoon dairy sour cream over; sprinkle with crumbled crisp bacon.

MICHIGAN BURGERS: Top with a sauce made of ¼ cup catsup, 2 tablespoons melted butter or margarine and 2 tablespoons bottled steak sauce.

NORTH DAKOTA BURGERS: Top with heated canned barbecue beans and shredded Cheddar cheese; grill just until cheese melts.

SOUTH DAKOTA BURGERS: Top with a sauce made of 1 to 3 teaspoons chili powder cooked in 1 tablespoon butter or margarine and ½ cup chili sauce.

KENTUCKY BURGERS: Top with mustard relish, then Swiss cheese, and grill until cheese melts.

LOUISIANA BURGERS: Top with RED PEPPER JAM (recipe, page 29) and crumbed bacon; grill until jelly melts.

MARYLAND BURGERS: Top with mango chutney and sprinkle with sliced green onions.

MISSISSIPPI BURGERS: Top with a slaw made by combining 2 cups shredded cabbage, ⅓ cup bottled coleslaw dressing and ¼ cup chopped peanuts.

OREGON BURGERS: Top with cranberry relish from a jar and chopped walnuts.

NEVADA BURGERS: Top with sliced peaches and raspberry jam and grill, just until jam melts.

UTAH BURGERS: Top with roasted red and green peppers and Monterey Jack cheese; grill until cheese melts.

IOWA BURGERS: Top with mashed potatoes, chopped green onion and shredded American cheese.

ALL-AMERICAN HOT DOGS

We have designed a different frankfurter or other sausage-dog recipe for each state in the Union. See how you like your state's special. Some are photographed on page 22.

FRANKFURTERS
Grill for 10 minutes.
Makes 8 servings.

2 packages (1 pound each) frankfurters
Zesty Tomato Sauce (recipe, page 114)
Sweet-Sour Sauce (recipe, page 115)
2 packages (8 buns each) hot dog buns, toasted

1. Build a hot fire, or set gas or electric grill to high, following manufacturer's directions.
2. Score frankfurters about ¾-inch deep. Brush with ZESTY TOMATO SAUCE or SWEET-SOUR SAUCE.

3. Grill, 6 inches from heat, turning and brushing once or twice with more sauce, 10 minutes, or until hot dogs are puffed and richly glazed.
Suggested Variations:
HAWAIIAN DOGS: Serve with grilled canned pineapple spears, chopped macadamia nuts and diced green pepper.

INDIANA DOGS: Make a slaw of 2 cups shredded cabbage, ¼ cup mayonnaise or salad dressing, 2 tablespoons sweet pickle relish and 1 tablespoon prepared mustard. Spoon on buns and place hot dogs on top.

MONTANA DOGS: Place slices of longhorn Cheddar cheese on hot dog buns and grill until melted. Add grilled hot dogs and top with catsup.

ARIZONA DOGS: Insert tiny pieces of white American cheese into scored hot dogs before grilling; spread mustard on hot dog buns and arrange slices of red and green pickled cherry peppers around hot dogs.

IDAHO DOGS: Line toasted hot dog buns with prepared home fried potatoes; place grilled hot dogs on top and coat with catsup.

UTAH DOGS: Top grilled hot dogs with corn relish and FABULOUS FRIED ONION RINGS (recipe, page 117).

WASHINGTON DOGS: Line hot dog buns with potato salad, add grilled hot dogs and top with crumbled bacon.

WYOMING DOGS: Melt American cheese on hot dog buns; add grilled hot dogs and top with sweet onion slices and catsup.

SOUTH DAKOTA DOGS: Spoon heated barbecue beans, flavored with chili sauce, over grilled hot dogs.

NORTH DAKOTA DOGS: Spread toasted hot dog buns with sharp mustard and coat with crushed potato chips; place grilled hot dogs on top.

MISSOURI DOGS: Line toasted hot dog buns with tomato slices and thin onion rings; place grilled hot dogs on and top with chopped peanuts.

IOWA DOGS: Melt American cheese on toasted hot dog buns; place grilled hot dogs on and top with corn relish.

ARKANSAS DOGS: Top grilled hot dogs in toasted buns with watermelon pickle and chopped pecans.

FLORIDA DOGS: Top grilled hot dogs in toasted buns with orange sections and sweet onion slices.

GEORGIA DOGS: Top grilled hot dogs in toasted buns with grilled peach slices and mango chutney.

MISSISSIPPI DOGS: Fill toasted hot dog buns with rice salad and place grilled hot dogs over; top with dairy sour cream seasoned with mustard.

MAINE DOGS: Wrap bacon around hot dogs before grilling and top with hot dog relish in toasted buns.

NEW HAMPSHIRE DOGS: Spread toasted hot dog buns with sharp mustard and top with thin slices of sharp Cheddar cheese; grill until melted; place grilled hot dogs over.

RHODE ISLAND DOGS: Line toasted hot dog buns with sauerkraut and top with grilled hot dogs, sharp mustard and roasted red peppers.

VERMONT DOGS: Brush maple syrup on apple slices and grill; line toasted hot dog buns with apple slices and place grilled hot dogs on top.

ILLINOIS DOGS: Line toasted hot dog buns with 3-bean salad from a jar; place grilled hot dogs over and top with mustard relish.

OKLAHOMA DOGS: Spread toasted hot dog buns with canned deviled ham; place grilled hot dogs over and top with chopped Bermuda onion.

TEXAS DOGS: Line toasted hot dog buns with sautéed red and green peppers seasoned with chili sauce.

NEW MEXICO DOGS: Top grilled hot dogs with mashed avocado, sliced ripe olives and crushed corn chips.

GERMAN SKILLET FRANKS

Beer-braised sauerkraut gives franks a Bavarian flavor. Great with mugs of beer.

Grill for 45 minutes.
Makes 4 servings.

 6 slices bacon, diced
 1 small onion, sliced
 1 can (1 pound, 14 ounces) sauerkraut, drained
 1 cup beer
 1 tablespoon brown sugar
 1 teaspoon caraway seeds
 1 medium-size red-skinned apple
 1 package (1 pound) frankfurters

1. Build a medium fire, or set gas or electric grill to medium, following manufacturer's directions.
2. Cook bacon in a large metal skillet with flameproof handle on grill, 6 inches from heat, until fat begins to melt; push bacon to one side; cook onion 2 to 3 minutes; add sauerkraut; cook 5 minutes.
3. Stir in beer, sugar and caraway seeds; grate in apple; cover; simmer 30 minutes.
4. Place frankfurters on top; cover; simmer 15 minutes, or until frankfurters are heated through; garnish with apple slices and serve with rye bread and a sharp mustard. Add a large tossed salad of iceberg and celery with blue cheese dressing.

HEALTH BURGERS

Wheat germ adds a nutty flavor, as well as extra nutrition to thick hamburgers.

Grill for 14 to 18 minutes.
Makes 4 servings.

 2 pounds ground beef
 ¼ cup plain wheat germ
 3 tablespoons milk
 2 tablespoons finely chopped green onion
 2 tablespoons finely chopped celery
 1 tablespoon catsup
 1 teaspoon salt
 Few drops bottled red pepper seasoning

1. Build a medium fire, or set gas or electric grill to medium, following manufacturer's directions.
2. Combine ground beef, wheat germ, milk, onion, celery, catsup, salt and red pepper seasoning in a medium-size bowl; mix lightly, just until blended. Shape into four 1-inch-thick patties.
3. Grill, 4 inches from heat, 7 to 9 minutes; turn with a pancake turner; grill 7 to 9 minutes longer, or until done as you like. Serve on toasted English muffins with French fried onion rings.

KING CHEESEBURGERS

Great for a kid's birthday party.

Grill for 20 minutes.
Makes 6 servings.

 1½ pounds ground beef
 ¼ cup chili sauce
 1 clove garlic, minced
 1½ teaspoons salt
 ⅛ teaspoon pepper
 1 loaf long thin French bread
 Prepared mustard
 Mayonnaise or salad dressing
 1 medium-size sweet onion, peeled, sliced and separated into rings
 1 package (8 ounces) sliced process American cheese, cut into strips

1. Build a medium fire in a kettle grill, or set electric or gas grill to medium, following manufacturer's directions.
2. Mix ground beef lightly with chili sauce, garlic, salt and pepper in a medium-size bowl.
3. Split French bread lengthwise; spread each half lightly with mustard and mayonnaise or salad dressing, then meat mixture.
4. Grill 6 inches from heat, with cover on grill, 15 minutes, or until beef is done as you like; top with onion rings and cheese strips. Grill 5 minutes longer, or just until cheese melts. Slice into thirds and serve with potato chips and coleslaw. Then choose a beverage from our selection on pages 98-99 to complete the menu.

SPICED BEEF SAUSAGE

Allspice, cloves and thyme flavor cylinder-shaped ground beef.

Grill for 10 minutes.
Makes 6 servings.

 2 pounds ground beef
 2 cloves garlic, minced
 2 teaspoons salt
 ½ teaspoon leaf thyme, crumbled
 ¼ teaspoon freshly ground pepper
 ¼ teaspoon ground allspice
 ¼ teaspoon ground cloves
 ½ cup beef broth
 Vegetable oil

1. Combine beef, garlic, salt, thyme, pepper, allspice and cloves in a large bowl until well blended. Beat in beef broth with a wooden spoon until light and fluffy.
2. Divide mixture into 18 parts and shape each into a 3-inch-long rope, dipping hands in cold water to ease shaping. Place on cookie sheet and chill until grill is ready.
3. Build a very hot fire, or set gas or electric grill to high, following manufacturer's directions.
4. Brush beef ropes with a generous coating of oil.
5. Grill, 4 inches from heat, turning often, 10 minutes, or until beef is done as you like. Serve on heated pita bread with roasted red peppers, if you wish.

CHEESEBURGER KABOBS

Blue cheese and mushrooms are the hidden treat inside each meatball kabob.

Grill for 20 minutes.
Makes 6 servings.

 18 small mushrooms
 2 pounds ground beef
 1 tablespoon finely chopped chives
 2 teaspoons salt
 ¼ teaspoon freshly ground pepper
 1 package (3 ounces) blue cheese

1. Remove stems from mushrooms and chop. Combine chopped caps with ground beef, chives, salt and pepper in a medium-size bowl; mix lightly, just until blended.
2. Divide blue cheese among mushrooms and press inside caps. Divide ground beef mixture into 18 portions and wrap a portion around each mushroom. Thread 3 meatballs onto each of 6 skewers and chill while heating grill.
3. Build a slow fire, or set electric or gas grill to low, following manufacturer's directions.
4. Grill, 4 inches from heat, turning several times, 20 minutes, or until meat is done as you like. Serve with rice pilaf and tall glasses of iced tea with mint, if you wish.

(Recipes continued on page 108.)

GARDEN-FRESH
Home-preserved pickles and relishes add the crowning touch to backyard barbecue fare. For recipes and names of condiments shown, see page 28.

HOME-DILLED PICKLE STICKS

When July brings a bumper crop of cucumbers, be sure to put up some of these. Photographed in San Diego and shown on page 26.

Makes 3 one-quart jars.

- 18 pickling cucumbers, cut into quarters, lengthwise (about 4 pounds)
- 4 cups cider vinegar
- 3 tablespoons salt
- 1 tablespoon mustard seed
- 6 cups sugar
- 2⅓ cups white vinegar
- 2¼ teaspoons celery seed
- 1 teaspoon whole allspice

1. Combine cucumbers, cider vinegar, salt, mustard seed and ¼ cup of the sugar in a large kettle. Bring to boiling; lower heat; cover kettle; simmer 10 minutes; drain and discard liquid. Pack cucumbers, lengthwise, into hot quart jars.
2. Combine remaining 5¾ cups sugar, white vinegar, celery seed and allspice in a large saucepan; bring to boiling; pour over cucumber sticks, leaving ½-inch headroom.
3. Seal and process 15 minutes in waterbath, following directions on page 29.
4. Store in cool, dry place at least 1 month to develop flavors.

TANGY MUSTARD RELISH

Great on franks or grilled sausages, this relish uses a bit of all the vegetables from your garden. Shown surrounded by foliage on page 26.

Makes 4 one-quart jars.

- 8 green tomatoes, cored and cut into wedges
- 8 cucumbers, cut into 1-inch pieces
- 4 large green peppers, halved, seeded and diced
- 4 large red peppers, halved, seeded and diced
- 3 large onions, quartered
- ⅓ cup kosher salt
- ½ cup firmly packed brown sugar
- 3 tablespoons dry mustard
- 2 teaspoons turmeric
- 2 teaspoons mustard seeds
- 2 teaspoons celery seeds
- 6 cups cider vinegar
- ½ cup all purpose flour
- 1 cup cold water

1. Chop green tomatoes, cucumbers, green and red peppers and onions by putting through a food processor or the fine blade of a food grinder.
2. Combine chopped vegetables and salt in a large ceramic or glass bowl; cover with plastic wrap and allow to stand at room temperature overnight; pour off liquid and spoon vegetables into a large heavy kettle.
3. Add sugar, mustard, turmeric,

mustard and celery seeds and vinegar.
4. Bring to boiling, stirring often; lower heat; simmer 15 minutes. Combine flour and cold water in a bowl; stir into bubbling mixture. Cook, stirring constantly, until mixture thickens and bubbles 5 minutes. Ladle into hot sterilized one-quart jars, leaving ½-inch headroom. Seal and process 15 minutes in water-bath, following directions on page 29.
6. Store in a cool, dry place at least 1 month before serving.

HOMEMADE CHILI SAUCE

It's spicy and tangy and the perfect topper for grilled hamburgers. Shown near a pond at Vacation Village, San Diego, page 26.

Makes 3 one-quart jars.

- 16 large tomatoes, peeled, cored and chopped (16 cups)
- 2 cups chopped onion
- 2 cups chopped sweet red pepper
- 3 hot red peppers, chopped
- 3 cups white vinegar
- 1 cup firmly packed brown sugar
- 2 tablespoons salt
- 1 teaspoon ground ginger
- 1 teaspoon ground nutmeg
- 1 teaspoon ground allspice
- 2 tablespoons crushed stick cinnamon
- 1 tablespoon mustard seed
- 1 tablespoon celery seed
- 1 teaspoon whole cloves
- 1 bay leaf

1. Combine tomatoes, onion, sweet and hot peppers, vinegar, sugar, salt, ginger, nutmeg and allspice in a large kettle. Tie stick cinnamon, celery and mustard seeds, cloves and bay leaf in cheesecloth; add to kettle.
2. Bring to boiling; lower heat; cook, stirring several times with a long wooden spoon, 2 hours, or until as thick as you want it; remove spice bag.
3. Ladle into hot one-quart jars, leaving ½-inch headroom. Seal and process 15 minutes in water-bath, following directions on page 29.
4. Store in cool, dry place 3 weeks.

LEMON TARTAR RELISH

Just as special on burgers as on fried fish.

Makes 1 cup.

- 2 hard-cooked eggs, chopped
- ⅓ cup mayonnaise or salad dressing
- 2 tablespoons sweet pickle relish
- 2 tablespoons lemon juice
- 1 tablespoon chopped green onion
- ¼ teaspoon paprika

Combine eggs, mayonnaise or salad dressing, pickle relish, lemon juice, green onion and paprika in a small glass or ceramic bowl; stir until well blended. Cover with plastic wrap; chill until ready to serve.

PICKLED YELLOW PEPPERS

They're hot, but so good with a slab of grilled steak or on a kabob. The photograph is on page 27.

Makes 3 one-quart jars.

- 12 cups yellow peppers (about 3 pounds)
- 2 tablespoons kosher salt
  Water
- 3 cups white vinegar
- ¾ cup sugar
- ½ teaspoon whole cloves
- 3 small bay leaves

1. Soak washed and trimmed peppers in salt and water to cover in a large glass or ceramic bowl 48 hours at room temperature; drain.
2. Bring vinegar, sugar and cloves tied in cheesecloth to boiling in a large kettle; add peppers; return to boiling; cook 3 to 5 minutes; remove spice bag.
3. Ladle into hot one-quart jars, leaving ½-inch headroom. Add a bay leaf to each jar. Seal and process 15 minutes in water-bath, following directions on page 29.
4. Store in cool, dry place at least 6 weeks to develop flavors.

ANTIPASTO RELISH

Pickled cauliflower, carrot, onion, peppers and cucumber can be the start of great antipasto platters. Shown with a flock of wild ducks, on page 27.

Makes 4 one-quart jars.

- 7 large cucumbers, sliced
- 6 medium-size white onions, sliced
- 3 large sweet red peppers, halved, seeded and chopped
- 2 cauliflowers, separated into flowerets
- 4 large carrots, pared and sliced
- ¼ cup kosher salt
  Cracked ice or ice cubes
- 2½ cups white vinegar
- 2½ cups sugar
- 1 tablespoon mustard seed
- 1 teaspoon celery seed
- ½ teaspoon ground cloves

1. Layer cucumbers, onions, peppers, cauliflower and carrots with salt in a large glass or ceramic bowl; cover with cracked ice or ice cubes.
2. Weight pickles down by placing a plate, just a little smaller than bowl, over ice cubes and stacking several large cans on top. Let stand 4 hours. Pour off liquid.
3. Bring vinegar, sugar, mustard and celery seeds and cloves to boiling in a large kettle; add drained vegetables and return to boiling. Ladle into hot quart jars, leaving ½-inch headroom. Seal and process 15 minutes in water-bath, following directions on page 29.
4. Store in a cool, dry place at least 1 month for flavors to develop.

RUBY GARDEN RELISH

A hot dog topping with a definite bite.

Makes 7 one-pint jars.

- 12-14 large beets, boiled, peeled and chopped (6 cups)
- 6½ cups chopped cabbage
- 1½ cups chopped celery
- ⅔ cup chopped green pepper
- 2 cups cider vinegar
- ¾ cup sugar
- ½ cup beet cooking liquid
- 2 tablespoons horseradish (or more to taste)
- 2 tablespoons salt
- ¼ teaspoon white pepper
- Dash cayenne pepper

1. Combine beets, cabbage, celery, green pepper, vinegar, sugar, beet liquid, horseradish, salt, pepper and cayenne in a large kettle.
2. Bring to boiling; ladle into hot one-pint jars, leaving ½-inch headroom. Seal and process 10 minutes in water-bath, following directions at right.
3. Store in cool, dry place at least 3 weeks, but it improves with age.

CALIFORNIA RELISH

A delicious accompaniment to steaks.

Makes 5 cups.

- 1 can (6 ounces) pitted ripe olives, chopped
- 1½ cups finely chopped celery
- 4 medium-size dill pickles, chopped (1 cup)
- 1 medium-size onion, chopped (½ cup)
- 1 clove garlic, minced
- 1 can (2 ounces) anchovy fillets
- ½ cup vegetable oil
- ¼ cup wine vinegar or cider vinegar
- ¼ teaspoon pepper

1. Combine olives, celery, dill pickles, onion and garlic in a large glass or ceramic bowl; toss lightly to mix.
2. Drain oil from anchovies into olive mixture; cut anchovies into tiny pieces and stir in with oil, vinegar and pepper; toss well to mix. Cover with plastic wrap; chill several hours.

TANGY HOT DOG RELISH

Just as delicious with hamburgers.

Makes 2¼ cups.

- 4 large stalks celery
- 2 large lemons, quartered
- 6 green onions
- 1 small green pepper, quartered and seeded
- ¼ cup parsley
- ½ cup sugar
- 1 teaspoon salt
- 1 teaspoon celery seed
- 1 teaspoon dry mustard
- ¼ teaspoon ground allspice

1. Process celery, lemons, green onions, pepper and parsley with the grating blade of an electric food processor, following manufacturer's directions, or work through food chopper, using coarse blade.
2. Combine vegetable mixture, sugar, salt, celery seed, mustard and allspice in a large glass bowl; stir until sugar dissolves; cover with plastic wrap. Refrigerate overnight to develop flavor. Spoon into a large jar with a screw top and store in refrigerator.

GENERAL DIRECTIONS FOR CANNING AND WATER-BATH PROCESS

Follow all the directions carefully and *do not* take any shortcuts. Your time is too valuable and food too costly to have your rows of preserves spoiled in a few months or so.

1. Place hot-water-bath canner onto surface burner; add water to half fill canner (a tea kettle does this job easily); cover canner; bring water to boiling while preparing jars and food.
2. Wash jars in hot sudsy water; rinse well; leave in hot water until ready to use.
3. Place new domed lids in a bowl and cover with boiling water; keep in water until ready to use.
4. Follow individual recipe directions.
5. Remove jars from water, one at a time; place on paper towels or a clean cloth; pack and/or ladle food into jars, leaving the headroom called for in the individual recipe.
6. Wipe top and outside rim of jar with a clean cloth; place domed lid on top; screw metal rings on tightly, but do not use force.
7. Place jars in canner rack and lower into rapidly boiling water, adding additional boiling water to kettle if the level of water is not 2-inches above the jars; cover kettle. Return to a full boil.
8. Process, following the times given in the individual recipes and calculated from the time that the water comes to the second boil.
Note: For those who live at altitudes above sea level, when recipe directions call for processing 20 minutes or less, add 1 minute for each 1,000 feet; when processing more than 20 minutes, add 2 minutes for each 1,000 feet.
9. Remove jars from canner and place on wire racks or cloth-lined surface at least 3-inches apart until cool, for about 12 hours.
10. Test all jars to be sure that they are sealed by tapping with a spoon. (A clear ringing sound means a good seal. If jars are not sealed properly, either store in refrigerator and plan to use within a month or pour contents of jar into a bowl and process

again from Step 5.)
11. Remove metal rings; wipe jars with a clean dampened cloth; label, date and store jars in a cool, dark, dry place.

GREEN PEPPER JAM

Use this same recipe with sweet red pepper for Red Pepper Jam.

Makes five ½-pint jars.

- 12 large green peppers
- 1 tablespoon kosher salt
- 3 cups sugar
- 2 cups white vinegar
- 2 three-inch sticks cinnamon
- 6 whole cloves

1. Quarter and seed peppers. Press through the medium blade of a food chopper, or process in your food processor.
2. Place chopped peppers in a large glass or ceramic bowl and mix with salt; cover with plastic wrap. Allow to stand at room temperature overnight. Drain through a colander.
3. Combine drained peppers with sugar and vinegar in a large kettle. Tie cinnamon and cloves in cheesecloth and press under liquid in kettle.
4. Bring to boiling, stirring several times; lower heat; cook 45 minutes stirring often, or until mixture thickens; remove spice bag.
5. Ladle into hot sterilized ½ pint jars; cover and seal, following manufacturer's directions. Cool on a cloth-lined tray. Allow to stand at least 1 week before serving with grilled hot dogs, barbecued beef and glazed spareribs.

QUICK CORN RELISH

Before your corn crop comes in, make this recipe with canned corn; later, use 3 cups cooked corn.

Makes 4 cups.

- ¾ cup vegetable oil
- ¼ cup cider vinegar
- 1 tablespoon prepared horseradish
- 1½ teaspoons Worcestershire sauce
- 1 teaspoon sugar
- ½ teaspoon salt
- ¼ teaspoon paprika
- 2 drops bottled red pepper seasoning
- 2 cans (12 or 16 ounces each) whole kernel corn, drained

1. Combine oil, vinegar, horseradish, Worcestershire sauce, sugar, salt, paprika and red pepper seasoning in a jar with a screw top; seal and shake.
2. Pour over corn in a medium-size glass or ceramic bowl; stir well; cover with plastic wrap; refrigerate at least 4 hours to blend flavors. ∎

Be your own butcher and save on your meat budget. Look for the specials at your supermarket that feature "family-size" pieces of beef, often at cents off per pound.

beef

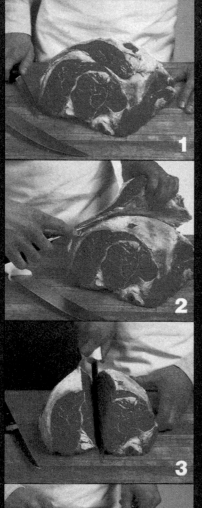

1. A whole sirloin tip with the cap on is that part of the beef loin from which steaks such as beef loin, sirloin and shell, or New York, steaks come. We show you how one sirloin roast can become a roast for the rotisserie, plus steaks and kabob cubes.

2. Using a 7-inch, very sharp knife, cut off the cap, following natural seam, leaving a slight covering of fat. (The cap meat can be cut into cubes for kabobs.) You now have a sirloin tip, or ball tip roast.

3. Using a long, sharp butcher knife, make a major cut, lengthwise, through center of beef. (This way each half will be part fore and part shank meat; if meat cut were made crosswise, half would be

tender and the second half all shank meat.)

4. Using a slip knot, tie up one half of beef at 1-inch intervals with cotton twine, to use on rotisserie. (This gives the beef a better shape and also shows the grain of the meat for easier carving after roasting.)

5. Cut second piece of beef into individual steaks at least 1-inch thick. (This is a good size for grilling. They can be cut in half at serving time if too large.) Cut shank end into cubes for kabobs and marinate before grilling.

6. The beef rib roast, small end, is delicious roasted whole; however, it is large, so when there are less people to serve, cut into steaks, some for now and some to freeze

for grilling later. Have market cut off chine bone. Continue cut made by market through cartilage and discard with backbones.

7. Following the natural seam of muscle, cut off top fat and cut into curve to remove fat. Following bones, cut beef from back ribs, leaving lean whole. You can grill the bones.

8. This is a rib eye roast. It can now be tied and cooked on rotisserie or in kettle-grill, if you wish. For rib eye steaks, cut off excess fat. (This can cause fat fires in grill, so trim meat well, then brush meat surface with oil just before grilling, or marinate in an oil-

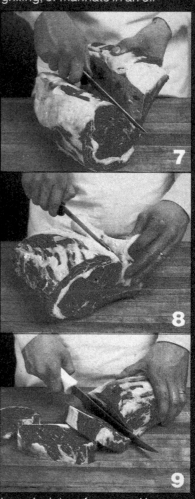

based mixture for several hours before grilling.)

9. Cut meat into 1-inch-thick steaks, using a long, sharp butcher knife. To freeze steaks, wrap individually in heavy-duty aluminum foil using the drugstore wrap (see page 47), label, date and freeze at 0° F immediately. Grill, following Frozen Steak Grilling Chart, page 53.

1. Pork loin roast is the most popular, and frequent, special cut of pork at your supermarket. With no special butchering tools and just a little practice, you can take two pork loin roasts and transform them into 3 different and delicious pork cuts for kabobs, grilling and roasting.

2. With a very sharp 7-inch knife, trim off all outer fat from 2 pork

Today's pork is the perfect choice for barbecuing because it's leaner and doesn't have to be cooked as long as in the past.

pork

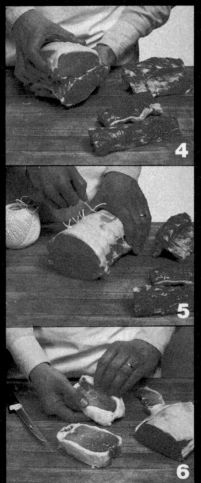

loin roasts. Cut along and against bones, feeling along with knife and fingers to remove meat from bones. Separate meat into muscles by cutting down long side of roast, following the natural seam, and pull into two sections.

3. You now have two large, lean muscles, two tenderloins, and the bones from both roasts which can go into a stock pot, or cut them into serving-size pieces and grill, 6 inches from heat, 40 minutes, then baste with barbecue sauce and grill 20 minutes longer.

4. There are two ways that the large, top muscle can be prepared for barbecuing. The first is the boneless pork roast. This is prepared by placing the 2 lean muscles together, fat-sides out.

(The muscles need not come from the same side of the animal; in fact, the final shape of the roast will be better if they are from the opposite sides of the animal.)

5. Tie boneless roast into shape by wrapping roast with strong cotton twine (never thread) and securing with butcher or square knots, tight enough to hold roast in place, but not tight enough to

change shape of roast while grilling, nor to force out meat juices.

6. The second way to prepare the top muscle is to prepare butterfly chops. Cut top muscle into 1-inch-thick slices with a very sharp 7-inch knife. Make a second cut down through center of slices, almost to the bottom, then force chop open and flatten.

7. The 2 tenderloins are ideal for kabob cooking; just cut into 1-inch cubes and thread onto metal or wooden skewers. Pork kabobs can be put together with vegetables, such as mushrooms, parboiled onions or sweet potatoes. Be sure to marinate pork in an oil marinade to keep the meat moist and juicy while grilling.

8. Three ways to prepare pork loin roasts: (top right) boneless pork roast—Marinate and kettle-roast (for recipe, see page 105); (bottom) butterfly pork chops—Brush with an oil and herb baste and grill; (top left) pork kabobs—Follow kabob recipes.

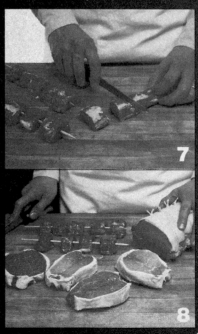

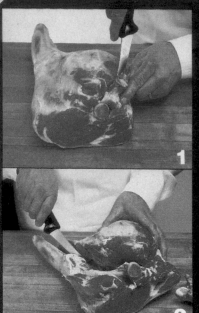

1. Have butcher cut off 4 sirloin steaks from full-trimmed leg of lamb. Using a sharp boning knife and starting at tip of femur bone to ball socket, cut along and against bone, feeling with knife, following direction of bones.

2. Repeat cutting on other side and along bottom of leg bones. (You can keep meat whole, cutting

thick muscle in half, crosswise, flattening for whole butterfly lamb.)

3. Separate leg muscles into 3 main parts by cutting along the natural seam to separate the thickest part of leg. Two of these muscles can be tied into tiny roasts and rotissed. Use one on grill; use bones in stock pot.

4. To cut lamb into more barbecue cuts: Slice off 4 cutlets from the thickest muscle. Cut rest of muscle into cubes for kabobs.

5. Cut part of second muscle into more cubes and remaining into thin strips for teriyaki or stroganoff. Above, going clockwise: (top center) sirloin steaks; (right top) kabob cubes; (right bottom) lamb cutlets; (bottom left) lamb strips, and (left top) butterfly lamb.

Grill a butterfly leg of American lamb, or cut into cutlets, kabobs and steaks.

lamb

the crown roast

Make your reputation as a gourmet barbecue chef extraordinaire with this Lamb Crown Roast.

1. Be sure to have a sharp knife (we used a 5-inch boning knife), a trussing needle or a carpet needle and cotton twine. Starting with 2 racks of lamb roasts, have butcher saw through rib bones. Remove excess from back of racks and remove back strap at rib bone end. To French ribs: Remove 1½- to 2-inches from top of ribs by cutting down to bones and removing fat.

2. Cut down both sides of each bone, so you can remove little tidbits of meat from between bones. (Marinate tidbits and grill quickly.) Score skin between each rib with tip of knife, so rack can bend into half circle.

3. Put Frenched racks flat on work surface, lining up rib bones.

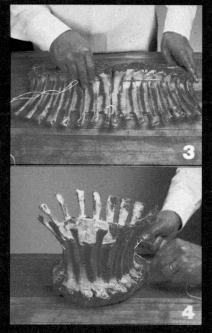

Thread a trussing needle (see Buyer's Guide) or use a carpet needle with strong cotton twine. Sew, going from under last rib of one rack to first rib of second rack; tie with a secure knot. Continue every 1-inch along ribs.

4. Bend racks backward to shape into crown and repeat sewing. Fill with stuffing (recipe, page 12).

CRESTLINE

Barbecue cooking has come a long way from its humble beginnings around an open campfire to the gourmet patio feasts served today. As barbecue cooking techniques have improved through the years, so have the "tools of the trade." In this chapter is a represent-ative sampling of the very latest equipment in outdoor cooking, from grills, such as the American-made hibachi shown here, to charcoal/water smokers for indoor/outdoor cooking. Plus, helpful guide-lines for both the amateur and experienced barbecue chef.

tools & techniques

SMOKED-IN FLAVOR
Charcoal/water smokers give all meats unbelievable succulence and a rich barbecue taste. A pan of simmering water, broth or other liquid evaporates above the coals, mixes with smoke and continuously bastes meat on the grill; you don't have to turn or baste the meat once. One more flavor bonus: Pan juices make a delectable sauce base.

SMOKE'N PIT

NECESSITIES at any barbecue are long-handled utensils. Knife and fork have tapered lines for roasting and carving; basting brush applies barbecue sauce evenly; tongs hold meat firmly for easy turning.

PORTABLE plastic canister holds up to 9 qts. of liquid. Or, filled with ice, it's a giant cooler.

Large plastic salt and pepper shakers have easy-grasp shape and hinged seal.

S P

Iced tea or fruit punches pour handily from this 2 qt. plastic pitcher.

STACKABLE bowls conserve space and are ideal for storing leftovers or individual servings. Measuring cup features a snap-cap pouring spout—great for barbecue sauces.

TABLETOP ELECTRIC GRILL lets you enjoy real cookout flavor all year round—without the bother of messy charcoal.

SIDE DISHES and main-dish casseroles cook beautifully in this 3-qt. oblong baking dish with serving basket. Use it to keep food warm at side of grill, too.

CUPS OZ. CUPS
4 — 32
3½ — 28 — 3⅓
3 — 24 — 2⅔
2½ — 20 — 2⅓
2 — 16 — 1⅔
1½ — 12 — 1⅓
1 — 8 — ⅔
½ — 4 — ⅓

FOLD-AWAY SIDE TABLES provide extra work space in a smoker grill. Adjusting knobs move cooking grid to four cooking heights and tilt grid left or right for cooking rare to well done at the same time.

BAKE AND SERVE moist and flavorful meals in a covered casserole with attractive serving basket.

GRAB-IT BOWL is perfect for single servings of your favorite casserole (holds 15 oz.). Keeps bastes and sauces warm at side of grill, too.

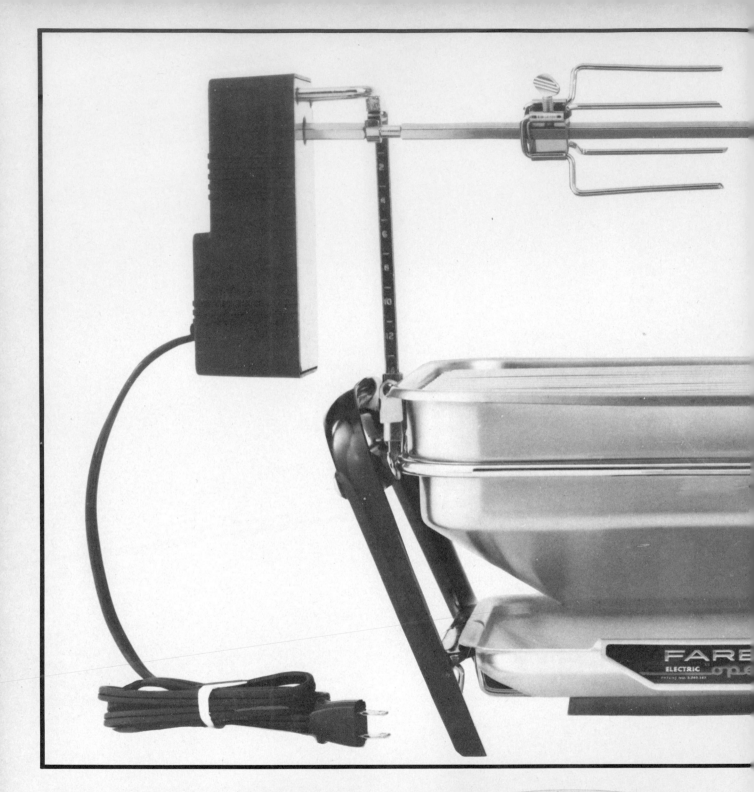

FARE
ELECTRIC *opel*

MARINATE
meat and poultry in
a leakproof plas-
tic container,
to avoid a metallic
taste. No need to
turn meat with a fork—
just flip sealed
dish once.

EN CASSEROLE
Oval-shaped, with a woodsy motif, travels
from side of grill to table.

COOK ON AN "OPEN HEARTH" Electric broiler with rotisserie attachment barbecues roasts, steaks and chops in your kitchen, all year round. Disassembles easily for quick clean-up. Motors for spit and grill operate on two separate circuits.

charcoal cooking pointers

For a successful barbecue, you must begin with a good fire. When cooking with charcoal, follow these simple steps to just the right fire, as called for in the individual recipe, for the food you're cooking.

- Stack the briquets in a pyramid and ignite with an electric or chimney-type starter, or place a wad of paper in the bottom of grill; top with a few wood chips and then stack the briquets over the chips; light paper with a match.
- Let briquets burn for at least 30 to 40 minutes, or until, in daylight, the coals are covered by a layer of gray ash and at night they have a bright red glow. Spread the briquets into a single layer with tongs and start grilling.
- For grilling a small steak, a few chops or some ham-

burgers or hot dogs, plan on using 12 to 24 briquets. For a roast, whole fish or poultry, plan on using 30 to 40 to start and adding more, if needed.

- For a quick temperature test, hold your hand at cooking height, palm-side down. If you can keep it there for 2 seconds, you have a hot fire, for 3 seconds, a medium-hot fire, 4 seconds a medium fire and 5 seconds a low heat.
- To lower the temperature of the grill, raise the grid or spread out the coals. To raise the temperature of the fire, tap ash from coals or push them closer together.
- When you need more coals, add them to the outer edge of hot coals until they are hot, then push into center of fire with long metal tongs.

DETACHABLE HOOD
protects items on spit or grill, while warming oven keeps other food hot. Swing-out spit lets you tend food away from heat.

TABLETOP BRAZIER
converts to a freestanding model in seconds. Features include a crank-up revolving grill, notched windguard and two skewers.

PORTABLE GRILL
with built-in exhaust system brings barbecue flavor indoors, for year-round use. It's electric.

SHARP knives are essential for neat, safe carving. They often come in matching sets, too.

make your barbecue a safe one

Unnecessary accidents can ruin an otherwise pleasurable barbecue. The National Safety Council offers outdoor chefs the following advice:

The Right Location
• *Never* use a charcoal grill in your home or garage, only equipment specially designed for indoor use.
• Set the grill in the open on level ground. Check for stability before lighting fire. Be extra cautious on windy days.

Proper Dress
• Roll up sleeves, tuck in shirttails and make sure scarves and apron strings won't dangle over the grill.
• Wear a large apron of denim or other heavy material and potholder-type gloves, as protection against sparks and grease splatters.

Start the Fire
• The safest way to start a fire is to spread charcoal over lighted wood shavings or kindling. There are also some commercially available products that are quite safe, if used as directed—electric starters with the UL label approval and "treated" solid starters.

Intensifying the Fire
• To freshen a fire, place more charcoal briquets around smoldering ones (see page 39 for more charcoal tips).
• We don't recommend liquid starters; however, if you prefer them, *never* use them once the fire is started, even if it appears to be out.

Barbecue Utensils
• Invest in a sturdy long-handled spatula or fork and a pair of long tongs; both keep the chef from getting too near the fire and hot grill.

Special Rotisserie Tips
• If the electric rotisserie cord on a charcoal grill has an ordinary two-prong plug (rather than a three-prong, grounding one), place the grill on a non-conductive surface—never on damp concrete or grass. Even when a three-prong plug is provided, extension cords also should be of the three-wire type.

Food Safety
• Plan on serving hearty appetizers and filling salads (see SALAD BAR, page 128), so that hungry guests won't drink too much while waiting for the grilled food.
• Keep cold foods in the refrigerator until ready to serve. Cool leftover foods immediately to keep them from spoiling.

ALL-WEATHER Portable, covered gas grill with rotisserie unit lets you grill outdoors all year round, regardless of weather conditions.

THERMAL container keeps both hot and cold beverages and soups at their proper temperature.

what you should know about knives

A barbecue chef can be no better than his tools and a few well-chosen, sharp knives can make all the difference when trimming raw meat or carving barbecued steaks.

There is no need to have a large collection of knives, just a few well-made ones that feel comfortable in your hand and will serve your purposes. Our experts from the National Live Stock and Meat Board and the American Lamb Council, shown on pages 30, 31 and 32, used just two knives, a 7-inch boning knife and a 10-inch butcher's knife. The additional tool shown in the photograph on page 4 is the steel which helps to keep the knives razor-sharp while in use. In addition to these basic tools, you will probably want to have a 5- to 6-inch paring knife, a 9- to 11-inch French knife and a long, slender carving knife.

Knives can be made of carbon steel or stainless steel and there are proponents of each metal. With carbon steel, the blade will hold a sharper edge a little longer, but many foods stain the blade and it can rust. However, if a stainless steel knife is sharpened on a hard enough stone, it too will hold a very sharp edge, while a wipe with a soapy steel-wool pad can remove the stain and rust from carbon steel blades.

You should always buy good knives, but that doesn't mean that they have to be expensive. In almost all cities there is a restaurant or butcher supply store where you can buy the same professional knives that chefs and butchers choose at a lower price than department stores. Check

yellow pages of your phone directory for the address.

The important qualities to look for in a knife are that the knife be well-balanced and feel comfortable in your hand and that the metal extension of the blade, called the tang, goes at least three divets deep into the handle, unless it is made of the molded polypropylene that bonds the metal to the handle permanently. This type of handle is becoming very popular with professionals since there is no danger of bacteria building up on the handle, as there is with a wooden handle.

To sharpen a knife: Use a sharpener that is harder than the metal of the knives and rub with vegetable oil to lubricate; place the back of the blade at a 20° angle to the stone, holding the stone in place with the other hand. Exert gentle pressure and draw the blade down and across the stone to the tip; turn and draw the other side of knife-blade down stone; repeat about 6 times.

Wash knives by hand in warm, but not hot, soapy water; store in a knife rack or on a magnetic rack and never keep knives in a jumble in a drawer or within the reach of children. To keep the sharp edge on a knife while carving, run blade along the steel every so often.

If you take the time to choose your knives carefully, sharpen them before each use and store them so that the blades are protected, you will have tools that will serve you with great satisfaction for many years.

PLUG-IN SMOKER
Electric smoker cooks an entire meal at one time, with very little effort on your part. Once closed, the unit seals in all steam and smoke, constantly basting food inside— there's no need to peek until cooking time is over. Old-fashioned flavor comes from aromatic hardwood chips.

COVERED KETTLE
cooks traditional barbecue favorites, as well as a large variety of specialties. The cover reflects heat, evenly cooking food and reducing preparation time. Kettles operate on charcoal, as shown, or gas. Both methods use fuel efficiently, with scrumptious results.

43

RECESSED WINDOW
lets you view what's cooking in this smoker wagon. Front, side and bottom shelves provide ample work space.

GAS-FIRED
unit ignites instantly, is ready for use in minutes. Air and gas adjustment assure controlled cooking with perfect results, no matter how bad the weather. Ceramic "briquets" replace charcoal.

Charmglow 3200

SHARPENERS such as the stone and steel shown here are absolute necessities for keeping all your knives razor-sharp.

meat & poultry on the grill

What You Should Know

Almost any cut of meat that's tender enough to roast, broil, pan-broil or pan-fry can also be cooked on the grill. Even the less tender cut can become ready for the barbecue, if you marinate it in one of the mixtures given in the Marinades & Glazes section of this book.

Roasts should be as even in shape as possible to insure even cooking. Steaks and chops should be at least ¾-inch thick and meat for kabobs should be cut into even-size cubes; all meat should be at room temperature.

Since people's appetites grow in the great outdoors, plan on extra-large portions of meat or poultry for each guest— at least ¾ pound per person for boneless cuts and 1½ pounds per person for bone-in cuts and poultry.

Plan your party-time schedule around the barbecued meat or poultry and give plenty of time for the grill to heat to temperature and for the extra cooking time that may be needed when roasting or grilling outdoors. It's better to start the barbecue a little early and have the meat ready ahead of time and "resting," than to have a crowd of hungry guests standing around for an hour while the roast comes to the right degree of doneness.

As in all meat and poultry cooking, low or slow heat is always best to insure moist, tender results. Coals should glow, rather than flame and the low or medium setting on the gas or electric grill should be used *unless* one of the recipes in this issue directs otherwise. You can control the heat during grilling by adjusting the height of the grids in relation to the coals, or by turning down the gas or electric grill, if the roast seems to be smoking, browning too quickly or giving other evidences of cooking too quickly.

Points on Rotisserie Cooking

Roasts, chickens, turkeys and Rock Cornish hens are even more moist and flavorful when cooked over the coals, turning slowly on a rotisserie. On page 81 you will find specific directions for using the rotisserie. Below in Fig. 1 you see how the roast or poultry should balance evenly on the rotisserie rod for even cooking. Fig. 2 shows how the holding forks should be inserted securely to prevent the meat from slipping while roasting. Fig. 3 illustrates how the gray coals should be piled to the back of the grill with the drip pan directly under the grilling meat or poultry to prevent fat flare-ups that give a burned, rather than a charcoal taste to foods.

To Roast in a Kettle Grill

Arrange gray coals around drip pan, following Fig. 4 and place trussed poultry or tied roast, fat-side up, on a meat rack or directly on grill, directly over drip pan. Cover kettle and arrange vents, following manufacturer's directions and recipe cooking times.

To Truss Poultry

Secure neck skin with a metal skewer; push tail into cavity and secure with a metal skewer. Press wings against side of breast and wrap a long piece of cotton twine twice around bird and tie securely; loop a second long piece of twine several times around drumsticks and tie. If poultry is stuffed, be sure to secure opening with small metal skewers and lace closed with twine.

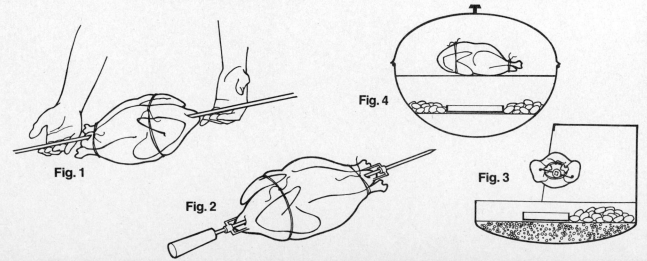

Fig. 1

Fig. 2

Fig. 4

Fig. 3

how to feed a crowd

Make Your Own Big Grill

When you have a large crowd to feed and a recipe that calls for a large, covered grill, finding such a grill doesn't have to be a difficult or expensive venture. The covered cooker shown below was easy and inexpensive to make with a 55-gallon steel drum and a few tools. A grill like this is perfect for cooking large quantities of meat for a crowd, as in JAY'S BARBECUE FOR A CROWD on page 104, and there's still room inside for a pan of barbecue sauce to simmer and absorb the flavor while the meat grills.

To make a barrel grill like the one illustrated on this page, start with a 55-gallon steel drum and cut it in half lengthwise, as shown. Strong steel hinges are bolted to the inside on each half along the back so the lid can open and close. As a safety measure, a strong brace could be added to either one or both sides to hold the lid in its open position. Bolt a steel drawer pull to the front of the top half as shown.

Weld a frame of steel pipe or angle iron to fit around the bottom half approximately four inches below the rim. (**Note:** As an alternate to welding, use angle irons and bolt the pieces together.) Weld pipe or angle iron lengths to the sides of the frame to form legs, as shown. Place the barrel inside the frame and weld at corners to reinforce, if desired, or leave the pieces separate for easier transporting. Protect the barrel by painting the outside with a paint designed for hot surfaces.

If desired, add a cutting board to one side by bracing a sturdy piece of lumber to the grill with large shelf brackets or a length of steel pipe underneath. The shelf is also useful for keeping your cooking utensils and serving dishes close at hand.

The actual grill surface is formed with old refrigerator or oven shelves you can often pick up at a garage sale or tag sale or from a junk shop or trade-in department of a major appliance distributor. The wire shelves can either be large enough to sit on top of the open barrel, or better still, in different sizes that are small enough to fit inside the barrel at different heights from the coals.

Using a mineral base insulation material (available at lumber stores), fill the bottom of the barrel to raise the fire bed to within five inches of the grilling grates. Place one layer of coals to cover the fire base when cooking for a large crowd; use less for cooking smaller quantities of meat.

Helpful Tools to Have

• Empty 46-ounce juice cans are great for holding basting sauces or glazes, or melting butter or margarine and heating butterscotch or chocolate sauce for dessert toppings.

• Plastic dish pans are great serving dishes for salads, slaws or an assortment of fresh fruits. Big plastic garbage pails are great for chilling beverages with plenty of ice.

• Ice cream scoops help to serve potato or rice salad, hot vegetables or pudding desserts quickly and evenly, while soup ladles serve punch, stews and bean dishes easily.

• Large colorful baskets are ideal for non-breakable holders for potato chips, raw relishes, cookies or fruits.

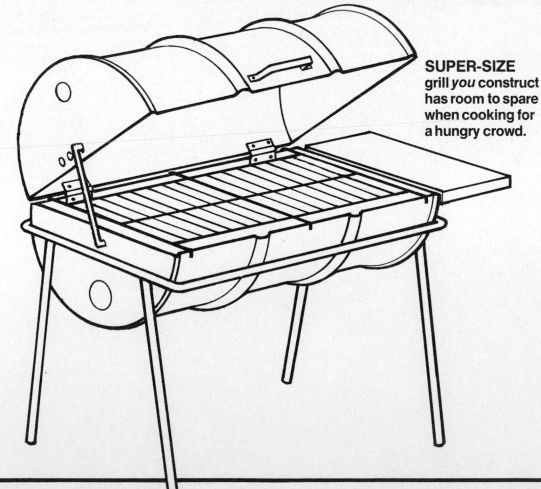

SUPER-SIZE grill *you* construct has room to spare when cooking for a hungry crowd.

CUSTOM-SIZE drip pans made from aluminum foil end fat flare-ups for good.

Fig. 1

Fig. 2

Fig. 3

Fig. 4

HINGED basket lets you grill whole fish with ease.

Fig. 5

Fig. 6

Fig. 7

foil to the aid of a barbecue

WRAPPED properly, food packets hold juices in while keeping air out.

Fig. 8

Fig. 9

Fig. 10

Fig. 11

COAT HANGERS and aluminum foil are used for a makeshift grill cover.

Outdoor cooking is supposed to be fun, not work for the patio chef, so here are a few ways that pieces of heavy-duty aluminum foil can come to the aid of the barbecue.

How to Make a Drip Pan

Fat flare-ups will be a problem of the past when you place a custom-size drip pan under the meat you are kettle-grilling or roasting on the rotisserie. Tear off three 24-inch pieces of 18-inch-wide heavy-duty aluminum foil. Fold in half to make a double thickness (Fig. 1). Turn up the edges 2-inches on each side and press edges firmly together to form mitered corners (Fig. 2). Press mitered corners inwards, towards pan sides, to make a firm pan (Fig. 3).**(Note:** This will give you an 8 x 14-inch drip pan. If this is not the right size for your needs, begin with the size pan you will need and then add 4 inches to both the length and the width and then double the measurement of the width.)

A Hinged Wire Basket

While a hinged wire basket (Fig. 4) is not exactly a barbecue utensil you make with foil, it is a very helpful tool to have when you want to grill small fish, such as trout, or a delicate hamburger mixture, or even a steak that seems a little too difficult to handle with tongs.

The Drugstore Wrap

This is the only way to wrap and seal packets of food for the barbecue or meats for the freezer. In either case, it is essential that the seal be tight, so that the cooking food juices won't spill over into the fire and the air won't get into the meat and cause freezer-burn. Start by placing the item to be wrapped in the center of a piece of heavy-duty aluminum foil that is large enough to go around the food and allow for folding at the top and sides. Bring the two long sides up and over the food and fold them over about 1-inch (Fig. 5). Make a crease the entire length; make one more tight fold to bring the wrapping down to the level of the food surface. Press out the air toward the ends (Fig. 6). Fold the ends up and over, pressing out air and shaping to contours of food (Fig. 7).

Coat Hanger Hood for Grill

This can turn any inexpensive grill into a covered barbecue. Clip the hooks off 8 or 9 coat hangers with a wire cutter and straighten the remaining wire with pliers (Fig. 8). Form 2 or more lengths of wire into a firm circle the same size as the circumference of your grill; bind ends together with picture wire (Fig. 9). Loop the remaining wires at the top, umbrella-fashion, and attach to the base circle, using pliers to twist the ends. Fasten all together with picture wire (Fig. 10). Cover with heavy-duty aluminum foil, leaving foil a little loose at the top for draft (Fig. 11).

Other Quick Tricks with Foil

• Line the firebox of your grill with a sheet of heavy-duty aluminum foil. This way spills, spatter and flames will not touch the bottom of the grill. Food cooks faster over foil because it reflects heat. Also, the clean-up will be much easier because all you have to do is gather the ends of the foil into a ball and then place into a metal container.

• For foil-grilled potatoes: Scrub potatoes and rub with butter or margarine and wrap in a double thickness of heavy-duty aluminum foil. Then place directly over coals, turning 2 or 3 times during cooking with long metal tongs, 50 minutes, or until tender when pierced with a two-tined fork. Split foil and potato and serve.

• For patio popcorn: Place ¼ cup popcorn, 2 tablespoons vegetable oil and 1 teaspoon seasoned salt in the center of an 18-inch square of heavy-duty aluminum foil; form into a loose bundle and wire to a long, sturdy stick; toss over coals until corn stops popping.

STEAKS, CHOPS & BUTTERS

To many people, a thick, juicy steak or chop is the quintessence of a memorable barbecue; this collection of recipes proves their luscious versatility. Try marinating them first, for extra flavor, or stir-fry thin slices for an Oriental treat. An assortment of savory butters will transform anything you grill to gourmet fare.

THREE *IS* A CROWD
Very romantic! Begin with Gorgonzola Salad
(page 90), then share T-Bone Steak for Two
(page 51). Grand finale: Champagne Strawberries
and spirited Coffee Italiano (page 98).
Don't forget wine!

T-BONE STEAK FOR TWO

Choose T-bone steak when you want an extra-special meal. Shown in a Pacific Beach home, on page 49.

Grill for 20 to 40 minutes.
Makes 2 servings.

- 1 T-bone or Porterhouse steak, cut 2-inches thick (about 3 pounds)
- ⅓ cup vegetable oil
- ¼ cup dry red wine
- 3 shallots, chopped
  OR: 1 small onion, chopped (¼ cup)
  Butter or margarine
  Salt and freshly ground pepper
  Duchesse Potatoes (recipe follows)
  Butter Braised Vegetables (recipe follows)
  Béarnaise Sauce (recipe, page 115)

1. Trim excess fat from steak; score remaining fat at 1-inch intervals. Place in a large shallow utility dish. Combine oil, red wine and shallots or onion in a 1-cup measure; pour over steak. Allow to marinate at room temperature at least 2 hours. Remove steak from marinade.
2. Build a medium fire, or set gas or electric grill to medium, following manufacturer's directions.
3. Grill, 5 inches from heat, 10 minutes on each side for rare, 15 minutes on each side for medium and 20 minutes on each side for well done.
4. Place on carving board; spread with a pat of butter or margarine and season with salt and pepper. Allow steak to "rest" 10 minutes. To carve steak, remove the T-bone and slice across, so that each slice will have back tenderloin and piece of loin strip. Serve with DUCHESSE POTATOES, BUTTER BRAISED VEGETABLES AND BÉARNAISE SAUCE.

DUCHESSE POTATOES: Makes 2 servings. Pare and quarter 2 large potatoes. Cook in salted boiling water in a small saucepan 15 minutes, or just until tender; drain water. Toss potatoes in pan 3 minutes to fluff and dry. Add 2 tablespoons butter or margarine, ¼ teaspoon salt, freshly ground pepper, 2 tablespoons milk and 1 egg and bring to boiling; remove from heat. Mash potatoes with a potato masher, then beat with electric mixer at low speed until very smooth. Fit a pastry tube with a large star tip; fill with potato mixture; shape into

Summer weekends are perfect for barbecue brunches. Brunch Chop Platter—an updated Victorian classic—stars lamb and pork chops grilled to eye-opening perfection.

two potato nests on a small cookie sheet. Sprinkle with grated Parmesan cheese. Bake in very hot oven (450°) 10 minutes, or until golden.
CHEF'S TIP: Potato nests can be made ahead of time and refrigerated on cookie sheet. Bake 15 to 20 minutes, or until golden.

BUTTER BRAISED VEGETABLES: Makes 2 servings. Wash and trim 1 pound fresh asparagus, or thaw 1 package (10 ounces) frozen asparagus spears. Wipe ¼ pound fresh mushrooms with a damp paper towel and cut into thin slices. Heat 3 tablespoons butter or margarine in a large skillet; add asparagus spears and mushroom slices in separate piles; sprinkle with 1 teaspoon sugar, 1 teaspoon mixed Italian herbs, crumbled, and ¼ cup water. Bring to boiling; lower heat; steam 10 minutes, or until asparagus is crisply-tender. Season with salt and freshly ground pepper, just before serving.

BRUNCH CHOP PLATTER

Grilled lamb and pork chops are sure to be the talk of your next patio brunch. Shown in La Jolla, California, on page 50.

Grill for 30 to 40 minutes.
Makes 6 servings.

- 6 rib lamb chops
- 6 thin pork chops
- ⅓ cup vegetable oil
- ⅓ cup cider vinegar
- 1 teaspoon salt
- ¼ teaspoon pepper
- 1 teaspoon pumpkin pie spice
- 3 large apples
- ¼ cup apple jelly

1. Build a medium fire, or set gas or electric grill to medium, following manufacturer's directions.
2. Trim excess fat from chops and score remaining fat around edges at 1-inch intervals.
3. Combine oil, vinegar, salt, pepper and pumpkin pie spice in a small bowl. Brush generously over chops.
4. Grill chops, 4 inches from heat, basting and turning several times, 30 to 40 minutes, or until chops are done as you like.
5. Core apples and cut into ¾-inch-thick slices. Stir apple jelly into remaining chop baste and pour into a metal cup; heat over grill until bubbly. Brush over apple slices.
6. Grill apple slices, basting and turning several times, 10 minutes.
7. Arrange chops and apple slices on a heated platter and garnish with lettuce. Serve with your favorite pancakes and fruit syrups.
CHEF'S TIP: Barbecue brunches are a great way for families with young children to entertain. For the kids, why not grill some turkey hot dogs?

DILLED LAMB CHOPS

Thick shoulder lamb chops are at their best when just grilled to rare—the French way.

Grill for 20 to 40 minutes.
Makes 6 servings.

- 6 shoulder lamb chops, 1½-inches thick (about 3 pounds)
- 4 shallots, chopped
  OR: ¼ cup sliced green onions
- 1 clove garlic, minced
- 3 tablespoons peanut or vegetable oil
- 3 tablespoons cider vinegar
- 1 tablespoon chopped dill
  OR: 1 teaspoon dillweed
- 1 teaspoon salt
- ¼ teaspoon freshly ground pepper

1. Trim excess fat from chops; score remaining fat at 1-inch intervals. Place in a large utility dish.
2. Combine shallots or green onions, garlic, oil, vinegar, dill, salt and pepper in a cup; pour over chops; turn chops to cover second side; cover dish with plastic wrap. Marinate at room temperature 1 hour.
3. Build a medium fire, or set electric or gas grill to medium, following manufacturer's directions.
4. Grill, 4 inches from heat, 10 minutes per side for rare, 15 minutes per side for medium, and 20 minutes per side for well done, or until lamb is done as you like it. Serve with boiled potatoes and herbed zucchini slices.

STEAK AU POIVRE

Cracked pepper covers steak in this French classic.

Grill for 30 to 50 minutes.
Makes 6 to 8 servings.

- 1 sirloin steak, 2-inches thick (about 4 pounds)
- 2 to 4 tablespoons cracked pepper
  Salt
- ¼ cup brandy

1. Wipe steak with damp paper towels. Press half of the pepper into each side of the steak, using your fingers and heel of hand. Let stand at room temperature for 1 hour.
2. Build a medium fire, or set electric or gas grill on medium, following manufacturer's directions.
3. Grill, 5 inches from heat 15 minutes per side for rare, 20 minutes per side for medium, and 25 minutes per side for well done, or until steak is done as you like it. Sprinkle with salt when removed from heat.
4. Transfer the steak to a hot sizzle-platter. Warm brandy in a small metal saucepan with flameproof handle over grill; pour over steak; ignite, using fireplace matches. Serve with French fried potatoes and grilled tomato halves.

SUGGESTED TIME & TEMPERATURE CHART
FOR
ROTISSERIE COOKING ROASTS ON CHARCOAL GRILLS

CUT OF MEAT	RARE	MEDIUM	WELL DONE
Beef Rib	135° F.	145° F.	160° F.
6½ pounds	2 - 2¼ hrs.	2½ - 3 hrs.	3½ hrs.
Rib Eye Roast	2-2½ hrs.	2½ - 3 hrs.	3½ - 4 hrs.
6 pounds			
Tenderloin Roast	45 min.	1 hr.	1¼ - 1½ hrs.
4 pounds			
Beef Round Tip	2-2½ hrs.	2½ - 3 hrs.	3 - 4 hrs.
Roast			
6 pounds			
Eye Round Roast	1¾ - 2 hrs.	2½ hrs.	3 hrs.
6 pounds			
Cross Rib Pot	2½ hrs.	3- 3½ hrs.	4 - 4½ hrs.
Roast (bone-less), or			
Rump Roast			

Important!! The above grilling times may differ according to amount of coals used, weather conditions, type of grill: Thus, we recommend these times be used only as a guide. For optimum results, use a meat thermometer, and remove roast when thermometer reaches 10° below desired doneness.

CHABLIS ROUND STEAK

Wine is a great meat tenderizer as well as a flavor additive for barbecued meats.

Grill for 15 to 30 minutes.
Makes 6 servings.

- **1 round steak, cut 1-inch thick (about 2½ pounds)**
- **1 cup Chablis wine**
- **½ cup lemon juice**
- **½ cup vegetable oil**
- **2 teaspoons salt**
- **1 teaspoon leaf oregano, crumbled**
- **2 cloves garlic, crushed**

1. Trim excess fat from steak; score remaining fat at 1-inch intervals; score surface of meat in diamond pattern, ⅛-inch deep with a sharp knife; place meat in a large plastic bag or shallow glass baking dish.
2. Combine wine, lemon juice, oil, salt, oregano and garlic in a small saucepan; bring to boiling; lower heat; simmer 10 minutes; cool marinade.
3. Pour marinade over steak; seal in plastic bag or cover dish with plastic wrap. Refrigerate 6 to 8 hours, or overnight. Let steak stand at room temperature 1 hour before grilling. Remove steak from marinade and reserve marinade to baste steak.
4. Build a medium-hot fire, or set gas or electric grill to medium-high, following manufacturer's directions.
5. Grill steak, 3 inches from heat, 8 minutes for rare, 12 minutes for medium, and 15 minutes for well done; brush with reserved marinade; turn

steak with tongs; grill 7 minutes for rare, 12 minutes for medium, and 15 minutes for well done, or until steak is done as you like it.
6. Place on wooden carving board and allow to "rest" 10 minutes; cut into thick slices and serve with shoestring potatoes.

LAMB STEAK AU POIVRE

Try these steaks just cooked to rare for a truly Continental touch.

Grill for 10 to 18 minutes.
Makes 4 servings.

- **4 lamb steaks, cut ½-inch thick (about 2 pounds)**
- **Instant unseasoned meat tenderizer**
- **Seasoned salt**
- **Peppercorns**

1. Build a hot fire, or set electric or gas grill to high, following manufacturer's directions.
2. Moisten steaks and sprinkle with meat tenderizer, following label directions; sprinkle lightly with seasoned salt.
3. Crush peppercorns with a rolling pin. (Easy if you place the peppercorns in a plastic bag.) Press onto each side of steaks.
4. Grill, 6 inches from heat, turning once, 5 minutes per side for rare, 7 minutes per side for medium, or 9 minutes per side for well done, or until meat is done as you like.

BEER-BASTED HAM STEAK

Ready-to-cook ham makes quick and flavorful patio grilling.

Grill for 25 minutes.
Makes 6 servings.

- **1 center-cut ham steak, cut 1½ inches thick (about 2 pounds)**
- **½ cup firmly packed brown sugar**
- **⅓ cup beer or apple juice**
- **2 tablespoons prepared sharp mustard**
- **1 teaspoon pumpkin pie spice**

1. Trim excess fat from steak; score remaining fat at 1-inch intervals.
2. Build a medium fire, or set electric or gas grill to medium, following manufacturer's directions.
3. Grill, turning once, 15 minutes.
4. While ham steak grills, combine sugar, beer or apple juice, mustard and pumpkin pie spice in a small metal saucepan with a flameproof handle. Heat on grill, stirring several times, until bubbly-hot.
5. Baste ham with beer mixture; grill 5 minutes, turn and baste again; grill 5 minutes longer, or until well glazed. Serve with baked sweet potatoes and mustard pickle.

BRITISH BROILED BEEF

Rosemary is a favored herb when English chefs grill beef.

Grill for 30 to 50 minutes.
Makes 8 servings

- **1 blade-bone chuck steak, cut 2-inches thick (about 4 pounds)**
- **Vegetable oil**
- **2 tablespoons leaf rosemary, crumbled**
- **Instant unseasoned meat tenderizer**
- **2 tablespoons butter or margarine**
- **2 tablespoons chopped chives**

1. Remove steak from refrigerator 1 hour before grilling. Trim off any excess fat, then score remaining fat edge at 1-inch intervals so meat will lie flat on grill.
2. Brush steak all over with vegetable oil; pat rosemary onto both sides. Let stand at room temperature 1 hour.
3. Build a medium fire, or set gas or electric grill to medium, following manufacturer's directions.
4. Moisten steak and sprinkle with tenderizer, following label directions.
5. Grill, 5 inches from heat, 15 minutes per side for rare, 20 minutes per side for medium, 25 minutes per side for well done, or until steak is done as you like it.
6. Remove to a cutting board or large platter; dot with butter or margarine; let melt into steak; sprinkle with chives. Slice steak ¼-inch thick and serve with home-fried potatoes.

CARIOCA ROUND STEAK

South-of-the-border barbecue chefs like to add a touch of coffee to beef bastes.

Grill for 12 to 22 minutes.
Makes 6 servings.

- **1 top round steak, cut 1½-inches thick (about 3 pounds)**
- **2 tablespoons instant coffee powder**
- **⅓ cup hot water**
- **1 can (6 ounces) frozen concentrate for orange juice, thawed**
- **2 tablespoons instant minced onion**
- **1 tablespoon lemon juice**
- **1 teaspoon salt**
- **¼ teaspoon ground cloves**
- **⅛ teaspoon bottled red pepper seasoning**

1. Trim excess fat from steak; score remaining fat around edge at 1-inch intervals; place in a large plastic bag or a shallow glass baking dish.
2. Dissolve coffee in hot water; combine with concentrated orange juice, instant onion, lemon juice, salt, cloves and red pepper seasoning in a small bowl; pour over steak, coating evenly.
3. Seal plastic bag or cover dish with plastic wrap. Refrigerate at least 4 hours, or overnight. Let stand 1 hour at room temperature. Remove from marinade and reserve.
4. Build a medium-hot fire, or set gas or electric grill to medium-high, following manufacturer's directions.
5. Grill steak, 5 inches from heat, 6 minutes for rare, 9 minutes for medium, and 11 minutes for well done; brush with reserved marinade; turn with tongs.
6. Grill 6 minutes for rare, 9 minutes for medium, and 11 minutes for well done, or until steak is done as you like it. Serve with an avocado and orange salad and toasted corn bread.

SAKE STEAK

Japanese rice wine, or dry Sherry adds an Oriental touch to grilled steak.

Grill for 6 to 10 minutes.
Makes 6 servings

- **6 individual chuck or round steaks, cut 1-inch thick (about 3 pounds)**
- **2 tablespoons sesame seeds**
- **½ cup teriyaki or soy sauce**
- **⅓ cup sake or dry Sherry**
- **1 bunch green onions, sliced**
- **1 clove garlic, minced**
- **1 teaspoon shredded ginger root OR: ½ teaspoon ground ginger**

1. Place steaks in a single layer in a large glass utility dish.
2. Sprinkle sesame seeds on a small skillet. Heat, stirring constantly, until sesame seeds turn golden brown. Remove from heat. Stir in teriyaki or soy sauce, sake or Sherry, green onions,

garlic and ginger; pour over steaks; cover dish with plastic wrap.
3. Marinate at room temperature 2 hours, or refrigerate from 4 hours to overnight, removing steak from refrigerator at least 1 hour before grilling. Remove steaks from marinade and reserve.
4. Build a medium fire, or set gas or electric grill to medium, following manufacturer's directions.
5. Grill, 4 inches from heat, 3 minutes per side for rare, 4 minutes per side for medium, or 5 minutes per side for well done, or until steaks are done as you like them. Serve with heated reserved marinade.

GRILLED LAMB CHOPS

Shoulder lamb chops are an economical, yet tender, barbecue meat.

Grill for 20 minutes.
Makes 6 servings.

- **6 shoulder lamb chops, cut 1-inch thick (about 2 pounds)**
- **Salt and pepper**
- **¼ cup (½ stick) butter or margarine, softened**
- **½ teaspoon leaf thyme, crumbled**

1. Trim excess fat from chops; score remaining fat around chops to prevent curling; let stand at room temperature for 1 hour.
2. Build a medium-hot fire, or set electric or gas grill to medium-high, following manufacturer's directions.
3. Grill chops, 4 inches from heat, 10 minutes; turn and grill 10 minutes longer. Sprinkle salt and pepper over chops and place on a heated platter.
4. Combine butter or margarine and thyme in a small bowl; spread over chops and serve with SPRINGTIME POTATO SALAD (recipe, page 122).

ALL-AMERICAN GRILLED STEAK

A super-thick cut of beef, grilled to a turn and topped with mushrooms and onions.

Grill for 30 to 50 minutes.
Makes 8 servings.

- **1 sirloin steak, cut 2-inches thick (about 4 pounds)**
- **⅔ cup olive or vegetable oil**
- **⅓ cup wine or cider vinegar**
- **1 teaspoon salt**
- **1 teaspoon leaf thyme, crumbled**
- **¼ teaspoon pepper**
- **2 large onions, peeled, sliced and separated into rings**
- **3 tablespoons butter or margarine**
- **1 pound mushrooms, sliced**

1. Remove steak from refrigerator 2 hours before cooking. Trim off any excess fat, then score remaining fat edge at 1-inch intervals so meat will lie flat on grill. Place steak in a shallow glass utility dish.
2. Mix oil, vinegar, salt, thyme and pepper in a small bowl; pour over steak; cover with plastic wrap. Let stand at room temperature 2 hours.
3. Build a medium fire, or set gas or electric grill to medium, following manufacturer's directions.
4. Grill, 5 inches from heat, brushing several times with marinade from pan, 15 minutes on each side for rare, 20 minutes on each side for medium and 25 minutes per side for well done, or until steak is done as you like it.
5. While meat cooks, sauté onion rings in butter or margarine until soft in a large metal skillet with a flameproof handle on grill; stir in mushrooms; sauté 5 minutes; season with salt and pepper; keep hot.
6. Remove steak to a cutting board or large platter; spoon onions and mushrooms around edge. Slice steak ¼-inch thick.

STEAK GRILLING CHART

THICKNESS	DONENESS	DISTANCE	TIME PER SIDE
1 inch	rare	2-3 inches	8 to 10 min.
	medium		10 to 13 min.
	well-done		12 to 15 min.
2 inches	rare	4-5 inches	15 to 18 min.
	medium		20 to 23 min.
	well-done		25 to 28 min.

FROZEN STEAK GRILLING CHART

THICKNESS	DONENESS	DISTANCE	TIME PER SIDE
¾ inch	rare	4 inches	8 to 10 min.
	medium		10 to 12 min.
	well-done		12 to 14 min.
1¼ inches	rare	5 inches	11 to 13 min.
	medium		13 to 15 min.
	well-done		15 to 18 min.
1½ inches	rare	6 inches	15 to 18 min.
	medium		18 to 20 min.
	well-done		23 to 25 min.

GOURMET GRILLED STEAKS

The tender muscle of a chuck makes individual steaks with more flavor than filet mignon and they're certainly less costly.

Grill for 6 to 10 minutes.
Makes 6 servings.

- 6 **individual chuck steaks, cut ½-inch thick (abut 3 pounds)**
  Instant unseasoned meat tenderizer
- ⅓ **cup butter or margarine**
- ¼ **cup chopped parsley**
- 2 **tablespoons finely chopped chives**
- 1 **teaspoon dry mustard**
- 2 **tablespoons bottled gravy coloring**
  Vegetable oil

1. Cut a slit about 3-inches wide and 2-inches deep in one side of each steak to form a pocket for stuffing. Moisten steaks and sprinkle with tenderizer, following label directions.
2. Blend butter or margarine, parsley, chives and mustard in a small bowl; spread inside pockets in steaks, dividing evenly. Brush steaks with gravy coloring.
3. Build a hot fire, or set gas or electric grill to high, following manufacturer's directions.
4. Grill, 4 inches from heat, 3 minutes per side for rare, 4 minutes per side for medium, or 5 minutes per side for well done, or until steaks are done as you like them. Serve on toasted split rolls with sautéed sliced mushrooms.

BELMONT STEAKS

Thick ground beef steaks are served with a tangy tomato-orange sauce.

Grill for 10 to 20 minutes.
Makes 4 servings.

- 1½ **pounds ground beef**
- 2 **tablespoons finely chopped green pepper**
- 2 **tablespoons finely chopped chives**
- 2 **tablespoons finely chopped parsley**
- 1 **teaspoon salt**
- ½ **teaspoon paprika**
- ¼ **teaspoon pepper**
- 2 **tablespoons all purpose flour**
  Vegetable oil
- ¼ **cup (½ stick) butter or margarine**
- ½ **cup chili sauce**
- ¼ **cup orange juice**
- 1 **teaspoon sugar**
- 1 **tablespoon lemon juice**
- 1 **teaspoon prepared mustard**
  Few drops bottled red pepper seasoning

1. Build a medium-hot fire, or set gas or electric grill to medium-high, following manufacturer's directions.
2. Combine ground beef, green pepper, chives, parsley, salt, paprika and pepper in a medium-size bowl; mix

lightly, just until blended. Shape into 4 patties about 1-inch thick. Dust with flour, then brush each with oil.
3. Grill, 4 inches from heat, 5 to 10 minutes on each side, or until beef is done as you like it.
4. While meat grills, melt butter or margarine in a small metal saucepan with a flameproof handle on grill; add chili sauce, orange juice, sugar, lemon juice, mustard and red pepper seasoning; heat just to boiling.
5. Place steaks on a heated serving platter; pour hot sauce over. Serve with French fried potatoes.

STUFFED FLANK STEAK

Can't find flank steak? Have the butcher "butterfly" a top round steak for this recipe.

Grill for 1 hour.

- 1 **flank steak (about 2 pounds)**
  OR: 1 top round steak (about 2 pounds)
- 4 **slices bacon, diced**
- 1 **medium-size onion, chopped (½ cup)**
- 4 **slices white bread, cubed**
- 3 **hard-cooked eggs, shelled and chopped**
- ½ **cup chopped stuffed green olives**
- ½ **cup vegetable or peanut oil**
- 2 **tablespoons bottled steak sauce**
- 1 **teaspoon seasoned salt**
- ¼ **teaspoon seasoned pepper**

1. Ask your meatman to split flank steak "butterfly fashion", or follow directions on page 32. Pound steak slightly with a mallet or rolling pin to make evenly thin.
2. Sauté bacon until crisp in a large skillet; remove with a slotted spoon and drain on paper towels. Stir onion into drippings in same pan; sauté until soft. Stir in bread cubes, eggs, olives and bacon; toss lightly until moist.
3. Lay steak flat on countertop; brush with part of the vegetable oil; spread stuffing over steak to within 1 inch of edges.
4. Starting at a long side of steak, roll up tightly, tucking in any loose stuffing; tie every 2 inches with strong white string.
5. Build a medium fire in a kettle grill, arranging coals around a foil drip pan, following directions on page 45, or set gas or electric grill to medium, following manufacturer's directions.
6. Grill, 6 inches from heat with cover on grill, 30 minutes.
7. Mix remaining oil, steak sauce, seasoned salt and pepper in a small cup; brush part over steak roll.
8. Continue grilling, brushing several times with oil mixture, 30 minutes, or until meat is tender.
9. Remove roll to a cutting board or large platter; snip off strings. Carve roll into 1-inch-thick slices. Serve with baked potatoes and avocado salad.

STEAK UNDER FOIL

Hearty chunks of round steak bubble in a mushroom-vegetable sauce sealed in packets of aluminum foil.

Grill for 1 hour, 30 minutes.
Makes 6 servings.

- 1 **round steak, cut ¾-inch thick (about 2½ pounds)**
- ¼ **cup all purpose flour**
- 1 **teaspoon salt**
- 1 **teaspoon paprika**
- ¼ **teaspoon pepper**
- 1 **can condensed cream of mushroom soup**
- 1 **package (10 ounces) frozen mixed vegetables, thawed**
- ⅓ **cup dry white wine**
- 1 **teaspoon leaf basil, crumbled**

1. Cut steak into 6 serving-size pieces. Combine flour, salt, paprika and pepper in a plastic bag; add beef pieces and shake to coat evenly.
2. Combine soup, mixed vegetables, wine and basil in a small bowl.
3. Tear six 18x12-inch sheets of heavy-duty aluminum foil. Place a portion of beef in center of each foil sheet; spoon soup mixture over, dividing evenly. Wrap foil packets, following directions on page 47.
4. Build a medium fire, or set gas or electric grill to medium, following manufacturer's directions.
5. Grill packets, 4 inches from heat, turning, 1 hour, 30 minutes.

BEEF INDONESIA

Cumin and coriander add a touch of the exotic to hearty beef kabobs.

Grill 15 to 30 minutes.
Makes 4 servings.

- 1 **chuck beef or top round steak, cut 1½-inches thick (about 2½ pounds)**
  Instant unseasoned meat tenderizer
- ½ **cup soy sauce**
- ½ **cup lemon juice**
- 2 **tablespoons brown sugar**
- 2 **teaspoons ground coriander**
- 2 **teaspoons ground cumin**
- 1½ **teaspoons salt**
- 1 **teaspoon pepper**
- 1 **large onion, chopped (1 cup)**
- 8 **small white onions, peeled**

1. Trim all fat from steak; cut into 1½-inch cubes; pierce all over with a two-tined fork. Place in a shallow dish. Sprinkle meat with tenderizer.
2. Mix soy sauce, lemon juice, brown sugar, coriander, cumin, salt, pepper and chopped onion in a small bowl; pour over meat. Cover dish with plastic wrap; refrigerate, turning several times, 2 hours.
3. Parboil small onions in boiling salted water in a small saucepan 5 minutes; drain.

4. Build a medium fire, or set electric or gas grill to medium, following manufacturer's directions.
5. Remove meat from marinade, reserving marinade. Thread cubes of meat and small onions alternately onto 4 long skewers.
6. Grill, 6 inches from heat, turning and brushing several times with reserved marinade, 15 minutes for rare, 22 minutes for medium and 30 minutes for well done, or until meat is done as you like it. Serve with rice pilaf and marinated cucumbers, tomatoes and onions, if you wish.

EAST-WEST STIR-FRY STEAK

Flank steak strips are stir-fried in a wok over the grill with crisp vegetables.

Grill for 15 minutes.
Makes 6 servings.

    1   flank steak (about 2 pounds)
    4   large carrots
    4   stalks celery
    ½   pound fresh mushrooms
    1   bunch green onions
    1   package (6 ounces) frozen
         Chinese snow peas, thawed
    4   tablespoons peanut or vegetable
         oil
    1   clove garlic, minced
    ½   cup beef broth
    1   tablespoon cornstarch
    2   tablespoons dry Sherry or white
         wine
    ¼   cup soy sauce

1. Freeze flank steak for about 30 minutes to firm-up; cut meat into long diagonal slices. Place in a pile on a large tray.
2. Slice carrots, celery, mushrooms and green onions and place in separate piles on tray; place snow peas in a pile on tray.
3. Build a hot fire, or set electric or gas grill to high, following manufacturer's directions.
4. Heat 2 tablespoons of the oil with garlic in wok, 3 inches from heat; add beef strips, part at a time, and stir-fry just until beef is done as you like it; remove to tray with slotted spoon.
5. Add remaining 2 tablespoons oil; add carrots, celery, mushrooms, green onions and snow peas; stir-fry until vegetables are coated with oil.
6. Pour broth into pan; cover wok; steam 5 minutes, or until vegetables are crisply tender; return meat to wok.
7. Combine cornstarch, Sherry and soy sauce in a cup; stir into wok. Cook, stirring constantly, until sauce thickens and bubbles 3 minutes. Serve over Chinese noodles or vermicelli.
CHEF'S TIP: This is a great dish to make when you are not sure of the dining time. The steak and vegetables can be prepared ahead and the tray covered with plastic wrap. Chill in refrigerator until ready to cook.

FAR EASTERN BARBECUE

Peaches and oranges alternate with robust chunks of beef in a sweet-sour glaze.

Grill for 10 to 16 minutes.
Makes 6 servings.

    3   pounds top sirloin or chuck steak
    2   teaspoons salt
    1   cup mango chutney
    ½   cup catsup
    ½   cup freshly squeezed lemon juice
    1   tablespoon Worcestershire sauce
    2   large eating oranges
    2   fresh peaches

1. Trim beef and cut into 1½-inch cubes; sprinkle with salt; place in a large glass or ceramic dish.
2. Combine mango chutney, catsup, lemon juice and Worcestershire sauce in container of an electric blender; cover and process on high 30 seconds, or until smooth; pour over beef; cover with plastic wrap; refrigerate 2 hours, or overnight.
3. Drain marinade from beef and reserve. Cut oranges and peaches into wedge-shaped pieces. Alternate beef, orange wedges and peach wedges on 12 long skewers.
4. Build a medium-hot fire, or set gas or electric grill to medium-high, following manufacturer's directions.
5. Grill, 4 inches from heat, basting and turning kabobs several times, 10 minutes for rare, 13 for medium and 16 for well done beef. Serve with tangy lemonade.

PARSLEY-BASTED STEAK

Tie a bunch of washed parsley and use instead of a brush to baste flank steak—fun and flavorful.

Grill for 10 to 18 minutes.
Makes 6 servings.

    1   cup tomato juice
    ¼   cup sliced green onion
    ¼   cup chopped green pepper
    ¼   cup chopped celery
    ¼   cup olive or vegetable oil
    1   tablespoon wine vinegar
    1 to 2 cloves garlic, minced
    1 to 3 teaspoons chili powder
    1   teaspoon salt
    1   flank steak (about 2 pounds)
         Unseasoned meat tenderizer
    1   bunch parsley

1. Combine tomato juice, green onion, green pepper, celery, olive oil, vinegar, garlic, chili powder and salt in a small saucepan. Bring to boiling; reduce heat; cover. Simmer 15 minutes; cool.
2. Sprinkle meat tenderizer on steak, following label directions. Place in a shallow glass utility dish and pour cooled marinade over meat. Marinate for 1 hour at room temperature.
3. Build a medium fire, or set electric or gas grill to medium, following manufacturer's directions.
4. Tie a large bunch of washed parsley with string. Pour marinade from steak into a bowl; add parsley to use as a brush.
5. Grill, 4 inches from heat, basting with reserved marinade 5 minutes per side for rare, 7 minutes per side for medium, and 9 minutes per side for well done, or until steak is done as you like it.
6. Carve on the diagonal into thin slices and serve with garlic bread and a Caesar salad.

CRUMB-COATED STEAK

Mustard adds tang and crumbs give crunch to this deliciously different steak.

Grill for 30 to 50 minutes.
Makes 8 servings.

    1   sirloin steak, cut 2-inches thick
         (about 4 pounds)
    ¼   cup prepared mustard
    2   large green peppers, sliced into
         rings and seeded
    2   large red peppers, sliced into
         rings and seeded
    2   tablespoons butter or margarine
    2   tablespoons vegetable oil
         Crumb Topping (recipe follows)

1. Trim off any excess fat from steak, then score remaining fat edge every inch so meat will lie flat on grill.
2. Spread steak with mustard; let stand at room temperature 1 hour to season.
3. Build a medium fire, or set electric or gas grill to medium, following manufacturer's directions.
4. Grill, 5 inches from heat, 15 minutes per side for rare, 20 minutes per side for medium and 25 minutes per side for well done, or until steak is done as you like. Remove from grill.
5. While meat cooks, sauté green and red pepper rings in butter or margarine until soft in a large metal skillet with flameproof handle on grill; keep hot.
6. Brush steak all over with vegetable oil; pat CRUMB TOPPING over top of meat; return to grill and heat just until crumbs are set.
7. Remove steak to a cutting board or large platter; place pepper rings around edge. Carve steak in ¼-inch-thick slices and serve with baked potatoes and marinated tomato slices, if you wish.

CRUMB TOPPING: Makes 3 cups. Place 6 slices white bread on a cookie sheet; toast in slow oven (300°) 30 minutes, or until dry, crisp and richly golden; cool. Crush with rolling pin. Heat ¼ cup olive or vegetable oil with 1 teaspoon crumbled mixed Italian herbs in a medium-size saucepan; add bread crumbs; toss to mix well.

NAPA VALLEY STEAK

Rosé wine sauce adds a gourmet touch to perfectly grilled steak.

Grill for 15 to 45 minutes
Makes 4 servings.

1 **sirloin steak, cut 1 to 2 inches thick (between 3 and 4 pounds)**
  Salt
  Pepper
  Rosé Sauce (recipe, page 114)

1. Build a medium-hot fire, or set electric or gas grill to medium-high, following manufacturer's directions.
2. Grill steak, for time and distance shown in chart on page 53; sprinkle with salt and freshly ground pepper. Turn steak with tongs.
3. Grill on second side, following chart; transfer to heated serving platter. Let "rest" 10 minutes before carving, and serve with ROSÉ SAUCE and a big Caesar Salad.

STEAK SORRENTO

Fresh tomato sauce adds an Italian flavor to your grilled beef.

Grill for 25 to 35 minutes.
Makes 6 servings.

1 **round steak, cut 1½-inches thick (about 3½ pounds)**
1 **envelope instant meat marinade**
⅔ **cup dry red wine**
3 **medium-size onions, chopped (1½ cups)**
1 **clove garlic, minced**
3 **tablespoons olive or vegetable oil**
4 **medium-size tomatoes, peeled and chopped**
1 **teaspoon salt**
1 **teaspoon leaf marjoram, crumbled**
¼ **teaspoon seasoned pepper**

1. Remove steak from refrigerator 1 hour before cooking. Trim off any excess fat, then score remaining fat edge at 1-inch intervals so meat will lie flat on grill. Place steak in a shallow glass utility dish.
2. Mix meat marinade and wine in a 1-cup measure; pour over steak; pierce steak all over with a fork. Let stand at room temperature to season. Remove meat from marinade, reserving marinade.
3. Build a medium fire, or set electric or gas grill to medium, following manufacturer's directions.
4. Grill, 5 inches from heat, 12 minutes on each side for rare, 15 minutes on each side for medium and 18 minutes on each side for well done, or until steak is done as you like it.
5. While meat cooks, sauté onions and garlic in oil until soft in a large metal skillet with a flameproof handle on grill; stir in tomatoes, salt, marjoram and pepper. Simmer 10 minutes; stir in reserved marinade.

6. Remove steak to a cutting board or large platter; carve into ¼-inch-thick slices; arrange slices in sauce. Serve from skillet with hot linguine and buttered zucchini.

STEAK NAPOLI

Skillet-grilled steaks on the barbecue are quick to cook—so great when you're entertaining a crowd.

Grill for 10 minutes
Makes 8 servings.

8 **individual boneless steaks (round or chuck), cut 1-inch thick**
  Instant unseasoned meat tenderizer
1 **clove garlic, halved**
2 **tablespoons olive or vegetable oil**
1 **cup bottled barbecue sauce**
½ **cup shredded mozzarella cheese**

1. Moisten steaks and sprinkle with tenderizer, following label directions.
2. Build a hot fire, or set electric or gas grill to high, following manufacturer's directions.
3. Rub the inside of a large skillet with flameproof handle with garlic clove; add oil.
4. Heat oil in pan, 4 inches from heat; add steaks; brown 3 to 5 minutes per side; add barbecue sauce. Cook 1 minute, or until bubbly-hot; sprinkle with grated cheese. Heat just until cheese starts to melt. Serve on toasted split rolls with an antipasto salad.

STEAK GRANADA

Sherry adds a Spanish touch to steak.

Grill for 30 to 50 minutes.
Makes 8 servings.

1 **chuck steak, cut 2-inches thick (about 3 pounds)**
1 **medium-size onion, chopped (½ cup)**
¼ **cup vegetable oil**
1 **tablespoon curry powder**
½ **cup dry Sherry**
½ **teaspoon ground ginger**
  Instant unseasoned meat tenderizer

1. Remove steak from refrigerator 1 hour before grilling. Trim off any excess fat; score remaining fat edge at 1-inch intervals so meat will lie flat on grill. Place steak in a shallow glass utility dish.
2. Sauté onion in vegetable oil until soft in a medium-size skillet; stir in curry powder; cook 1 minute; remove from heat. Stir in Sherry and ginger; pour over steak; cover with plastic wrap. Let stand at room temperature, turning several times, 1 hour.
3. Build a medium fire, or set electric or gas grill to medium, following manufacturer's directions.

4. Remove steak from marinade; reserve marinade. Sprinkle with tenderizer, following label directions.
5. Grill, 6 inches from heat, brushing several times with marinade, 15 minutes per side for rare, 20 minutes per side for medium and 25 minutes per side for well done, or until steak is done as you like it.
6. Remove to a cutting board or large platter. Carve into ¼-inch-thick slices and serve with polenta and sautéed red and green pepper rings.

STEAK 'N' APPLE ROLLS

Spicy applesauce makes a deliciously different topping for beef.

Grill for 8 minutes.
Makes 6 servings

6 **cubed beef steaks (about 1½ pounds)**
1 **jar or can (1 pound) applesauce**
2 **teaspoons Worcestershire sauce**
2 **teaspoons lemon juice**
1 **teaspoon ground cinnamon**
½ **teaspoon salt**
6 **Kaiser rolls, split and toasted**

1. Let steaks stand at room temperature for at least 30 minutes.
2. Build a hot fire, or set gas or electric grill to high, following manufacturer's directions.
3. Combine applesauce, Worcestershire sauce, lemon juice, cinnamon and salt in a small metal saucepan with flameproof handle; stir to blend. Heat over grill while cooking steaks.
4. Grill steaks, 3 inches from heat, 4 minutes; season with salt and pepper; turn with tongs; grill 4 minutes longer, or until steaks are done as you like.
5. Place steaks on toasted Kaiser rolls and top with spicy applesauce. Serve with tossed salad.

CHUCK WAGON STEAKS

Chuck steaks are an economical, as well as flavorful, cut for barbecuing.

Grill for 8 to 15 minutes.
Makes 6 servings.

2 **beef blade steaks cut ¾-inch thick (about 3 pounds)**
1 **cup catsup**
1 **medium-size onion, chopped (½ cup)**
⅓ **cup cider vinegar**
2 **tablespoons light brown sugar**
2 **teaspoons salt**
1 **clove garlic, crushed**
1 **bay leaf**
  Few drops bottled red pepper seasoning

1. Trim excess fat from steaks; score remaining fat around edges at 1-inch intervals; place in a large plastic bag or a shallow glass baking dish.
2. Combine catsup, onion, vinegar,

sugar, salt, garlic, bay leaf and red pepper seasoning in a small saucepan; bring to boiling; simmer 5 minutes; cool to lukewarm.

3. Pour over steaks, coating evenly; seal plastic bag or cover dish with plastic wrap. Refrigerate at least 4 hours, or overnight; let stand at room temperature for 1 hour. Remove from marinade, reserving marinade.

4. Build a medium-hot fire, or set electric or gas grill to medium-high, following manufacturer's directions.

5. Grill steaks, 3 inches from heat, 4 minutes for rare, 6 minutes for medium, and 8 minutes for well done; brush with reserved marinade; turn with tongs.

6. Grill 4 minutes for rare, 6 minutes for medium, and 8 minutes for well done, or until steak is done as you like it. Serve with baked beans.

SPICY PORK CHOPS

Choose thick, meaty chops to grill, then glaze in a clove-mustard sauce.

Grill for 50 minutes.
Makes 6 servings.

---

12 loin pork chops, cut 1-inch thick
 1 cup orange marmalade
⅓ cup bottled smoke-flavored barbecue sauce
¼ cup light corn syrup
 1 tablespoon prepared mustard
 1 teaspoon ground cloves

1. Build a medium fire, or set gas or electric grill to medium, following manufacturer's directions.

2. Trim excess fat from chops; score remaining fat at 1-inch intervals.

3. Grill, 6 inches from heat, turning several times, 30 minutes.

4. Combine marmalade, barbecue sauce, corn syrup, mustard and cloves in a small metal saucepan with a flameproof handle. Heat over grill until bubbly. Brush sauce generously on chops.

5. Grill, turning and brushing several times with remaining sauce, 20 minutes, or until chops are tender and richly glazed. Serve with spiced pear halves and buttered green beans.

FLORENTINE GRILLED STEAK

Oregano and garlic give a special flavor.

Grill for 16 to 30 minutes.
Makes 4 servings.

---

 1 porterhouse or sirloin steak, cut 1½-inches thick (about 3 pounds)
½ cup olive or vegetable oil
¼ cup red wine vinegar
¼ cup chopped parsley
 1 clove garlic, minced
 2 teaspoons leaf oregano, crumbled
   Salt and freshly ground pepper

1. Trim fat around edge, then score remaining fat at 1-inch intervals to keep steak from curling while grilling. Place steak in a large shallow glass or ceramic dish.

2. Combine oil, vinegar, parsley, garlic and oregano in a cup; pour and spread over steak. Allow steak to marinate at least 1 hour at room temperature, turning once.

3. Build a very hot fire, or set gas or electric grill to high, following manufacturer's directions.

4. Grill, 3 inches from heat, 8 minutes for rare, 12 minutes for medium and 15 minutes for well done; turn steak with tongs and brush with remaining marinade; grill 8 to 15 minutes longer, or until steak is done as you like it. Place on heated carving platter and sprinkle with salt and pepper; allow to "rest" 5 minutes before carving. Serve with hot Italian bread and MARINATED MUSHROOMS (recipe, page 88), if you wish.

CHEF'S TIP: A center chuck steak can be substituted for porterhouse or sirloin steak in this recipe. Sprinkle with unseasoned meat tenderizer, following label directions.

CAMPERS' SUPPER

Make up these pork and sweet potato foil packets before you start and carry them in a thermal container.

Grill for 1 hour.
Makes 4 servings.

---

 4 thick rib or loin pork chops
 2 large sweet potatoes, parboiled
 1 medium-size onion
 2 large tart apples
 2 teaspoons salt
½ teaspoon leaf sage, crumbled
¼ teaspoon pepper
¼ cup pancake syrup

1. Trim excess fat from chops. Brown chops on both sides in a large skillet. Place each chop in the center of a heavy-duty aluminum foil square.

2. Peel and slice potatoes; place potatoes over chops. Peel and slice onion and place over potatoes. Quarter and core apples. Cut into thin wedges and arrange over onion slices. Combine salt, sage and pepper in a small cup; sprinkle over apples; drizzle pancake syrup over top.

3. Wrap and seal foil packets, following directions on page 47. Pack into an ice chest or other portable thermal container.

4. Build a medium fire, or set gas or electric grill to medium, following manufacturer's directions.

5. Grill, 4 inches from heat, turning packets several times, 1 hour, or until pork is tender when pierced with a two-tined fork. Serve with celery and cucumber sticks and iced tea.

MAITRE D'HÔTEL BUTTER

Lemon juice and herbs in butter are a classic topping for grilled beef or lamb.

Makes ⅔ cup.

½ cup (1 stick) butter or margarine, softened
 2 tablespoons finely chopped parsley
 2 tablespoons finely chopped chives
 2 tablespoons lemon juice

1. Blend butter or margarine, parsley and chives in a small bowl. Add lemon juice, a little at a time, and beat well.

2. Turn butter mixture out onto wax paper; shape into a 2-inch roll. Wrap tightly and refrigerate until firm. Cut into slices and serve on meat.

Suggested Variations:

CARAWAY BUTTER—Omit chives and add ½ teaspoon caraway seeds, crushed.

CHIVE BUTTER—Omit parsley.

ANCHOVY BUTTER—Omit herbs. Add 2 anchovy fillets, rinsed and mashed.

HORSERADISH BUTTER—Omit chives. Add 3 tablespoons prepared horseradish.

LEMON BUTTER—Add 1 teaspoon grated lemon rind.

MUSTARD BUTTER—Omit herbs. Add 1 tablespoon prepared mustard.

BLUE-CHEESE BUTTER

Serve on grilled burgers to raise them to the gourmet class.

Makes ¾ cup.

½ cup blue or Roquefort cheese
¼ cup (½ stick) butter or margarine, softened
 2 tablespoons Sherry, white wine, brandy or cream

1. Remove cheese and butter or margarine from refrigerator. Crumble the cheese. Allow both to stand at room temperature about 1 hour.

2. Mash cheese with butter in a small bowl with a fork. Stir in Sherry, wine, brandy or cream and mix to a smooth paste. Turn into a bowl. Serve at room temperature on beef or chicken breasts.

Suggested Variations:

ALMOND-CHEESE BUTTER—Add ¼ cup ground almonds.

GREEN ONION BUTTER—Add 1 green onion, finely chopped.

(Recipes continued on page 112.)

It's so easy to add delicious character to any cut of beef, poultry or seafood with the simple addition of a marinade, glaze or baste. From mild and delicate to pungent and spicy, here are quick and easy recipes that can work flavor magic and earn you a reputation as an exciting barbecue chef.

POUR ON THE FLAVOR
and improve the taste of any barbecue: (left to right) Plum Chutney Glaze—onion, green pepper and orange add tang; Tomato-Beer Baste— excellent on steaks and hot dogs; Lemon-Pineapple Glaze—the perfect combo with chicken or fish. Recipes begin on page 97.

MARINADES & GLAZES

POULTRY SEAFOOD

All-time barbecue favorites, poultry and seafood, take on exciting personalities with the simple addition of a baste or marinade. Here are fast and flavorful recipes for the best barbecues ever!

TANTALIZING TRIO of barbecued meals are, from the left, Sausalito Scampi, Tiburon Chicken and Chioppino. Recipes, page 63.

PHOTOGRAPHED AT BAKER BEACH, SAN FRANCISCO, CALIFORNIA

SAUSALITO SCAMPI

Sunset over San Francisco Bay is the perfect setting for our new twist on a classic dish. Shown on page 60.

Grill for 10 minutes.
Makes 6 servings.

 3 **whole chicken breasts**
 1 **pound fresh or frozen shrimp**
 ⅓ **cup butter or margarine**
 ⅓ **cup olive or vegetable oil**
 2 **cloves garlic, minced**
 1 **teaspoon salt**
   Freshly ground pepper
   Juice of 1 lemon
   Freshly chopped parsley

1. Build a hot fire, or set gas or electric grill to high, following manufacturer's directions.
2. Remove chicken meat from bones; cut into 1-inch pieces. Shell and devein shrimp.
3. Heat butter or margarine and oil in a large metal skillet with a flameproof handle on grill, 4 inches from heat.
4. Add garlic and sauté 2 minutes; add chicken and cook, stirring constantly, until brown; push to one side; add shrimp and cook, stirring constantly, until shrimp turns pink; season with salt and pepper; sprinkle with lemon juice and top with chopped parsley. Cook 1 minute longer. Serve with a dry red wine.

CHICKEN NAPOLI

So simple to fix, you'll want to prepare a dramatic salad to accompany it.

Grill for 40 minutes.
Makes 8 servings.

 8 **whole chicken breasts, split**
   (about 12 ounces each)
 ½ **cup olive or vegetable oil**
 2 **envelopes (about 5 ounces each)**
   Italian salad dressing mix
 ¼ **cup lime juice**

1. Place chicken breasts in a large glass utility dish. Combine oil, Italian salad dressing mix and lime juice in a cup; pour over chicken. Marinate 1 hour.
2. Build a medium fire or set electric or gas grill to medium, following manufacturer's directions.
3. Grill, 6 inches from heat, basting with marinade and turning several times, 40 minutes, or until chicken is richly glazed.

Baker Beach Grilled Fish, paired with a summertime salad, is the perfect "catch" at a seaside picnic. Tastes twice as good cooked over the coals in the great outdoors. Recipe is on this page.

DEVILED CHICKEN LEGS

Finger food is fun outdoor eating and these chicken legs are finger-lickin' good.

Grill for 40 minutes.
Makes 4 servings.

 12 **chicken legs (about 2 pounds)**
 ¼ **cup vegetable oil**
 1 **teaspoon salt**
 ¼ **teaspoon cayenne pepper**
   Tomato-Soy Sauce (recipe page 115)

1. Rub chicken legs with a mixture of oil, salt and cayenne.
2. Build a medium fire, or set electric or gas grill to medium, following label directions.
3. Grill, 4 inches from heat, turning several times, 20 minutes. Brush generously with TOMATO-SOY SAUCE. Grill 20 minutes longer, or until well glazed. Serve with French fried potatoes sprinkled with seasoned salt.

CHIOPPINO

All the foods of the sea—crab, shrimp, clams and bass—simmer in a tomato-clam broth. Shown with San Francisco in the background on page 61.

Grill for 45 minutes.
Makes 6 servings.

 1 **large onion, chopped (1 cup)**
 1 **clove garlic, minced**
 3 **tablespoons olive or vegetable oil**
 1 **can (2 pounds, 2 ounces) Italian tomatoes in tomato purée**
 2 **tablespoons chopped fresh basil**
   OR: 2 teaspoons leaf basil, crumbled
 2 **teaspoons salt**
 1 **bay leaf**
 2 **bottles (8 ounces each) clam broth**
 1 **Dungeness crab, cracked and cleaned (about 3 pounds)**
   OR: 2 pounds fresh or frozen King crab
 2 **dozen clams**
 1 **pound shrimp or prawns**
 1 **pound bass fillets**
   OR: 1 package (1 pound) frozen halibut

1. Build a medium fire, or set gas or electric grill to medium, following manufacturer's directions.
2. Sauté onion and garlic in oil in a large, heavy metal pot, 6 inches from heat, until soft. Stir in tomatoes in tomato purée, basil, salt, bay leaf and clam broth; simmer 30 minutes.
3. While sauce simmers, cut crab into 3-inch pieces; scrub clams; shell and devein shrimp or prawns; cut bass or halibut into small pieces.
4. Add fish and shellfish to kettle, being sure sauce covers seafood completely. Simmer 15 minutes. Serve in deep soup bowls with sourdough bread and a hearty red California wine, if you wish.

BAKER BEACH GRILLED FISH

What could be better than the deep-sea flavor of a fish you catch and grill right on the beach? Shown at Baker Beach in San Francisco, on page 62.

Grill for 40 minutes.
Makes 8 servings.

 1 **whole rock cod, sea bass, haddock or blue fish, dressed and boned (about 5 pounds)**
 1 **cup lemon juice**
 1 **cup vegetable oil**
 2 **teaspoons salt**
 2 **teaspoons dillweed**
 ¼ **teaspoon pepper**

1. Build a medium fire, or set gas or electric grill to medium, following manufacturer's directions.
2. Wash fish well in cold water; pat dry with paper towels.
3. Combine lemon juice, vegetable oil, salt, dillweed and pepper in a bowl; brush fish generously with mixture. Place fish in a fish grilling rack, if you have one.
4. Grill, 6 inches from heat, turning and basting several times, 40 minutes, or until fish flakes easily. Place on a heated fish platter and garnish with flat-leafed spinach and scored lemon slices and serve with a crisp salad, if you wish.

TIBURON CHICKEN

Chicken roasted to perfection with a pungent baste. Shown on the deck of Slinkey's El Monte in Sausalito, page 61.

Rotis 1 hour, 30 minutes.
Makes 4 servings.

 1 **roasting chicken (about 5 pounds)**
   Tomato-Beer Baste (recipe, page 114)
   Buttered Beans Italiano (recipe, page 118)

1. Build a hot fire in a grill with a rotisserie, positioning coals around drip pan, following directions on page 45, or set electric or gas grill to high, following manufacturer's directions.
2. Wash chicken and pat dry with paper towels. Truss, following directions on page 45. Insert spit through center of chicken, lengthwise, and test for balance by rotating spit on hands. Fasten chicken with holding forks, so it won't slip while roasting.
3. Brush chicken generously with TOMATO-BEER BASTE. Place rotisserie rod into position, following manufacturer's directions, with drip pan in proper position.
4. Rotis, basting every 20 minutes, 1 hour, 30 minutes, or until chicken legs move easily. Allow to "rest" 20 minutes on a heated serving platter. Serve with BUTTERED BEANS ITALIANO and a full Italian red wine.

CURRIED SWORDFISH

Simmer swordfish steaks in a skillet over your barbecue for a gourmet treat.

Grill for 15 minutes.
Makes 4 servings.

1½ pounds swordfish
  OR: 2 packages (12 ounces each)
    frozen halibut steaks
2 cups water
1 teaspoon salt
¼ teaspoon pepper
1 tablespoon lemon juice
1 bay leaf
1 tablespoon vegetable oil
1 tablespoon chopped onion
1 tablespoon chopped green
    pepper
1 to 2 teaspoons curry powder
1 tablespoon cornstarch

1. Build a medium-hot fire or set electric or gas grill to medium-high, following manufacturer's directions.
2. Cut fish into 4 pieces. Heat water to boiling in a large metal skillet with a flameproof handle; add fish, salt, pepper, lemon juice and bay leaf; simmer 15 minutes on grill, or until fish flakes easily; remove fish to a metal au gratin dish; cover with aluminum foil and push to back of grill to keep warm.
3. Strain cooking liquid into a 2-cup measure. Add oil to skillet; sauté onion and green pepper 2 minutes; add curry powder and cook 1 minute.
4. Pour 1 cup of the strained cooking liquid into skillet and bring to boiling. Combine cornstarch and 2 tablespoons cold water in a cup; stir into skillet. Cook, stirring constantly, until sauce thickens and bubbles 3 minutes; pour over fish and garnish with chopped green onion and parsley. Serve with hot rice.

GRILLED SWORDFISH

Thick swordfish or halibut steaks are bathed in a lemon and dill baste.

Grill for 20 minutes.
Makes 4 servings.

4 swordfish or halibut steaks, cut 1-
    inch thick (about 2 pounds)
¼ cup vegetable oil
2 tablespoons lemon juice
1 tablespoon chopped fresh dill
  OR: 1 teaspoon dillweed
1 tablespoon paprika
1 teaspoon salt
¼ teaspoon pepper

1. Place swordfish or halibut in a single layer in a large glass utility dish.
2. Combine oil, lemon juice, dill, paprika, salt and pepper in a cup; pour over steaks; cover with plastic wrap. Allow to stand at room temperature 1 hour.
3. Build a medium fire, or set electric or gas grill to medium, following label

directions.
4. Grill, 4 inches from heat, basting with marinade and turning once, 20 minutes, or until fish flakes easily with a fork. Serve with parslied boiled potatoes and buttered peas.

FRENCH GRILLED SALMON

Dry vermouth and thyme give a Continental aroma to fresh salmon steaks.

Grill for 12 to 15 minutes.
Makes 6 servings.

6 salmon steaks, cut ¾-inch thick
    (about 3 pounds)
½ cup dry vermouth or white wine
¼ cup peanut or vegetable oil
2 tablespoons chopped chives
1 teaspoon leaf thyme, crumbled
1 teaspoon salt
¼ teaspoon freshly ground pepper

1. Place salmon steaks in a large glass utility dish.
2. Combine vermouth or wine, oil, chives, thyme, salt and pepper in a cup; pour over salmon; cover dish with plastic wrap. Allow to marinate at room temperature 1 hour.
3. Build a medium fire, or set gas or electric grill to medium, following label directions.
4. Grill, 4 inches from heat, turning and basting with marinade, 12 to 15 minutes, or until fish flakes easily with a fork. Serve with crusty French bread and a romaine salad with a lemon and oil dressing.

CHICKEN FOR THE GANG

Here is a simple, yet finger-lickin' good way to grill chicken for a crowd.

Grill for 1 hour, 15 minutes.
Makes 12 servings.

6 broiler-fryers, split
    (2½ pounds each)
2 cups vegetable oil
½ cup lime or lemon juice
2 tablespoons salt
1 teaspoon seasoned pepper
1 teaspoon leaf rosemary, crumbled
1 teaspoon leaf sage, crumbled
¼ cup honey

1. Wash chicken halves, then dry. Mix oil, lime or lemon juice, salt, seasoned pepper, rosemary and sage in a small bowl; brush part over chicken.
2. Build a medium fire in a large grill, or set electric or gas grill to medium, following manufacturer's directions.
3. Grill, 6 inches from heat, turning every 10 minutes and basting with oil mixture, 1 hour. Add honey to remaining oil mixture. Baste and turn chicken halves 15 minutes, or until well glazed. Serve with potato salad and tomato slices.

GRILLED CLAM BAKE

First dip the steamed clams in melted butter, then drink the rich clam broth.

Grill for 10 minutes.
Makes 4 servings.

4 dozen small clams
1 cup water
1 clove garlic, minced
  Chopped parsley
½ cup (1 stick) butter or margarine

1. Build a medium fire, or set electric or gas grill to medium, following label directions.
2. Scrub clams with a stiff brush under cold running water. Place in a large metal kettle with flameproof handles. Add water, garlic and parsley; cover kettle.
3. Grill, 4 inches from heat, until water steams, then time 5 minutes, or until shells open.
4. Serve clams to dip in melted butter, then strain broth through a triple layer of cheese cloth into cups. Serve with chowder crackers.

FISHERMAN'S SOUP

Start with a flavorful stock and add the fish you catch in a stream—or supermarket.

Grill for 45 minutes.
Makes 6 servings

¼ cup olive or vegetable oil
1 large leek, washed well and
    chopped
  OR: 1 large onion, chopped (1 cup)
1 clove garlic, minced
1 can (2 pounds, 3 ounces) Italian
    tomatoes
2 tablespoons chopped fresh basil
  OR: 2 teaspoons leaf basil,
    crumbled
2 teaspoons salt
2 bottles (8 ounces) clam juice
2 dozen clams
  OR: 1 can (10 ounces) whole clams
2 pounds fresh or frozen king crab,
    in the shell
1 package (1 pound) frozen cod,
    haddock or turbot fillet

1. Build a medium-hot fire, or set gas or electric grill to medium-high, following manufacturer's directions.
2. Heat oil in a large metal kettle on grill; add leeks or onion and garlic and sauté until soft; add tomatoes, basil, salt and clam juice; bring to boiling; cover and push kettle to side of grill; simmer 15 minutes.
3. While sauce simmers, scrub clams; cut frozen fish into 1-inch cubes.
4. Add shell fish and fish to kettle and simmer 15 minutes. Serve in deep soup bowls with chunks of crusty French bread and a romaine salad, if you wish.

CHEF'S TIP: If fresh fish fillets are used, add to kettle, just for the last 5 minutes of cooking.

TURKEY TERIYAKI

Turkey with an Oriental taste—what a great way to feed a crowd on a holiday.

Rotis for 3 hours.
Makes 12 servings.

- **1 fresh or frozen turkey, thawed (about 8 pounds)**
- **2 cups dry white wine**
- **½ cup peanut or vegetable oil**
- **½ cup soy sauce**
- **¼ cup lemon juice**
- **1 clove garlic, minced**
- **2 teaspoons salt**
- **½ teaspoon freshly ground pepper**

1. Truss turkey, following directions on page 45. Place turkey in a large plastic bag. Add wine, oil, soy sauce, lemon juice, garlic, salt and pepper. Tie bag and turn turkey in bag to coat evenly. Allow to marinate at room temperature 1 hour.
2. Build a slow fire in a grill with rotisserie, positioning coals around a foil drip pan, following directions for rotisserie cooking on page 45, or set gas or electric grill to low, following manufacturer's directions.
3. Insert spit through center of turkey, lengthwise, and test for balance by rotating spit on hands. Fasten turkey with holding pins; place rotisserie rod into position. Add 1 cup water to foil drip pan; cover grill.
4. Rotis, basting often with marinade, 3 hours, or until meat thermometer inserted in thickest part of thigh registers 180°. Serve with cranberry chutney.
Suggested Variations: For *TURKEY VERMOUTH,* substitute 2 cups dry vermouth and ½ cup bottled steak sauce for the white wine and soy sauce in this recipe.

SEASAME CHICKEN BREASTS

Toasted sesame seeds give a crunchy coating to delicate chicken breasts.

Grill for 45 minutes.
Makes 6 servings.

- **6 whole chicken breasts, split (about 10 ounces each)**
- **1 jar (about 1 ounce) sesame seeds**
- **½ cup dry white wine**
- **½ cup peanut or vegetable oil**
- **2 teaspoons lemon salt**
- **¼ teaspoon freshly ground pepper**

1. Place chicken breasts in a large glass utility dish.
2. Sprinkle sesame seeds in a large skillet. Heat, stirring often, until sesame seeds turn a golden brown; remove from heat; stir in wine, oil, lemon salt and pepper; spoon over chicken to coat. Allow to stand at room temperature while grill heats.
3. Build a medium fire, or set electric or gas grill to medium, following label directions.
4. Grill, 4 inches from heat, turning and basting with sesame mixture several times, 45 minutes, or until breasts are golden brown. Serve with spiced peaches and boiled rice.

CLAMS ITALIANO

Great as a first course or as part of a seafood barbecue along with a grilled whole fish.

Grill for 10 minutes.
Makes 24 appetizers.

- **2 dozen large clams**
- **1 cup marinara sauce**
- **2 tablespoons lemon juice**
- **2 tablespoons chopped Italian parsley**
- **2 tablespoons chopped green onion**
- **Butter or margarine**

1. Build a medium fire, or set gas or electric grill to medium, following label directions.
2. Scrub clams well with a stiff brush under cold running water.
3. Grill, 4 inches from heat, 5 minutes, or until shells open; remove with tongs to a wooden board; twist off top shell.
4. Combine marinara sauce and lemon juice in cup; spoon over clams in shell; sprinkle with parsley and green onion; dot with butter or margarine.
5. Grill 5 minutes, or until clams are bubbly-hot. Serve with cocktail forks or wooden picks.

GRILLED TROUT

Black olives and capers bubble in a buttery sauce to spoon over delicately grilled fish.

Grill for 15 minutes.
Makes 4 servings.

- **4 fresh or frozen rainbow trout (about 2 pounds)**
- **⅓ cup butter or margarine**
- **2 tablespoons lemon juice**
- **1 teaspoon salt**
- **1 teaspoon leaf rosemary, crumbled**
- **¼ teaspoon freshly ground pepper**
- **2 tablespoons drained capers**
- **2 tablespoons slivered black olives**

1. Build a hot fire, or set electric or gas grill to high, following manufacturer's directions.
2. Split trout; thaw frozen trout, if used; wipe with paper towels.
3. Melt butter or margarine in a small saucepan; add lemon juice, salt, rosemary and pepper; brush over trout to coat well.
4. Grill trout, 4 inches from heat, 8 minutes; turn with tongs and brush with butter mixture; grill 7 minutes longer, or until fish flakes easily. Place trout on a heated serving platter. Add capers and ripe olives to remaining butter mixture; spoon over trout.

HUNTING HILLS CHICKENS

Bottled Italian dressing is the basis of this quick and easy way to grill split chickens.

Grill for 40 minutes.
Makes 6 servings.

- **3 broiler-fryers, cut up (2½ pounds each)**
- **¾ cup bottled Italian dressing**
- **¼ cup (½ stick) butter or margarine**
- **¼ cup dry white wine**
- **1 teaspoon leaf tarragon, crumbled**

1. Remove excess fat from chickens and allow to stand at room temperature while grill heats.
2. Build a medium fire, or set gas or electric grill to medium, following manufacturer's directions.
3. Combine Italian dressing, butter or margarine, wine and tarragon in a small bowl. Brush mixture generously over chickens.
4. Grill, 6 inches from heat, turning and basting several times, 40 minutes, or until drumsticks move easily. Serve with baked potatoes and coleslaw.

SCALLOPS EN COQUILLE

You can use sea shells, metal au gratin dish or individual foil pans to serve this definitely French dish.

Grill for 20 minutes.
Makes 6 servings.

- **2 pounds fresh or frozen sea scallops**
- **⅔ cup dry white wine**
- **¼ cup peanut or vegetable oil**
- **¼ cup lemon juice**
- **2 tablespoons chopped chives**
- **1 teaspoon salt**
- **¼ teaspoon white pepper**
- **Buttered Bread Crumbs (recipe follows)**

1. Build a medium fire in a grill with a cover, or set electric or gas grill to medium, following label directions.
2. Thaw frozen scallops, if used. Divide scallops among 6 scallop shells, au gratin dishes or foil pans. Drizzle first with wine, then oil and lemon juice. Spinkle with chives, salt and pepper. Top with BUTTERED BREAD CRUMBS.
3. Grill, 6 inches from heat in covered grill, 20 minutes, or until crumbs are golden. Serve with buttered Italian green beans and yellow squash.

BUTTERED BREAD CRUMBS: Makes 2 cups. Place 4 slices white bread, quartered, 1 slice at a time in container of an electric blender. Process on high for 15 minutes; empty into a medium-size bowl. Drizzle 3 tablespoons melted butter or margarine over; add 1 teaspoon paprika. Toss with a fork until crumbs are evenly coated.

GINGERED CORNISH HENS

When Cornish hens are on special at the supermarket, try this recipe and get ready for delicious barbecue eating.

Grill for 1 hour, 30 minutes.
Makes 8 servings.

- 4 frozen rock Cornish hens, thawed (about 1½ pounds each)
- 1 medium-size onion, chopped (½ cup)
- 1 tablespoon grated fresh ginger OR: 1 teaspoon ground ginger
- ½ cup dry white wine
- ½ cup soy sauce

1. Remove giblets from hens and use in soup. Place hens in a large plastic bag in a glass utility dish.
2. Add onion, ginger, wine and soy sauce to hens; tie bag tightly; turn bag several times to coat hens evenly with marinade. Allow hens to marinate for 1 hour at room temperature.
3. Build a fire for kettle-roasting around aluminum foil pan, following directions on page 45, or set gas or electric grill to low, following manufacturer's directions.
4. Grill, 5 inches from heat with cover on grill, basting and turning hens several times, 1 hour, 30 minutes, or until hens are golden brown. Place hens on heated platter and allow to "rest" 10 minutes. Halve hens with poultry shears and serve over shredded lettuce; heat remaining marinade and spoon over. Serve with a dry white wine.

MINTED CHICKEN

Coriander, as well as mint, flavors chicken as the bird whirls around.

Rotis for 1 hour, 30 minutes.
Makes 4 servings.

- 1 broiler-fryer (about 3 pounds)
- 1 large onion, sliced
- ½ cup chopped mint
- 1 tablespoon chopped fresh coriander
- 2 tablespoons vegetable oil
- 1 clove garlic, minced
- 1 teaspoon salt
- ¼ teaspoon freshly ground pepper

1. Build a hot fire in a grill with rotisserie spit, following directions on page 81, or set electric or gas grill to high, following manufacturer's directions.
2. Wipe chicken with a damp paper towel; stuff with sliced onion, mint and coriander. Truss, following directions on page 45. Insert spit through center of chicken, and test for balance by rotating spit on hands. Fasten chicken with holding forks. Place rotisserie rod in position.
3. Combine oil, garlic, salt and pepper in a cup. Rub into chicken surface

to coat generously.
4. Rotis on spit 1 hour, 30 minutes, or until juices run clear and not pink when thigh is pierced with a two-tined fork. Serve with TUNISIAN RELISH.

ITALIAN BARBECUED CHICKEN

Start with bottled Italian salad dressing; add the punch of sharp mustard and you have delectable chicken in less than an hour.

Grill for 40 minutes.
Makes 8 servings.

- 2 broiler-fryers, quartered (about 2½ pounds each)
- 1 bottle (8 ounces) Italian salad dressing
- 2 green onions, chopped
- 2 tablespoons Dijon mustard
- ¼ cup dry white wine

1. Place chicken skin-side down in a large shallow glass dish.
2. Combine salad dressing, green onions, mustard and wine in a small bowl; pour over chicken; cover dish with plastic wrap.
3. Refrigerate and marinate at least 2 hours, or overnight.
4. Build a medium-hot fire or set electric or gas grill to medium-high, following label directions.
5. Grill, 6 inches from heat, turning every 10 minutes and basting with marinade 40 minutes, or until chicken is golden brown and pieces are tender when pierced with a two-tined fork. Serve with GRILLED CORN (recipe on page 120).

RAINBOW TROUT FRY

Sweet and tender trout are "farmed" in southern Idaho, so every fisherman can have fish for his campfire.

Grill for 15 minutes.
Makes 6 servings.

- 6 fresh or frozen rainbow trout (about 3 pounds)
- ½ pound sliced bacon
- 1 teaspoon salt
- ¼ teaspoon pepper
- ¼ cup all purpose flour

1. Split trout; thaw frozen fish, if used; wipe with paper towels.
2. Build a hot fire, or set electric or gas grill to high, following manufacturer's directions.
3. Fry bacon until crisp in a large metal skillet with a flameproof handle, 4 inches from heat; remove bacon and keep warm.
4. Season fish with salt and pepper; coat lightly with flour on wax paper.
5. Fry trout in bacon fat 8 minutes, or until golden; turn with pancake turner; fry 7 minutes longer, or until fish flakes easily. Serve with bacon and wedges of lemon.

SCALLOPED SCALLOPS

Sea scallops simmer in a tomato sauce with a toasty crumb topping.

Grill for 20 minutes.
Makes 4 servings.

- 1 pound fresh or frozen sea scallops, halved
- 3 tablespoons butter or margarine
- 1 clove garlic, minced
- ¼ cup dry white wine
- 2 large tomatoes, cored and chopped
- 3 tablespoons chopped parsley
- 1 teaspoon salt
- ¼ teaspoon freshly ground pepper
- 2 cups soft white bread crumbs, toasted (4 slices)
- 2 tablespoons melted butter or margarine
- 2 tablespoons grated Parmesan cheese

1. Build a medium fire, or set gas or electric grill to medium, following manufacturer's directions.
2. Cook scallops in the 3 tablespoons butter or margarine in a large metal skillet with a flameproof handle on grill, 4 inches from heat 5 minutes. Add garlic and wine and simmer 3 minutes.
3. Add tomatoes, parsley, salt and pepper; heat to bubbling; push skillet to side of grill; simmer 10 minutes.
4. Toss bread crumbs with the melted butter and cheese in a small bowl until evenly coated. Sprinkle on scallops. Serve immediately.

PUNGENT CHICKEN

Red pepper and garlic give character to charcoal-broiled chicken quarters.

Grill for 40 minutes.
Makes 8 servings.

- 2 broiler-fryers, quartered (about 2½ pounds each)
- ⅓ cup butter or margarine
- ¼ teaspoon dried red pepper, crushed
- ¼ cup olive or vegetable oil
- 1 small onion, chopped (¼ cup)
- 1 clove garlic, minced
- ¼ cup chopped parsley
- ¼ cup lemon juice
- 2 teaspoons salt

1. Wipe broiler-fryers with damp paper towels; remove any excess fat and reserve for frying. Let chicken stand at room temperature for at least 1 hour before grilling.
2. Melt butter or margarine with red pepper in a small saucepan; add oil, onion, garlic, parsley, lemon juice and salt; simmer 5 minutes. Brush generously over chicken pieces.
3. Build a medium-hot fire or set electric or gas grill to medium-high, following manufacturer's directions.
4. Grill, 6 inches from heat, turning

every 10 minutes and basting with butter mixture, 40 minutes, or until chicken is golden brown and pieces are tender when pierced with a two-tined fork.

GRILLED SALMON STEAKS

Serve on the 4th of July with creamed peas for a traditional barbecue, New England-style.

Grill for 15 minutes.
Makes 4 servings

  4 salmon steaks, 1-inch thick (about
       2 pounds)
  ⅓ cup butter or margarine, softened
  2 tablespoons chopped shallots or
       green onions
  1 clove garlic, minced
  1 tablespoon chopped dill
       OR: 1 teaspoon dillweed
  1 teaspoon salt
  ¼ teaspoon freshly ground pepper

1. Wipe salmon steaks well with paper towels.
2. Combine softened butter or margarine, shallots or green onions, garlic, dill, salt and pepper in a cup.
3. Build a medium-hot fire or set electric or gas grill to medium-high, following manufacturer's directions.
4. Spread a generous layer of butter mixture on salmon steaks.
5. Grill steaks, 4-inches from heat, 8 minutes; spread steaks with butter mixture; turn with pancake turner and grill 7 minutes longer, or until steaks are firm; place on heated serving platter; spread with remaining butter mixture and serve with lemon wedges.

PEACHY CHICKEN

Grilled chicken breasts and peach halves are gourmet-fare for any night in the week.

Grilled for 40 minutes.
Makes 4 servings.

  4 whole chicken breasts (about 12
       ounces each)
  1 can (1 pound) peach halves
  ¼ cup rum
  2 tablespoons bottled steak sauce

1. Arrange chicken, breast-side up, in a large glass utility dish. Drain peach syrup into a 2-cup measure and add rum and steak sauce. Pour mixture over chicken breasts and marinate at room temperature while grill heats.
2. Build a medium fire, or set gas or electric grill to medium, following manufacturer's directions.
3. Grill, 6 inches from heat, turning and basting with marinade, 30 minutes. Add peach halves to grill and baste with marinade. Grill 10 minutes longer, or until chicken and peaches are well glazed. Serve with rice salad and buttered whole green beans.

TANGY CHICKEN QUARTERS

First take a survey and find out who likes which part of the bird, then buy just the right number of those parts.

Grill for 1 hour.
Makes 6 servings.

  6 broiler-fryer chicken quarters
       (about 4½ pounds)
  ¼ cup (½ stick) butter or margarine,
       melted
  2 tablespoons grated onion
  ¾ cup catsup
  ¼ cup corn syrup
  2 tablespoons cider vinegar
  1 tablespoon prepared mustard
  1 tablespoon Worcestershire sauce

1. Build a medium fire, or set electric or gas grill to medium, following manufacturer's directions.
2. Brush chicken quarters with a mixture of melted butter or margarine and grated onion.
3. Grill, skin-side down, 6 inches from heat, turning pieces often, 40 minutes.
4. While chicken grills, combine catsup, corn syrup, vinegar, mustard and Worcestershire sauce in a small metal saucepan with a flameproof handle; heat on side of grill.
5. Brush chicken with barbecue sauce and grill, turning and basting several times, 20 minutes longer, or until chicken is tender and well glazed. Serve with plenty of paper napkins and tall glasses of minted iced tea.

HIBACHI SHRIMP

Grill shrimp in the shell in an Oriental sauce for the perfect party appetizer.

Grill for 10 minutes.
Makes 4 appetizer servings.

  1 pound fresh or frozen large raw
       shrimp in shell
  ½ cup peanut or vegetable oil
  ½ cup lemon juice
  1 teaspoon seasoned salt
  ½ teaspoon seasoned pepper
  ¼ cup soy sauce
  ¼ cup thinly sliced green onions

1. Wash shrimp under cold running water, thawing frozen shrimp, if used; remove feelers but do not shell; drain on paper towels. Place in a medium-size glass bowl.
2. Stir in oil, lemon juice, seasoned salt and pepper and soy sauce. Let stand at room temperature, turning several times, 30 minutes.
3. Build fire in a hibachi, following manufacturer's directions.
4. Lift shrimp from marinade with a slotted spoon, reserving marinade. Grill, turning once and brushing with more marinade, 10 minutes, or until shrimp turn pink.
5. Pour remaining marinade into a

small bowl; add green onions. Serve as dipping sauce. Let each guest shell his own shrimp and then dip in sauce. Pass warm moist towels for wiping hands after eating, the Oriental way.

GRILLED HALIBUT STEAKS

You can substitute thawed frozen haddock or turbot for the halibut in this recipe.

Grill for 15 minutes.
Makes 4 servings.

  4 halibut steaks, cut 1-inch thick
       (about 2 pounds)
       OR: 2 packages (1 pound each)
       frozen haddock or turbot fillets,
       thawed
  ⅓ cup vegetable oil
  ¼ cup lemon juice
  ¼ cup soy sauce
  1 teaspoon garlic salt
  ½ teaspoon ground ginger
  ¼ teaspoon pepper

1. Place halibut steaks in a large glass utility dish, or halve haddock or turbot fillets and place in dish.
2. Combine oil, lemon juice, soy sauce, garlic salt, ginger and pepper in a cup; pour over fish; cover dish with plastic wrap; let marinate at room temperature 1 hour.
3. Build a slow fire, or set gas or electric grill to low, following label directions.
4. Grill, 4 inches from heat, basting with marinade and turning over, 15 minutes, or until fish flakes easily with a fork. Serve with shoestring potatoes and pickled beets.

LOUISIANA GRILLED CHICKEN

Bottled red pepper seasoning and butter make a pungent, yet simple, basting sauce for your next chicken barbecue.

Grill for 45 minutes.
Makes 4 servings.

  1 broiler-fryer, cut up (about 3
       pounds)
       Louisiana Sauce (recipe, page 115)
  1 teaspoon salt
  1 teaspoon poultry seasoning
       Paprika

1. Build a medium-hot fire, or set electric or gas grill to medium-high, following label directions.
2. Brush chicken generously with LOUISIANA SAUCE.
3. Grill, 6 inches from heat, turning every 10 minutes and basting with sauce, 40 minutes, or until pieces are golden brown and tender when pierced with a two-tined fork.
4. Turn chicken pieces skin-side up, sprinkle with salt, poultry seasoning and paprika; baste with remaining LOUISIANA SAUCE. Grill 5 minutes longer. Serve with hot fluffed rice.

GRILLED ROCK LOBSTER TAILS

Make your barbecue an event with zesty lobster tails.

Grill for 8 minutes.
Makes 4 servings.

- **1 pound frozen South African rock lobster tails, thawed**
- **¼ cup (½ stick) butter or margarine, melted**
- **2 tablespoons lemon juice**
  Few drops bottled red pepper seasoning
  Salt and pepper

1. Build a medium-hot fire, or set electric or gas grill to medium-high, following manufacturer's directions.
2. Cut underside membrane around edge of lobster tails and remove membrane; bend tail backwards towards shell-side to crack. (This prevents lobster tails from curling.)
3. Combine butter or margarine, lemon juice and red pepper seasoning in a cup; brush generously over lobster tails.
4. Grill, 4 inches from heat, flesh-side down, 5 minutes; brush with butter mixture; turn with tongs; grill 3 minutes longer, or until meat turns white. Brush with remaining butter sauce and season with salt and pepper. Serve with peas and pine nuts.

COHO SALMON

"This game fish of the Great Lakes makes great salmon steak for grilling. You could substitute halibut or swordfish steaks, if you live in other parts of the country," suggests Joe Walsh, Detroit barbecue expert.

Grill for 20 minutes.
Makes 4 servings.

- **4 Coho salmon steaks, cut 1-inch thick (about 3 pounds)**
  OR: 4 halibut or swordfish steaks
- **1 medium-size onion, chopped (½ cup)**
- **1 small green pepper, halved, seeded and chopped**
- **1 clove garlic, minced**
- **¼ cup vegetable oil**
- **1 can (8 ounces) tomato sauce**
- **2 tablespoons lemon juice**
- **1 tablespoon Worcestershire sauce**
- **1 tablespoon sugar**
- **2 teaspoons salt**
- **¼ teaspoon coarsely ground pepper**
  Herbed Tomatoes (recipe follows)

1. Place salmon steaks in a large glass utility dish.
2. Sauté onion, green pepper and garlic in oil until soft in a medium-size skillet; stir in tomato sauce, lemon juice, Worcestershire sauce, sugar, salt and pepper. Simmer 5 minutes; cool slightly and pour over steaks. Allow to marinate while heating grill.
3. Build a medium fire, or set gas or electric grill to medium, following

manufacturer's directions.
4. Spray a hinged wire basket with Pam® or Mazola Spray-On® and arrange steaks in basket; close basket.
5. Grill, 4 inches from heat, basting with marinade, 10 minutes on each side. Serve with HERBED TOMATOES.

HERBED TOMATOES: Makes 4 servings. Wash and stem 1 basket (1 pint) cherry tomatoes. Place in a metal pan with 2 tablespoons melted butter or margarine, 1 teaspoon lemon salt and ½ teaspoon leaf basil, crumbled. Place pan on grill and cook tomatoes, stirring several times, 3 minutes, or just until skins burst.

CHINESE DUCK

Marinated duck cooks slow and moist in the new charcoal water smoker for an exotic barbecue treat.

Smoke 8 hours.
Makes 4 servings.

- **1 frozen duckling, thawed (about 5 pounds)**
- **¼ cup dry Sherry**
- **¼ cup soy sauce**
- **¼ cup honey**
- **¼ teaspoon freshly ground pepper**
- **1 teaspoon anise seeds**

1. Prepare charcoal water smoker, using hickory wood chips, following directions on page 81, or use your owner's manual.
2. Remove neck and giblets from thawed duck and use to make stock. Wash and pat duck dry with paper towels.
3. Combine Sherry, soy sauce, honey and pepper in a small bowl and brush generously over duck.
4. Fill water pan with boiling water and anise seeds. Place duck on cooking grill; cover smoker.
5. Smoke 8 hours, checking water pan after 5 hours, and adding more, if needed, or until leg moves easily.
6. Place duck on platter and allow to "rest" 15 minutes. Carve into thin slices and serve with boiled rice and duck sauce.

CURRANT GLAZED CHICKEN

Roast chicken is the perfect bird for your rotisserie since it's ready so quickly.

Rotis for 1 hour, 30 minutes.
Makes 4 servings.

- **2 cups ready-mix bread stuffing (from an 8-ounce bag)**
- **½ cup (1 stick) butter or margarine, melted**
- **1 cup frozen chopped onion**
- **⅔ cup water**
- **½ cup sliced almonds**
- **1 roasting chicken (about 4 pounds)**
- **½ cup currant jelly, melted**

1. Build a hot fire in grill with rotisserie spit, positioning coals around drip pan, following directions on page 45, or set gas or electric grill to hot, following manufacturer's directions.
2. Prepare stuffing mix with ⅓ cup of the melted butter or margarine, onion, water and almonds, following label directions.
3. Stuff chicken neck and body cavities lightly; skewer neck skin to body; tie legs tightly to tail.
4. Insert spit through center of chicken, lengthwise, and test for balance by rotating rod in hands. Fasten chicken with holding forks. Place rotisserie rod in position; brush with remaining melted butter or margarine.
5. Rotis, checking several times while turning, 1 hour, 15 minutes.
6. Brush with melted jelly. Rotis, brushing several times, 15 minutes longer, or until richly glazed. Remove to heated serving platter and serve with spinach salad.

STUFFED RED SNAPPER

This recipe would be delicious with trout, pollock, cod or whitefish as well.

Grill for 40 minutes.
Makes 6 servings

- **1 whole red snapper, cleaned and scaled (about 3 pounds)**
- **¼ cup (½ stick) butter or margarine**
- **1 small onion, chopped (¼ cup)**
- **1 package (10 ounces) fresh spinach, well washed, stemmed and finely chopped**
- **½ cup dry white wine**
- **2 cups soft white bread cubes (4 slices)**
- **1 teaspoon salt**
- **¼ teaspoon freshly ground pepper**
  Vegetable oil

1. Build a medium-hot fire, or set electric or gas grill to medium-high, following manufacturer's directions.
2. Wipe fish inside and out with paper towels.
3. Melt butter or margarine in a medium-size skillet; sauté onion until soft; add spinach and cook 2 minutes; add wine and bring to boiling; stir in bread cubes, salt and pepper until well blended.
4. Stuff fish with spinach mixture; close opening with wooden food picks laced with cord; rub skin well with oil. Place fish in a fish grilling rack, if you have one.
5. Grill, 4 inches from heat, 20 minutes, brushing several times with oil; turn grilling rack, or turn fish with 2 pancake turners; grill 20 minutes longer, or until fish is firm. Place on heated platter; serve with CUCUMBER-LETTUCE SALAD (page 122).

CHICKEN CACCIATORE

Take a kitchen favorite out to the grill for special outdoor cooking.

Grill for 40 minutes.
Makes 4 servings.

1 broiler-fryer, cut up (3 pounds)
¼ cup vegetable or olive oil
1 large onion, sliced
1 clove garlic, minced
2 large tomatoes, chopped
½ cup dry red wine
1 teaspoon salt
1 teaspoon leaf basil, crumbled
¼ teaspoon freshly ground pepper

1. Wipe chicken with damp paper towels; remove excess fat and reserve for frying. Rub chicken with part of oil. Let stand at room temperature.
2. Build a medium-hot fire or set electric or gas grill to medium-high, following manufacturer's directions.
3. Grill chicken pieces, 6 inches from heat, turning often, 20 minutes, or until beginning to brown.
4. While chicken grills; heat oil in a large metal skillet with a flameproof handle on grill; sauté onion and garlic until soft; add tomatoes, wine, salt, basil and pepper; heat to bubbling.
5. Add chicken pieces to skillet; spoon sauce over; cook, stirring often, 20 minutes, or until chicken is tender when pierced with a two-tined fork. Serve over fluffy hot rice, if you wish.

CALICO CHICKEN

Chicken quarters and colorful vegetables cook to moist tenderness in individual aluminum foil packets.

Grill for 1 hour, 15 minutes.
Makes 4 servings.

1 broiler-fryer, quartered
    (about 3 pounds)
1 can (12 ounces) whole kernel
    corn, drained
1 can (1 pound) tomatoes, drained
    and chopped
1 small onion, grated
1 large green pepper, cut into rings
2 tablespoons butter or margarine
1 teaspoon salt
¼ teaspoon seasoned pepper
¼ cup grated Parmesan cheese

1. Build a medium fire, or set electric or gas grill to medium, following manufacturer's directions.
2. Grill chicken quarters, skin side down, 4 inches from heat, 10 minutes; turn with tongs; grill 5 minutes longer.
3. While chicken browns, combine corn, tomatoes, onion and green pepper in a small bowl. Tear four 18-inch squares of heavy-duty aluminum foil and spoon vegetable mixture into center of foil squares, dividing evenly; dot vegetables with butter or margarine.
4. Place a chicken quarter in each foil

square; season with salt and pepper and sprinkle with Parmesan cheese. Wrap foil with drug store wrap, following directions on page 47.
5. Grill, 4 inches from heat, turning every 10 minutes, 1 hour, or until chicken is tender. Serve with fluffy mashed potatoes.

GRILLED THIGHS AND DRUMSTICKS

"This is great to prepare when you have children among your guests. Every kid loves finger food," says patio chef Joe Walsh.

Grill for 40 minutes.
Makes 8 servings.

2 packages (about 2 pounds each)
    chicken thighs and drumsticks
1 can (6 ounces) frozen lemon
    concentrate, thawed
½ cup soy sauce
¼ cup rum
2 teaspoons seasoned salt
1 teaspoon celery salt
½ teaspoon garlic powder
    Few drops bottled red pepper
    seasoning

1. Remove any bits of fat from thighs. Place chicken pieces in a large glass utility dish.
2. Combine lemon concentrate, soy sauce, rum, seasoned salt, celery salt, garlic powder and red pepper seasoning in a 2-cup measure; pour over chicken. Allow to marinate at room temperature while heating grill.
3. Build a medium fire, or set gas or electric grill to medium, following manufacturer's directions.
4. Grill, 6 inches from heat, turning and basting with marinade several times, 40 minutes, or until chicken is tender and well glazed. Serve with French fries and carrot and celery sticks for an all-finger-food menu.

ROAST TURKEY SEVILLE

Dry Sherry and garlic give turkey a Spanish touch. Leftover meat is extra tasty.

Grill for 2 hours.
Makes 10 servings.

1 frozen turkey breast, thawed
    (about 6 pounds)
¼ cup olive or vegetable oil
3 shallots, chopped
    OR: 1 small onion, chopped
    (¼ cup)
1 clove garlic, minced
½ cup dry Sherry or white wine
2 tablespoons salad seasoning for
    oil and vinegar dressing (see
    Cook's Guide)

1. Place thawed turkey breast in a large plastic bag in a large bowl.
2. Add oil, shallots or onion, garlic, Sherry or wine and salad seasoning to bag; tie bag securely; turn several

times to coat turkey evenly with marinade.
3. Marinate in refrigerator, turning several times, 4 hours, or overnight. Allow to stand at room temperature at least 1 hour before grilling.
4. Build fire for kettle-roasting around aluminum foil pan, following directions on page 45, or set gas or electric grill to low, following manufacturer's directions.
5. Grill, 5 inches from heat, basting often with marinade, 2 hours, or until turkey is golden brown. Place on heated serving platter and allow to "rest" 15 minutes before slicing. Serve with spiced cranberries and toasted corn bread.

SAVORY STUFFED TROUT

Individually stuffed and bacon-wrapped trout make great outdoor eating.

Grill for 15 minutes.
Makes 6 servings.

6 fresh or frozen rainbow trout
    (about 3 pounds)
1 cup sliced mushrooms
½ cup quartered cherry tomatoes
2 tablespoons chopped green
    pepper
1 tablespoon chopped celery
1 tablespoon chopped onion
1 clove garlic, minced
¼ teaspoon salt
¼ teaspoon leaf thyme, crumbled
    Dash pepper
6 slices bacon
⅓ cup butter or margarine

1. Split trout; thaw frozen trout, if used; wipe with paper towels.
2. Combine mushrooms, tomatoes, green pepper, celery, onion, garlic, salt, thyme and pepper in a small bowl; divide filling among trout; tie and wrap a slice of bacon around each trout, securing with wooden picks.
3. Build a hot fire, or set electric or gas grill to high, following manufacturer's directions.
4. Brush trout generously with melted butter or margarine.
5. Grill, 4 inches from heat, 8 minutes; brush with butter; turn with tongs, grill 7 minutes longer, or until fish flakes easily. Serve with crispy French fried potatoes and wedges of lemon, if you wish.
CHEF'S TIP: When grilling fish, thick fish steaks or fillets can be placed right on the grill. Smaller, serving-size fillets or small, whole fish, however, are best held firmly together during cooking in a hinged wire basket placed on the grill. Or, look for ones with feet that can be placed directly over the coals. Some baskets are even made fish-shaped; but whatever their shape, they can also hold hamburger patties and other easily-damaged foods during grilling. ∎

Casseroles, kabobs and other international dishes offer the perfect opportunity for imaginative barbecue chefs to create delectably different combinations of meat, seafood and vegetables. You'll find the recipes in this chapter, from exotic Smoked Turkey Orientale to Classic Lamb Shish Kabobs, to be the most delicious mingling of ingredients ever!

CROWD-PLEASING KABOBS
start with chunks of garden-fresh vegetables and juicy cubes of meat or seafood: (left to right) Prawn Kabobs; Sausage Kabobs; Napa Valley Beef Kabobs; Spanish Lamb Kabobs; Mustard Chicken Kabobs. Recipes start on page 75.

KABOBS & CASSEROLES

ARROZ CON MARISCOS, an internationally famous casserole, features a mouth-watering combination of seafood, ham and rice in a flavorful broth. Recipe appears on page 75.

ARROZ CON MARISCOS

California Dungeness crabs simmer with rice and ham in this San Francisco version of a Spanish classic. You can substitute King crab, shrimp or rock lobster tails for the Dungeness crab in this recipe. Shown on terrace in San Francisco, page 71.

Grill for 1 hour.
Makes 8 servings.

- ¼ cup olive or vegetable oil
- 1½ cups long grain rice
- 1 large onion, chopped
- 2 cloves garlic, minced
- 16 thin slices cooked ham
- 2 cans condensed chicken broth
- 1 cup water
- 2 teaspoons salt
- ¼ teaspoon pepper
- 1 tablespoon lemon rind
- 1 bay leaf
- 1 Dungeness crab, cleaned and cracked (about 3 pounds)
  OR: 3 pounds King crab legs in shell,
  1½ pounds fresh or frozen shrimp, shelled and deveined,
  8 small rock lobster tails, thawed and membrane removed
- 1 package (10 ounces) frozen peas, thawed
- 1 jar (4 ounces) pimento, diced

1. Build a medium fire in a kettle grill, or set electric or gas grill to medium, following manufacturer's directions.
2. Heat oil in a 12-cup shallow heavy saucepan with a flameproof handle or casserole on grill or on range.
3. Sprinkle raw rice over oil and brown, stirring often, until grains turn toasty-brown; remove with slotted spoon and reserve.
4. Sauté onion and garlic in pan until soft; push to one side; brown ham slices, part at a time in same pan; remove and reserve.
5. Add chicken broth, water, salt, pepper, lemon rind and bay leaf to pan; bring to boiling.
6. Add toasty rice and sautéed onion and garlic; add shellfish and ham slices; cover pan.
7. Cook in covered grill, 10 inches from heat, 50 minutes; arrange peas and pimiento over rice; cover. Grill 10 minutes longer, or until rice is tender and liquid is absorbed. Serve with Sangria and an avocado salad, if you wish.

The internationally-famous Chinese method of charcoal-smoke cooking turns out a juicy and delicious Smoked Turkey Orientale. Shown here with Basque Vegetable Bowl and fluffy-light Pilaf Amandine, it's a cook-out feast to please the hungriest crowd. Recipe is on this page.

MUSTARD CHICKEN KABOBS

Try this tangy mustard and honey glaze on other kabobs you cook this summer. Shown fanned in a small watermelon on page 71.

Grill for 20 minutes.
Makes 6 servings.

- 6 small white onions
- 12 chicken wings
- 6 small artichokes
- 6 cherry tomatoes
- ½ cup bottled oil and vinegar dressing
- ½ cup honey
- ¼ cup prepared mustard
- 6 crab apples

1. Build a medium fire, or set gas or electric grill to medium, following manufacturer's directions.
2. Peel onions and cook in a small amount of boiling salted water 15 minutes, or just until tender; drain.
3. Thread 6 long skewers with chicken wings, white onions, artichokes and cherry tomatoes. Brush generously with dressing.
4. Grill, 4 inches from heat, turning several times, 10 minutes. Combine honey and mustard in a cup; brush kabobs with mixture. Grill 10 minutes longer, or until well glazed. Top each kabob with a crab apple.

SMOKED TURKEY ORIENTALE

Here's an old-time cooking method that's making a return to popularity with the new charcoal water smokers. Shown in Rancho Sante Fe on page 74.

Smoke for 10 hours.
Makes 12 servings, plus leftovers.

- 1 frozen turkey (about 12 pounds), thawed
- 1 cup bottled barbecue sauce
- ¼ cup dry Sherry
- 2 tablespoons bottled gravy coloring or steak sauce
  Pilaf Amandine (recipe, page 116)
  Basque Vegetable Bowl (recipe, page 116)

1. Prepare charcoal water smoker, using hickory wood chips, following directions on page 81, or use your owner's manual.
2. Remove neck and giblets from thawed turkey and use to make stock. Wash and pat turkey dry with paper towels.
3. Combine barbecue sauce, Sherry and gravy coloring or steak sauce in a small bowl and brush generously over bird.
4. Fill water pan with boiling water and a handful of leaf rosemary. Place turkey on cooking grill; cover smoker.
5. Smoke 10 hours, checking water pan after 5 hours and adding more, if needed, or until leg moves easily.
6. Place turkey on platter and allow to "rest" 20 minutes. Serve with PILAF AMANDINE and BASQUE VEGETABLE BOWL.

CHEF'S TIP: A SALAD BAR (directions, page 128) is an excellent choice for the meal opener with this menu. Sometimes winds or weather conditions can extend the cooking time an hour or so, and with guests nibbling away on crisp greens and all the toppings, no one will starve.

Suggested Variation: You can also prepare this recipe in a covered grill. Build a medium fire around an aluminum foil pan, following directions on page 45 and roast turkey 3 hours, or until leg moves easily.

BRITISH MIXED GRILL

Veal, sausages and chicken livers give a decidedly chophouse flavor to these kabobs.

Grill for 25 minutes.
Makes 6 servings.

- 2 pounds veal shoulder, cut into 1½-inch cubes
  Instant unseasoned meat tenderizer
- ½ cup mayonnaise or salad dressing
- ¼ cup unsweetened grapefruit juice
- 2 tablespoons Worcestershire sauce
- 1 clove garlic, minced
- 1 teaspoon paprika
- 1 teaspoon celery salt
- ¼ teaspoon lemon pepper
- 12 pork sausage links
- 1 pound chicken livers
- 3 medium-size tomatoes, quartered
- 1 small eggplant, pared, quartered lengthwise and cut into 1-inch slices
- ¼ cup vegetable oil
  Salt and pepper

1. Moisten veal and sprinkle with tenderizer, following label directions. Thread onto 3 long skewers.
2. Blend mayonnaise or salad dressing, grapefruit juice, Worcestershire sauce, garlic, paprika, celery salt and lemon pepper in a small bowl. Brush over veal cubes.
3. Build a medium fire, or set electric or gas grill to medium, following manufacturer's directions.
4. Grill, 4 inches from heat, turning often and brushing with more sauce, 25 minutes, or until tender.
5. While veal cooks, place sausages and chicken livers alternately on 2 long skewers and tomatoes and eggplant slices on 2 additional skewers. Brush meats and vegetables with oil and sprinkle with salt and pepper.
6. Grill, turning several times, 15 minutes, or until tender.
7. Slide meats and vegetables off skewers onto a heated chop plate. Serve with shoestring potatoes and mugs of cold ale.

75

SRANISH LAMB KABOBS

Pimiento-stuffed olives add just the right salty touch to lamb cookery. Shown with a variety of kabobs on page 71.

Grill 10 to 15 minutes.
Makes 6 servings.

- **2 pounds lean lamb, cut into 1½-inch cubes**
  Mediterranean Marinade (recipe, page 115)
- **1 large yellow squash**
- **6 small white onions**
- **1 green pepper, halved, seeded and cut into sixths**
- **12 pimiento-stuffed olives**
- **6 cherry tomatoes**

1. Place lamb cubes in a glass utility dish; pour MEDITERRANEAN MARINADE over; cover with plastic wrap; allow to stand at room temperature at least 2 hours.
2. Build a medium fire, or set gas or electric grill to medium, following manufacturer's directions.
3. Trim squash and cut into 6 pieces; peel onions; cook together in a small saucepan with a small amount boiling salted water for 10 minutes, or just until tender; drain.
4. Remove lamb from marinade and reserve marinade. Thread 6 long skewers with lamb, squash, green pepper and white onions; top kabobs with stuffed olives. Brush generously with reserved marinade.
5. Grill, 3 inches from heat, turning and basting often, 10 minutes for rare and 15 minutes for medium, or until lamb is done as you like. Top each kabob with a cherry tomato.

PRAWN KABOBS

West Coasters call shrimp, prawns—no matter which term you use, here is a delicious way to serve them. Shown in a garden in San Rafael, California, on page 71.

Grill for 10 minutes.
Makes 4 servings.

- **1 small bunch broccoli**
- **4 small patty pan squash**
- **1 pound prawns or shrimp, shelled and deveined**
- **4 fresh mushrooms**
  Pickled Yellow Peppers (recipe, page 28)
  Lemon Butter Baste (recipe, page 97)
  Pickled corn on the cob (from a 6-ounce jar)

1. Build a medium fire, or set electric or gas grill to medium, following manufacturer's directions.
2. Wash and tip broccoli and separate into flowerets. Scrub patty pan squash. Cook together in a small amount boiling salted water, 10 minutes, or until almost tender, drain.
3. Thread 4 long skewers with broc-

coli, patty pan squash, prawns or shrimp, mushrooms and PICKLED YELLOW PEPPERS. Brush generously with LEMON BUTTER BASTE.
4. Grill, 4 inches from heat, turning and basting often, 10 minutes, or until kabobs are well glazed. Top each kabob with a pickled corn on the cob. Serve with sourdough bread and a crisp green salad.

STEAK EN BROCHETTE

Thin strips of beef are threaded on kabobs with colorful vegetables and basted with tangy Russian dressing.

Grill for 7 to 10 minutes.
Makes 6 servings.

- **1 round steak, cut 1½-inches thick (about 2 pounds)**
- **1 bottle (8 ounces) Russian salad dressing**
- **2 tablespoons lemon juice**
- **18 small mushrooms**
- **18 cherry tomatoes**

1. Place steak in freezer for 30 minutes to "firm-up"; cut steak into ¼-inch-thick strips. Place in a shallow glass baking dish; drizzle Russian salad dressing and lemon juice over; cover with plastic wrap.
2. Refrigerate and marinate 4 hours, or overnight. Let stand at room temperature 1 hour before grilling.
3. Build a medium fire, or set electric or gas grill to medium, following manufacturer's directions.
4. Remove beef strips from marinade and thread alternately with mushrooms and tomatoes on 6 long skewers; brush with marinade.
5. Grill, 4 inches from heat, turning and basting with marinade, 7 to 10 minutes, or until beef is done as you like it. Serve with long loaves of French bread and a hearty red wine.

KIELBASA KABOBS

Polish sausage chunks are threaded with cubes of eggplant, dill pickle and tomatoes for a colorful kabob.

Grill for 15 minutes.
Makes 4 servings.

- **1 Polish sausage (about 1 pound)**
- **1 small eggplant, cut into 1-inch cubes**
- **1 green pepper, halved, seeded and cut into squares**
- **12 mushrooms**
- **12 cherry tomatoes, stemmed**
- **½ cup vegetable oil**
- **½ cup lemon juice**
- **2 tablespoons chopped parsley**
- **1 teaspoon salt**
- **1 teaspoon leaf marjoram, crumbled**
- **1 teaspoon leaf oregano, crumbled**
- **2 Polish dill pickles, cut into chunks**

1. Cut Polish sausage into 1-inch

pieces and place in a large glass bowl with eggplant, green pepper, mushrooms and cherry tomatoes.
2. Combine oil, lemon juice, parsley, salt, marjoram and oregano in a small bowl; pour over sausage and vegetables; toss carefully to coat evenly; cover bowl with plastic wrap; let stand at room temperature 2 hours, turning several times.
3. Build a medium fire, or set gas or electric grill to medium, following manufacturer's directions.
4. Thread Polish sausage alternately with eggplant, green pepper, mushrooms, cherry tomatoes and dill pickle chunks onto 8 skewers, dividing evenly; reserve marinade.
5. Grill, 4 inches from heat, turning and basting with marinade, 15 minutes, or until golden. Serve with wedges of ripe melon and lime.

CLASSIC LAMB SHISH KABOBS

Ancient Persians roasted cubes of lamb marinated in herbs over desert campfires.

Grill for 15 minutes.
Makes 8 servings.

- **4 pounds lamb shoulder, trimmed and cut into 1-inch cubes**
- **1¼ cups dry red wine**
- **½ cup olive or vegetable oil**
- **1 large onion, chopped (1 cup)**
- **1 clove garlic, minced**
- **1½ teaspoons salt**
- **½ teaspoon leaf basil, crumbled**
- **½ teaspoon leaf marjoram, crumbled**
- **½ teaspoon leaf rosemary, crumbled**
- **¼ teaspoon pepper**
- **2 large green peppers, halved, seeded and cut into cubes**
- **1 pound small mushrooms**
- **2 cans (1 pound each) small white potatoes**

1. Place lamb cubes in a large glass or ceramic bowl. Add wine, oil, onion, garlic, salt, basil, marjoram, rosemary and pepper; stir to coat lamb evenly. Cover with plastic wrap; refrigerate overnight.
2. Build a medium-hot fire, or set gas or electric grill to medium-high, following manufacturer's directions.
3. Remove lamb from marinade; reserve marinade. Thread lamb on 8 skewers, dividing evenly; divide peppers, mushrooms and potatoes among 8 additional skewers; brush all with marinade.
4. Grill lamb kabobs, 4 inches from heat, 5 minutes; turn. Add vegetable kabobs to grill. Cook 10 minutes longer for rare and 15 minutes for medium, basting several times with marinade. Serve one meat and one vegetable kabob to each guest, accompanied by pita bread and an orange-pomegranate salad.

NAPA VALLEY BEEF KABOBS

Wine-marinated beef cubes are threaded with tiny artichokes and eggplant for an exceptional meal. Shown on page 71.

Grill for 10 to 20 minutes.
Makes 6 servings.

1 top round steak, cut 1½-inches thick (about 2 pounds)
Lemon-Herb Marinade (recipe, page 97)
1 small eggplant
1 small head cauliflower
6 tiny artichokes
6 cherry tomatoes

1. Trim excess fat from beef; cut into cubes; place in a glass utility dish; pour LEMON-HERB MARINADE over; cover with plastic wrap; allow to stand at room temperature at least 2 hours.
2. Build a medium fire, or set gas or electric grill to medium, following manufacturer's directions.
3. Cut eggplant into 2-inch cubes; separate cauliflower into flowerets. Combine vegetables with artichokes in a large saucepan with a small amount boiling salted water. Bring to boiling; lower heat and simmer 10 minutes, or just until tender; drain. Remove beef from marinade and reserve marinade.
4. Thread 6 long skewers with beef, eggplant, cauliflower and artichokes. Brush generously with marinade.
5. Grill, 4 inches from heat, basting and turning often, 10 minutes for rare, 15 minutes for medium and 20 minutes for well done, or until beef is done as you like. Top each kabob with a cherry tomato. Serve with hot buttered linguine, if you wish.

FIESTA CASSEROLE

Beans and ground beef make hearty campfire fare.

Grill for 1 hour.
Makes 6 servings.

1 large onion, chopped (1 cup)
½ cup chopped celery
1 to 3 teaspoons chili powder
2 tablespoons vegetable oil
1½ pounds meatloaf mixture
OR: 1½ pounds ground beef
1 teaspoon leaf oregano, crumbled
1 can (8 ounces) tomato sauce
2 cans (about 1 pound each) baked beans
1 cup shredded Cheddar cheese (4 ounces)

1. Build a slow fire, or set gas or electric grill to low, following manufacturer's directions.
2. Sauté onion and celery with chili powder in oil in a metal Dutch oven, 4 inches from heat, just until soft; push to one side.
3. Shape meatloaf mixture or ground beef into a large patty in same pan; brown 5 minutes on each side; break up into chunks. Stir in oregano and tomato sauce; heat to boiling. Stir in beans and cover kettle.
4. Cook on grill, 6 inches from heat, stirring occasionally, 40 minutes; sprinkle top with cheese; cover. Cook 5 minutes longer, or until cheese melts. Serve with heated corn bread and an avocado-orange salad.

MUSTARD SAUSAGE KABOBS

Peppers and tomatoes layer with breakfast sausages for hearty eating.

Grill for 15 minutes.
Makes 4 servings.

1 package (8 ounces) brown 'n' serve sausages
8 slices bacon, halved crosswise
8 thick slices Bermuda onion
3 green peppers, quartered and seeded
3 tomatoes, quartered
8 fresh or canned mushrooms
Mustard Glaze (recipe follows)

1. Build a medium fire, or set gas or electric grill to medium, following manufacturer's directions.
2. Wrap sausages with bacon; fasten with wooden food picks.
3. Thread meat on 4 long skewers, alternating with onion slices, green pepper pieces, tomatoes and mushrooms; brush with MUSTARD GLAZE.
4. Grill, 4 inches from heat, basting with glaze and turning, 15 minutes, or until bacon is crisp. Serve on club rolls with coleslaw.

MUSTARD GLAZE: Makes 1½ cups. Combine ½ cup sugar, ½ cup cider vinegar, ½ cup honey, 2 tablespoons vegetable oil, 2 teaspoons dry mustard and ¼ teaspoon ground cloves in a small saucepan; cook over low heat 10 minutes, or until thick and bubbly.

VEGETABLE KABOBS

Here's a sextet of garden-fresh vegetables —so perfect for kabob cooking.

Grill for 20 minutes.
Makes 8 servings.

8 small new potatoes
4 medium-size zucchini
4 medium-size yellow squash
8 large fresh mushrooms
2 large tomatoes
2 large green peppers
¼ cup (½ stick) butter or margarine
2 teaspoons chopped chives
1 teaspoon dillweed
1 teaspoon salt
¼ teaspoon lemon pepper

1. Scrub potatoes; cut off a band of skin around middle of each. Trim zucchini and yellow squash, but do not pare; cut into 1-inch-thick slices
2. Parboil potatoes in boiling salted water 10 minutes; add zucchini and squash and cook 5 minutes; drain.
3. While potatoes, zucchini and squash cook, wash mushrooms, trim ends and halve each. Cut each tomato into 8 wedges. Halve green peppers; remove seeds; cut peppers into strips. Thread potatoes, zucchini and squash onto 4 long skewers. Thread mushrooms, tomato wedges and pepper strips onto 4 long skewers.
4. Melt butter or margarine in a small saucepan; stir in chives, dillweed, salt and lemon pepper.
5. Grill potato-squash kabobs 6 inches from heat, turning and brushing several times with butter mixture, 15 minutes; place tomato-mushroom kabobs alongside. Continue grilling 15 minutes, or until tender.

LEMONY KABOBS

Tangy lemon and pungent plums bring a touch of Persia to your barbecue.

Grill for 15 minutes.
Makes 4 servings.

2 pounds lamb shoulder or pork shoulder, cut into 1-inch cubes
Lemon-Herb Marinade (recipe, page 97)
1 can (1 pound) small white onions, drained
1 large green pepper, halved, seeded and cut into strips
2 small firm tomatoes, quartered
2 small zucchini, cut into 1-inch pieces
1 cup plum preserves
¼ cup (½ stick) butter or margarine

1. Trim lamb or pork cubes and place in a large glass or ceramic bowl. Add LEMON-HERB MARINADE; toss to coat well; cover with plastic wrap and refrigerate at least 2 hours, or overnight.
2. Build a medium-hot fire, or set electric or gas grill to medium-high, following manufacturer's directions.
3. Remove meat from marinade, reserving marinade. Divide meat among 4 skewers; alternate onions, pepper strips, tomato quarters and zucchini on 4 skewers.
4. Add ⅓ cup LEMON-HERB MARINADE to plum preserves in a small metal saucepan with a flameproof handle; add remaining marinade and butter or margarine to a second saucepan and heat both saucepans on grill.
5. Brush meat with plum mixture and vegetables with butter mixture.
6. Grill, 4 inches from heat, 10 minutes, turning several times. Baste meat kabobs with plum mixture and vegetables with butter mixture. Cook 5 minutes longer, or until kabobs are golden and well glazed.

MOROCCAN LAMB KABOBS

Lemon wedges and plump olives grill to perfection with spicy lamb chunks.

Grill for 10 to 15 minutes.
Makes 6 servings.

    2 pounds lean lamb, cut into 1-inch
         cubes
    ½ cup olive or vegetable oil
    ¼ cup lemon juice
    1 large clove garlic, minced
    2 tablespoons chopped parsley
    1 teaspoon salt
    1 teaspoon ground ginger
    ½ teaspoon ground cumin
    ¼ teaspoon freshly ground pepper
   12 small white onions
    3 lemons
   12 large stuffed Spanish olives

1. Place lamb cubes in a large shallow glass or ceramic dish; add oil, lemon juice, garlic, parsley, salt, ginger, cumin and pepper; toss to coat well. Cover with plastic wrap and marinate at room temperature 2 hours, or overnight in refrigerator, removing lamb from refrigerator at least 1 hour before grilling.
2. Peel onions; cut an "X" in stem end; cook in salted boiling water 10 minutes, or until crisply tender. Cut lemons into quarters.
3. Build a medium-hot fire, or set electric or gas grill to medium-high, following manufacturer's directions.
4. Remove lamb from marinade, reserving marinade; thread on 6 skewers, alternating with onions, lemon wedges and olives; brush generously with marinade.
5. Grill, 4 inches from heat, turning and basting often, 10 minutes for pink lamb or 15 minutes for medium meat. Serve with a rice pilaf, if you wish.

KABOBS ITALIANO

Zucchini, eggplant and artichoke hearts are grilled with tender pieces of beef in a robust marinade.

Grill for 10 to 15 minutes.
Makes 6 servings.

    2 pounds beef sirloin tip
    1 bottle (8 ounces) Italian salad
         dressing
    1 teaspoon leaf oregano, crumbled
    1 small eggplant, cut into 1-inch
         cubes
    2 medium-size zucchini, cut into
         1-inch slices
    1 package (9 ounces) frozen
         artichoke hearts, thawed

1. Cut beef into 1-inch cubes; place in a shallow glass baking dish; pour Italian dressing and oregano over beef cubes and toss to coat evenly; cover with plastic wrap.
2. Refrigerate for 2 hours, or overnight; let stand at room temperature

1 hour before grilling.
3. Place eggplant, zucchini and artichoke hearts in separate piles in a large skillet; pour in boiling water to a depth of 1 inch. Bring to boiling; lower heat; simmer 5 minutes, or until crisply tender; drain vegetables.
4. Build a medium fire, or set electric or gas grill to medium, following manufacturer's directions.
5. Remove beef cubes from marinade; reserve marinade. Thread meat alternately with zucchini, eggplant and artichoke hearts on 6 long skewers; brush with marinade.
6. Grill, 4 inches from heat, turning and basting with marinade, 10 to 15 minutes, or until beef is done as you like it. Serve with an antipasto salad, if you wish.

RIBS-AND-ORANGE KABOBS

Spareribs seem to be designed for threading on long skewers for impressive cooking.

Grill for 1 hour, 30 minutes.
Makes 6 servings.

    6 pounds fresh spareribs
    1 bottle (12 ounces) lemon-lime
         carbonated beverage (see
         Cook's Guide)
    1 cup freshly squeezed orange juice
    ⅓ cup hickory-flavored catsup
    ¼ cup lemon juice
    3 tablespoons light brown sugar
    1 tablespoon instant minced onion
    1 tablespoon soy sauce
    ¼ teaspoon salt
    3 small eating oranges
    1 large green pepper
    1 can (1 pound) small white onions

1. Build a slow fire, or set electric or gas grill to low, following manufacturer's directions.
2. Trim excess fat from spareribs; brush generously with lemon-lime beverage.
3. Grill, 6 to 8 inches from heat, turning and basting with lemon-lime beverage, 1 hour, or until tender when pierced with a two-tined fork.
4. Combine orange juice, catsup, lemon juice, brown sugar, instant minced onion, soy sauce and salt in a small saucepan with a flameproof handle.
5. Place on side of grill and cook, stirring often, 20 minutes, or until sauce thickens.
6. Thread spareribs onto two long skewers. Cut oranges into wedges; halve, seed and cut green pepper into large squares; drain onions. Alternate orange wedges, pepper squares and onions on two long skewers. Brush all skewers generously with sauce to coat evenly.
7. Grill, turning and basting often, 30 minutes, or until richly glazed. Serve with a cucumber salad.

PIZZA PACKAGES

Perfect to make ahead of time and pack in a cooler to cook at a beach picnic.

Grill for 45 minutes.
Makes 4 servings.

    1½ pounds ground beef
    ⅓ cup old-fashioned or quick oats
    1 small onion, chopped (¼ cup)
    1 egg
    ¼ cup catsup
    2 envelopes or teaspoons instant
         beef broth
    ⅛ teaspoon pepper
    1 can (8½ ounces) cut green
         beans, drained
    1 can (7 ounces) whole-kernel
         corn, drained
    1 jar (2½ ounces) sliced
         mushrooms, drained
    1 can (10 ounces) pizza sauce
    1 cup shredded Cheddar cheese
         (4 ounces)

1. Combine ground beef, oats, onion, egg, catsup, instant beef broth and pepper in a medium-size bowl; mix lightly, just until blended. Shape into 16 meatballs.
2. Tear four 12-inch squares of heavy-duty aluminum foil; place 4 meatballs in center of each piece. Divide green beans, corn and mushrooms among foil squares; spoon pizza sauce over and top with cheese.
3. Seal packets, following directions on page 47.
4. Build a low fire, or set electric or gas grill to slow, following manufacturer's directions.
5. Grill, 4 inches from heat, turning packets several times with tongs, 45 minutes. Open packets and serve with chunks of crusty bread and carrot and celery sticks with cream cheese.

POLYNESIAN KABOBS

Fresh pineapple and shrimp team with beef in a soy-ginger sauce.

Grill for 6 to 12 minutes.
Makes 6 servings.

    1 top round steak, (about 2 pounds),
         cut 1¼-inches thick
    ½ cup pineapple juice
    2 tablespoons peanut or vegetable
         oil
    1 tablespoon bottled meat sauce
    1 clove garlic, crushed
    1 teaspoon ground ginger
    ½ teaspoon anise seeds, crushed
    1 pound fresh or frozen deveined
         shelled raw shrimp, thawed
    1 small pineapple, pared, cored,
         and cut into small wedges

1. Pierce steak deeply all over with a two-tined fork; place in a shallow glass utility dish.
2. Mix pineapple juice, oil, meat sauce, garlic, ginger and anise seeds

in a 1-cup measure; pour over steak. Cover dish with plastic wrap; refrigerate, turning steak once, 30 minutes; remove from marinade to a cutting board, reserving marinade.

3. Cut meat diagonally into long slices about ¼-inch thick; thread, accordion-style, with shrimp and pineapple wedges onto 6 long kabobs.

4. Build a medium fire, or set gas or electric grill to medium, following manufacturer's directions.

5. Grill, 6 inches from heat, turning once and basting with marinade, 6 minutes for rare, 9 minutes for medium and 12 minutes for well done, or until steak is done as you like it. Serve with pita bread and a spinach and blue cheese salad.

RANCHO CASSEROLE

Cornmeal is a delicious contribution from the Americas to international cooking.

Grill for 1 hour.
Makes 6 servings.

- 1 cup yellow cornmeal
- 6 slices bacon
- 2 pounds ground beef
- 2 teaspoons salt
- ¼ teaspoon seasoned pepper
- ¼ cup chopped parsley
- 1 large onion, chopped (1 cup)
- 1 to 4 teaspoons chili powder
- 1 teaspoon cumin
- ½ cup chopped celery
- 1 clove garlic, crushed
- 1 can (1 pound) tomatoes
- 1½ cups grated Cheddar cheese
      (6 ounces)

1. Stir cornmeal slowly into 4 cups boiling water in a large saucepan; cook until thick, about 30 minutes. Pour into a greased 13x9x2-inch baking dish. Chill at least 4 hours, or overnight.

2. Build a slow fire in a grill with a cover, or set electric or gas grill to slow, following manufacturer's directions.

3. Cook bacon until crisp in a large metal skillet with a flameproof handle, on grill, 6 inches from heat; drain. Crumble and set aside. Pour off all but 2 tablespoons fat.

4. Mix ground beef lightly with 1 teaspoon of the salt, pepper and parsley in a medium-size bowl; shape into 24 small balls. Brown in drippings in pan; push to one side.

5. Stir onion, chili powder, cumin, celery and garlic into pan; sauté just until onion is soft. Stir in tomatoes, cheese and remaining 1 teaspoon salt. Remove from heat.

6. Remove chilled cornmeal mush from dish by turning upside down on a cutting board; cut into 2-inch blocks. Place half of the cornmeal blocks in the bottom of a greased 12-cup metal casserole. Top with half

each of the meat balls and sauce and crumbled bacon; repeat to make another layer.

7. Grill, 6 inches from heat, 40 minutes, or until bubbly hot. Serve with buttered tacos and a sliced avocado and orange salad.

ANTIPASTO KABOBS

All the good flavors of the Italian classic salad, heated on kabobs over the coals.

Grill for 5 minutes.
Makes 12 servings.

- 1 package (8 ounces) mozzarella
      cheese
- 1 package (4 ounces) sliced salami
- 24 cherry tomatoes
- 24 small mushrooms, trimmed
- 1 jar (4 ounces) marinated
      artichoke hearts
- 24 pitted ripe olives
- ¾ cup olive or vegetable oil
- ¼ cup wine vinegar
- 1 teaspoon salt
- 1 teaspoon dry mustard
- 1 teaspoon leaf oregano, crumbled
- ¼ teaspoon freshly ground pepper

1. Cut mozzarella cheese in thick slices, then cut slices lengthwise into sticks. Wrap each stick inside a slice of salami; cut in half crosswise; fasten each half with a wooden pick.

2. Thread 2 tomatoes, 2 mushrooms, 1 artichoke heart, 3 salami rolls, and 2 olives onto each of 12 short skewers; place in a large shallow utility dish.

3. Combine oil, vinegar, salt, mustard, oregano and pepper in a jar with a screw top; cover; shake well to mix. Drizzle dressing over kabobs. Let stand about an hour to season and blend flavors.

4. Build a medium fire, or set electric or gas grill to medium, following manufacturer's directions.

5. Grill, 4 to 6 inches from heat, 5 minutes, or until kabobs are heated through. Serve as the first course of a grilled steak dinner.

BARBECUE STROGANOFF

Tender pieces of beef or lamb make a superb stroganoff to make in your wok over the grill. Truly, it's an international dish.

Grill for 20 minutes.
Makes 6 servings.

- 2 pounds beef for stroganoff
      OR: 2 pounds lamb for kabobs
- 3 tablespoons peanut or vegetable
      oil
- 3 tablespoons butter or margarine
- 2 large onions, thinly sliced
- ½ pound fresh mushrooms
- 1 cup beef broth
- ¼ cup soy sauce
- 1 container (8 ounces) dairy sour
      cream
      Freshly ground pepper

1. Cut beef or lamb into ¼-inch-thick slices and let stand at room temperature while fire heats.

2. Build a medium fire, or set gas or electric grill to medium, following manufacturer's directions.

3. Heat oil and butter or margarine in a wok or a large metal skillet with a flameproof handle on grill, 4 inches from heat.

4. Brown meat, part at a time, quickly in pan; remove with slotted spoon and keep warm.

5. Sauté onions until soft in pan; add mushrooms and cook 2 minutes. Add beef broth and soy sauce; cover pan and simmer 5 minutes.

6. Spoon 1 cup hot mixture into sour cream in a small bowl; stir back into pan; return meat slices to pan. Heat, stirring constantly, 3 minutes, or until heated through; do *not* allow to boil. Season with pepper. Spoon over fluffy rice and serve with CUCUMBER-LETTUCE SALAD (recipe, page 122).

BEACHCOMBER CASSEROLE

Pop this hearty beef and vegetable dish into your covered grill, then take a leisurely walk along the beach.

Grill for 1 hour, 10 minutes.
Makes 8 servings.

- 2 pounds ground beef
- 1 large onion, chopped (1 cup)
- 1 large green pepper, halved,
      seeded and chopped
- 2 teaspoons salt
- 1 teaspoon mixed Italian herbs,
      crumbled
- ¼ teaspoon pepper
- 1 can (1 pound) tomatoes
- 1 can (15 ounces) tomato sauce
- 1 can (12 ounces) whole-kernel corn
- 1 package (7 or 8 ounces) small
      pasta shells, cooked and
      drained

1. Build a medium fire in a covered grill, or set electric or gas grill to medium, following manufacturer's directions.

2. Shape ground beef with palm of hand into a large patty in a 12-cup flameproof casserole.

3. Brown beef in casserole on grill, 4 inches from heat, 5 minutes; cut into quarters; turn with a pancake turner; brown on second side 5 minutes; remove from casserole and break into tiny pieces.

4. Sauté onion until soft in pan drippings; stir in green pepper; sauté 2 minutes. Return meat to casserole; season with salt, Italian herbs and pepper; stir in tomatoes, tomato sauce, corn and cooked shells; cover casserole; lower temperature of electric or gas grill to low. Place dome or lid on grill.

5. Simmer on grill, 6 inches from heat, 1 hour, or until bubbly-hot.

SHASHLYK

From Georgia, in Southern Russia, comes this classic skewered lamb dish.

Grill for 10 to 15 minutes.
Makes 6 servings.

- 2 pounds lean lamb, cut into 1-inch cubes
- ¼ cup olive or vegetable oil
- 2 tablespoons lemon juice
- 1 small onion, grated
- 1 teaspoon salt
- ¼ teaspoon freshly ground pepper
- 1 Bermuda onion
- 2 large ripe tomatoes, sliced
- 1 bunch green onions, sliced
- 1 lemon, cut into wedges

1. Combine lamb, oil, lemon juice, grated onion, salt and pepper in a plastic bag in a large bowl; seal plastic bag; toss lamb in marinade. Allow to marinate for 2 hours at room temperature, turning plastic bag several times.
2. Peel and halve Bermuda onion, crosswise; quarter each half lengthwise; separate onion into sections.
3. Build a very hot fire, or set electric or gas grill to very hot, following manufacturer's directions.
4. Remove lamb from marinade; reserve marinade. Thread lamb and onion alternately onto 6 skewers; brush with remaining marinade.
5. Grill, 4 inches from heat, turning twice, 10 minutes for pink lamb and 15 minutes for medium. Serve with an accompaniment of sliced tomatoes, green onions and lemon wedges to squeeze over meat.

CHEDDAR-BEEF KABOBS

Cheddar cheese cubes are hidden in spicy meatballs and kabobed with dill pickles and cherry tomatoes.

Grill for 12 to 20 minutes.
Makes 6 servings.

- 2 pounds ground beef
- ½ cup bottled barbecue sauce
- 1 small onion, grated
- ¼ cup all purpose flour
- 1 tablespoon prepared mustard
- 1 teaspoon salt
- ¼ teaspoon pepper
- 1 package (10 ounces) sharp Cheddar cheese
- 4 large dill pickles, cut into 1-inch pieces
  Bottled barbecue sauce
  Cherry tomatoes

1. Combine ground beef, the ½ cup barbecue sauce, onion, flour, mustard, salt and pepper in a medium-size bowl; mix lightly, just to blend. Divide into 24 portions.
2. Cut cheese stick into 24 cubes, about ¾-inches; wrap meat mixture around cubes to make 24 balls.
3. Thread 4 meatballs and three dill pickle slices on each of 6 skewers. Refrigerate while heating grill.
4. Build a medium fire, or set electric or gas grill to medium, following manufacturer's directions.
5. Grill, 4 inches from heat, 12 to 20 minutes, turning and basting with barbecue sauce; add 2 cherry tomatoes to each kabob for the last 3 minutes of grilling. Serve with a bean salad and slices of crusty bread, if you wish.

SAUSAGE KABOBS

Chunky pieces of Polish sausage add a spicy touch to kabob cookery. Photograph, taken in an Oriental garden, is on page 71.

Grill for 10 minutes.
Makes 6 servings.

- 2 sweet potatoes
- 6 small white onions
- 6 small white turnips
- 2 packages (12 ounces each) Polish sausage, cut into 2-inch pieces
  Molasses Barbecue Sauce (recipe, page 114)
  Pickled watermelon rind

1. Build a medium fire, or set electric or gas grill to medium, following manufacturer's directions.
2. Pare potatoes and cut into 1-inch pieces; peel white onions; scrub white turnips. Place vegetables in a medium-size saucepan with a small amount of boiling salted water. Cook 15 minutes, or until almost tender; drain.
3. Thread 6 long skewers with Polish sausage, sweet potatoes, white onions and white turnips. Brush generously with MOLASSES BARBECUE SAUCE.
4. Grill, 3 inches from heat, turning and basting several times, 10 minutes, or until kabobs are well glazed. Top each kabob with a piece of pickled watermelon rind.

TOASTED CHEESE KABOBS

Alternate slices of bread and cheese grill on the barbecue along with a steak or burgers.

Grill for 10 minutes.
Makes 8 kabobs.

- 1 loaf firm white bread
- ¼ cup (½ stick) butter or margarine, melted
- 1 package (8 ounces) process American cheese
  Pimiento-stuffed olives

1. Trim crusts from bread; cut each slice of bread into 4 squares; brush with melted butter or margarine. Cut cheese slices into squares.
2. Thread bread and cheese squares onto small skewers, beginning and ending with bread.
3. Grill, turning kabobs often, 10 minutes, or until cheese melts and bread toasts. Garnish with olives.

SEA SCALLOP KABOBS

Succulent scallops grill deliciously with bacon and mushrooms.

Grill for 10 minutes.
Makes 6 servings.

- 2 pounds fresh or frozen sea scallops
- ½ pound bacon, cut into 2-inch pieces
- 1 pound mushrooms, halved
- 2 lemons, sliced
  Cherry tomatoes
- ½ cup bottled oil and vinegar salad dressing

1. Thaw frozen scallops, if used. Thread on 6 skewers, alternately, with bacon pieces, mushrooms, lemon slices and cherry tomatoes.
2. Place kabobs in a large shallow utility dish; drizzle dressing over; cover dish with plastic wrap; let marinate at room temperature 1 hour.
3. Build a medium fire, or set electric or gas grill to medium, following label directions.
4. Grill, 3 inches from heat, turning and basting with dressing often, 10 minutes, or until scallops and bacon are done.

BAVARIAN KABOBS

Nutritious liver makes an excellent choice for kabob cooking.

Grill for 15 minutes.
Makes 6 servings.

- 1 pound small white onions, peeled
- 1 pound beef, lamb or pork liver, thinly sliced
- 12 slices bacon
- 2 large sweet red peppers, seeded and cut into squares
- 2 large green peppers, seeded and cut into squares
  Bavarian Sauce (recipe follows)

1. Build a medium fire, or set electric or gas grill to medium, following manufacturer's directions.
2. Parboil onions in boiling salted water in a small saucepan 5 minutes; drain and cool.
3. Cut liver slices into strips. Cut bacon slices in half.
4. Thread 6 long skewers with liver and bacon, laced accordion-style onto skewer, alternately with onions and red and green pepper squares. Brush with BAVARIAN SAUCE.
5. Grill, 5 inches from heat, turning and brushing often with BAVARIAN SAUCE, 15 minutes, or just until bacon is crisp. (Do not overcook.)

BAVARIAN SAUCE: Makes 2 cups. Combine 1 can (12 ounces) beer with ¼ cup mustard, ¼ cup firmly packed brown sugar and ¼ teaspoon caraway seeds, crushed, in a small bowl. ∎

charcoal-grilling tips

Rotisserie Cooking—roast on a spit:

Rotisserie cooking on a charcoal grill can be keyed to the most economical use of your time and money.

The following will provide basic tips for all rotisserie meat cookery including suggested cooking times, temperatures, seasonings and marinades for six different cuts of meat.

Tips to Successful Rotisserie Cooking Over Charcoal

1. Know the number of guests you're planning to serve. You'll need 8 ounces per serving for a boneless roast; 1 pound each for a roast with bone. How much will your roast cost? If the cost is of great importance, get a less expensive cut such as a chuck roast, and allow time to marinate.

2. First things first—be sure to build and start your charcoal fire properly. Rotisserie cooking *must* be done over a hot fire. For a quick temperature test, hold your hand at cooking height, palm side down. If you can keep it in position for only 2 seconds, the temperature is high (or hot). A 4-6 pound roast will take at least 5 pounds of charcoal briquets in a pyramid in the center of the grill bottom (or coal pan, if your unit has one.) Use a good starter. Try the electric or chimney type, or solid fibrous cubes. Be patient! Let the briquets burn to just the right stage before putting the roast on the spit. They'll generally require between 20-40 minutes. In daylight, your fire is ready when the briquets are covered with a layer of grey ash; at night they'll have a bright red glow. At this stage, spread the briquets into a single layer with tongs.

3. Remove all excess fat from roast and season roast as desired. Let it stand at room temperature for at least one hour before cooking. Be sure roast is well tied into a uniform shape to prevent uneven cooking and to allow it to rotate evenly. Push rotisserie spit, length-wise, through the center of the roast, and fasten both ends in place with holding forks. If roast is off balance, remount.

4. Always use a drip pan when rotissing. To make, see page 47. The pan is important, as it will catch fatty drippings, control fat flareups, and eliminate excessive smoke. Place rotisserie rod into rotor and watch the turning of the roast. If it has an irregular shape and the top of the roast rotates away from you, place the drip pan at the front of the coal pan and push the hot coals to the back. Reverse if the roast rotates toward you. If the roast is well-balanced, place the drip pan in the center and arrange the coals around it.

5. The use of a meat thermometer when rotissing is helpful. The cooking times are only guides, as wind and weather can affect actual cooking time. After placing the meat on the rotisserie rod, push the meat thermometer into the thickest part, not touching bone or the rod. Remove the roast when the thermometer registers 10 degrees below the desired degree of doneness. Remove roast from spit, and allow to "rest" for 20 minutes.

6. Many people like the taste of a marinade and use one with meats for the rotisserie for just that reason. Marinades should be used for at least 1 hour, but overnight is best for less expensive cuts such as a chuck roast. Basting depends on the recipe, but a good rule of thumb is: Baste every 30 minutes during cooking.

Rotisserie Cooking Reminders

• Keep your grill in a sheltered spot, as much away from wind as possible.

• Tap the coals occasionally to remove the coating of gray ash. It will be necessary to add briquets during rotissing, and they should be buried within the coals to burn properly.

• If any part of your roast over-browns, cover the spot with foil to prevent further browning.

• It is not necessary to keep the grill rack on during rotissing, but you can cook other food during the rotisserie process. Just arrange it on the grill away from where the roast drips into the pan. This is best for long-cooking items, like potatoes or acorn squash.

How to Use the Charcoal Water Smoker

These are the basic directions and may vary slightly with different charcoal water smokers—so it's important to read the manufacturer's directions.

• Remove the smoker's dome (lid), grill and water pan.

• Build the charcoal fire properly. You'll need at least one pound of briquets for every hour of cooking time. Stack briquets in a pyramid; they'll light faster since air can circulate around them. Use a good starter. Try the electric or chimney type, or choose solid fibrous cubes. Let the briquets burn to the right stage (about 20-40 minutes, depending on wind and weather).

• Place wood on top of hot coals.

• Replace water pan and fill to level specified by manufacturer.

• Place seasoned meat on rack. If you're cooking more than one piece, be sure they do not touch.

• Replace dome. Remove it only to check water level according to recipe or manufacturer's instructions. Refill if necessary to level suggested by manufacturer.

During cooking, the meat bastes itself, and you should never turn or baste the meat once you've begun cooking. Don't peek! This is a closed cooking concept, and you should only lift the lid after 5-6 hours (according to recipe or manufacturer's instructions) to check the water level.

Here are some handy tips to successful charcoal water smoking:

• Be sure meat is completely thawed before cooking.

• For double rack smokers, increase charcoal and cooking time slightly, according to manufacturer's directions.

• Increase charcoal and cooking time in colder weather.

• Cooking time should be increased about 1 hour for altitudes over 4,000 feet.

• Keep smoker in protected area and away from wind.

• Wood sticks used should be 3-4″ long and ½″ in diameter. Soaked chips may be used if you prefer.

For Cold Weather Barbecues

A grill with a cover and good hot fire are the secrets to successful winter barbecuing. Be sure to stack the briquets in a pyramid so there is good circulation while the coals heat. Use an electric starter, which can start the fire in just 8 minutes. The coals will reach proper cooking temperature in about 20 to 40 minutes. The signal for cooking is the color of the coals. During the day they will have a gray ash covering them; at night, they'll glow red-hot.

Depending on the size of the meat, charcoal briquets may have to be added to keep the fire hot enough to thoroughly cook the meat inside and out. Colder days will call for more briquets. A good idea, if you live in a particularly windy area, is to build a wind shield around the grill to keep the cold drafts off the side of the grill.

Once the coals are burning, let the flames die down until the briquets become ash gray. To judge the temperature of the fire, try the hand-held test. Hold hand, palm side down, over the briquets (near the grill rack and at cooking height). If you can hold it there for 2-3 seconds, the fire is very hot; 3-4 seconds means a medium-hot fire and 4-5 seconds means low. ■

VEGETABLES & BAKE-ALONGS

The star of your barbecue—whatever delectable meat or fish it is—needs a supporting cast. In this chapter you'll find side dishes to complement many entrées, from traditional baked potatoes and corn on the cob to more exotic fare. There's also a selection of bread recipes using mixes or store-bought loaves— a boon for the summer cook.

UP-FRONT SIDE DISHES
Clockwise from upper right, La Mesa Pepper Cups,
filled with a bean trio; Zucchini Coronado, in a rich
tomato-mushroom sauce; stir-fried Chinatown
Vegetable Bowl, with a hint of rosemary. Recipes
start on page 116.

VEGETABLES & BAKE-ALONGS

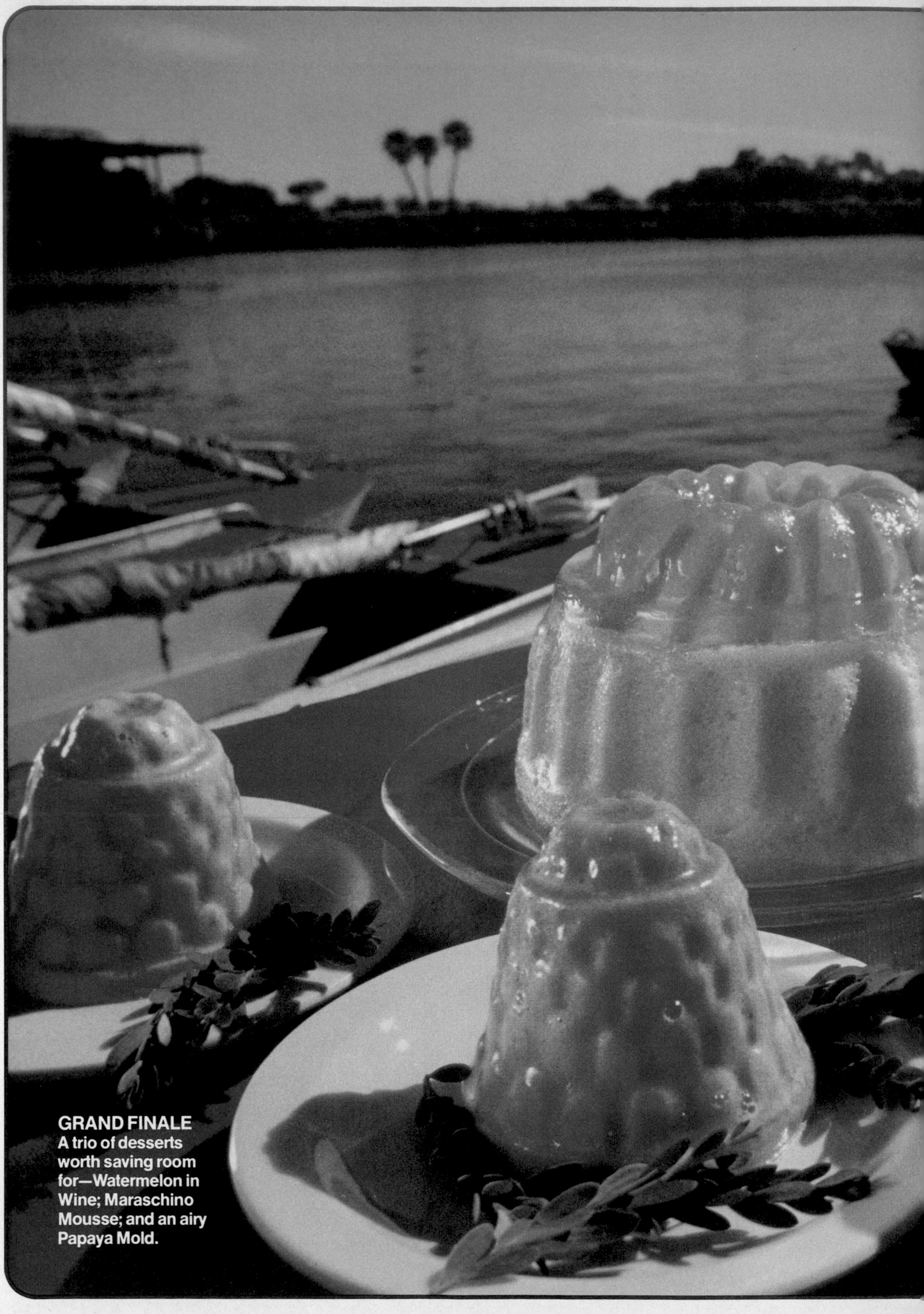

GRAND FINALE
A trio of desserts worth saving room for—Watermelon in Wine; Maraschino Mousse; and an airy Papaya Mold.

PHOTOGRAPHED AT VACATION VILLAGE, SAN DIEGO, CALIFORNIA

A collection of sweet
endings to cool and refresh—
many you make ahead.
Plus drinks for all,
from tropical punches to
homey fruit ades.

DESSERTS
&
BEVERAGES

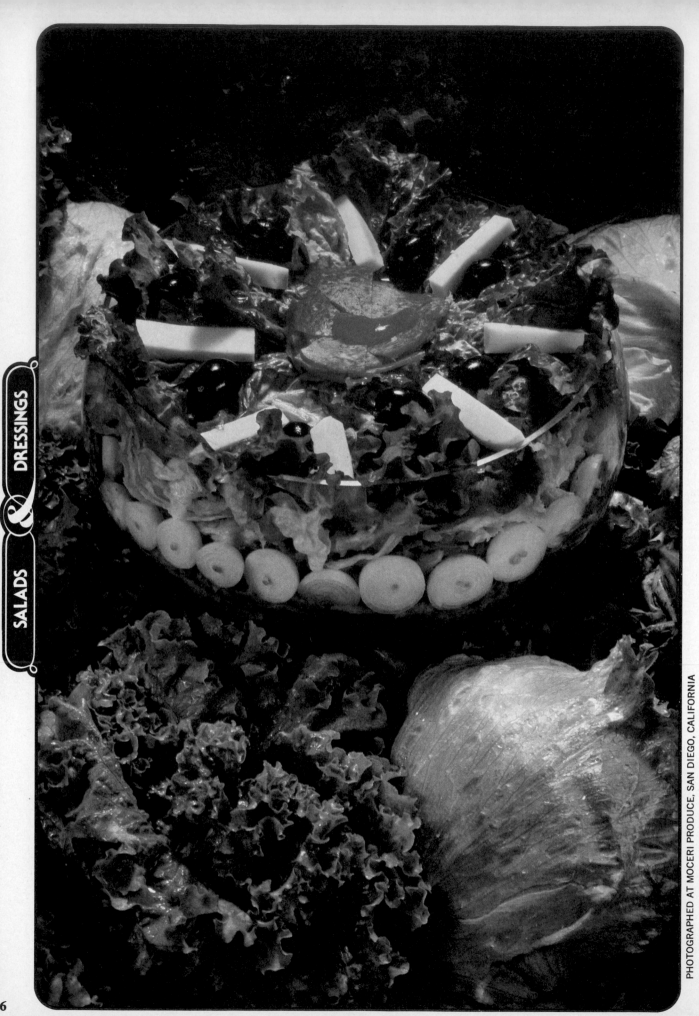

PHOTOGRAPHED AT MOCERI PRODUCE, SAN DIEGO, CALIFORNIA

Summer days are salad days, offering an almost endless variety of tender greens and crisp, colorful vegetables. Take advantage of nature's gifts and use your imagination—the best salads are made from the freshest produce available. Don't forget fruit combinations, either; they're super for curbing outdoor appetites, too.

FIT FOR A KING
Chef's salad with an Italian accent, Imperial Salad
Bowl features the best greens and vegetables from
California's Imperial Valley, crowned with salami
pieces and Provolone cheese. Recipe, page 94.

TOP-YOUR-OWN-SALADS

Your guests will enjoy their salads even more, when you let them assemble their own.

Makes 4 servings.

- 1 large head iceberg lettuce
  Sour Cream Dressing (recipe follows)
- 2 ripe tomatoes
- 1 can (8¾ ounces) chick peas
- 1 can (15 ounces) small whole carrots
- 1 can (1 pound) cut green beans
- 1 pound shrimp, shelled, deveined and cooked

1. Core, rinse and thoroughly drain lettuce; refrigerate in plastic bag or crisper. Shortly before serving, cut lettuce head crosswise into four rafts; cover with plastic wrap and chill.
2. Prepare and refrigerate SOUR CREAM DRESSING. Refrigerate tomatoes, chick peas, carrots, beans, still in their cans, and shrimp.
3. At serving time, slice tomatoes; drain chick peas, carrots and beans. Arrange vegetables with iceberg rafts and shrimp on a chilled platter. Serve with SOUR CREAM DRESSING.

SOUR CREAM DRESSING: Makes 1¼ cups. Combine 1 cup dairy sour cream with 2 tablespoons bottled chili sauce, 2 tablespoons chopped green onion, 2 tablespoons blue cheese seasoning for salads (see Cook's Guide), 2 tablespoons vinegar, ¼ teaspoon salt, dash white pepper and dash garlic powder in a small bowl until well blended; cover with plastic wrap and refrigerate to blend flavors.
CHEF'S TIP: For a thinner dressing, blend in 2 tablespoons dry white wine or milk at serving time.

APPLELAND POTATO SALAD

Slices of red-skinned apple and crumbled blue cheese make a distinctive addition to smooth and creamy potato salad.

Makes 8 servings.

- 6 large boiling potatoes
- ⅓ cup lemon juice
- 3 tablespoons vegetable oil
- 2 teaspoons salt
- ½ cup mayonnaise or salad dressing
- ¼ cup dairy sour cream
- 2 tablespoons light cream
- 1 large red apple, quartered, cored and thinly sliced
- ¼ to ½ cup crumbled blue cheese
  Iceberg lettuce

1. Cook potatoes 30 minutes, or just until tender, in boiling salted water in a large saucepan; drain. Peel potatoes and cut into thin slices; place in a large glass bowl.
2. Combine lemon juice, oil and salt in a jar with a screw top; cover jar

and shake well. Pour over potato slices and toss to coat. Cover bowl with plastic wrap; chill at least 3 hours.
3. Just before serving, combine mayonnaise or salad dressing, sour cream and light cream in a small bowl until smooth; pour over potatoes and toss well. Add apple slices and cheese; toss lightly.
4. Line a salad bowl with iceberg lettuce; spoon salad into bowl; garnish with slices of apple.

MARINATED MUSHROOMS

The perfect accompaniment to your barbecue, Italian-style.

Makes 8 servings.

- 1 pound fresh mushrooms
- ½ cup olive or vegetable oil
- ½ cup water
- ¼ cup lemon juice
- 1 clove garlic, halved
- 1 teaspoon salt
- ¼ teaspoon freshly ground pepper

1. Wipe mushrooms with a damp paper towel; cut large mushrooms into quarters; keep smaller ones whole.
2. Combine oil, water, lemon juice, garlic, salt and pepper in a large saucepan. Bring to boiling; lower heat; simmer 10 minutes.
3. Add mushrooms to saucepan and simmer 5 minutes. Pour mushrooms and marinade into a large glass or ceramic bowl; cover with plastic wrap. Refrigerate at least 2 days to blend flavors.

BEAN AND EGG SALAD

Two kinds of beans mix with hard-cooked eggs in a dill-flavored dressing.

Makes 6 servings.

- 6 hard-cooked eggs, chopped
- 1 can (8½ ounces) red kidney beans, well drained
- 1 can (8½ ounces) sliced green beans, well drained
- 1 small onion, chopped (¼ cup)
- 2 tablespoons minced green pepper
- ⅓ cup vegetable oil
- ¼ cup cider vinegar
- 1½ tablespoons sugar
- ¾ teaspoon salt
- ¾ teaspoon dry mustard
- ½ teaspoon dillweed
- ¼ teaspoon pepper
  Hard-cooked egg slices
  Parsley

Place chopped eggs, kidney and green beans, onion and green pepper in a large glass or ceramic bowl. Stir together oil, vinegar, sugar, salt, mustard, dillweed and pepper in a small bowl until well blended; pour

over bean mixture and mix gently until well blended. Cover with plastic wrap and refrigerate at least 2 hours to blend flavors. Garnish with egg slices and parsley just before serving.
CHEF'S TIP: For perfect hard-cooked eggs, follow this method: Put eggs in saucepan and add enough tap water to come at least 1-inch above eggs. Cover; bring rapidly to boiling. Remove pan from heat to prevent further boiling. Let eggs stand in hot water, 12 minutes for medium, 15 minutes for large, 18 minutes for extra large and 21 minutes for jumbo eggs. Cool immediately and thoroughly in cold water. (This prevents darkening around yolks and makes shells easier to remove.) To remove shell: Crackle it by tapping gently all over. Roll egg between hands to loosen shell; peel, starting at large end. Hold egg under running cold water, or dip in bowl of water to help ease off shell.

ICEBERG ORIENTALE

Unusual served hot or cold, this sweet and sour salad teams deliciously with barbecued chicken or grilled fish.

Makes 6 servings.

- 1 medium-size head iceberg lettuce
- ¼ cup shredded carrot
- 3 green onions, thinly sliced
- 1 small clove garlic, minced
- 1 teaspoon grated ginger root
  OR: 1 slice candied or preserved ginger, rinsed and finely chopped
- 2 tablespoons peanut or vegetable oil
- 1 can (13¼ ounces) pineapple tidbits in heavy syrup
- 1 envelope or teaspoon instant chicken broth
- 1 tablespoon cornstarch
- 1 tablespoon soy sauce
- ¼ cup cider vinegar
- ¼ cup brown sugar, packed
- 1 can (1 pound) bean sprouts, rinsed and drained
  OR: 1 pound fresh bean sprouts, rinsed and drained
- 1 medium-size green pepper, halved, seeded and cut into thin strips
- 1 can (6 ounces) water chestnuts, drained and sliced
  Chopped toasted almonds or peanuts

1. Core, rinse and thoroughly drain lettuce; refrigerate in plastic bag or large salad crisper.
2. Sauté carrot, green onions, garlic and ginger in oil in a large saucepan with a flameproof handle over medium heat on grill until limp.
3. Measure syrup from pineapple and add water to make 1 cup; stir into vegetables with chicken broth; bring to boiling and simmer 5 minutes.
4. Mix cornstarch with soy sauce in

a 1-cup measure; stir into hot mixture along with vinegar and brown sugar. Heat, stirring often, until mixture thickens and bubbles 3 minutes.
To serve hot: Cut head of lettuce in half, lengthwise; with cut sides down, prepare 4 cups shredded lettuce. Arrange lettuce on large serving platter. Mix pineapple, bean sprouts, green pepper and water chestnuts into bubbling sauce; simmer until heated through. Pour sauce over shredded lettuce; top with chopped nuts.
To serve cold: Cool sauce. At serving time, arrange outside leaves of lettuce on plates; shred remainder. Combine shredded lettuce, pineapple, bean sprouts, green pepper and water chestnuts in a large bowl, tossing lightly until well blended. Arrange mixture on lettuce-lined plates. Spoon part of sauce over each plate and sprinkle with chopped nuts. Pass soy sauce and remaining dressing.

BEAN SALAD

Sweet pickle relish gives a tangy taste to a bean duet.

Makes 6 servings.

- 1 can (16 ounces) cut green beans, drained
- 1 can (16 ounces) pinto beans, drained
- ½ cup sweet pickle relish
- ¼ cup vegetable or soybean oil
- 1 tablespoon lemon juice
- ¼ teaspoon garlic salt
- ⅛ teaspoon ground ginger

Combine green beans, pinto beans, pickle relish, oil, lemon juice, garlic salt and ginger in a large glass or ceramic bowl until well blended. Cover bowl with plastic wrap and refrigerate at least 2 hours to blend flavors.

FARM-STYLE POTATO SALAD

Make it up in the cool of the morning and chill through the day so you can serve it with your barbecue supper.

Makes 6 servings.

- 6 large boiling potatoes
- ¼ cup vegetable oil
- ¼ cup cider vinegar
- 1 medium-size onion, chopped
- 2½ teaspoons salt
- ¼ teaspoon pepper
- ¾ cup mayonnaise or salad dressing
- ¼ cup light cream
- 3 hard-cooked eggs, peeled and diced
- 1 cup sliced celery
  Boston lettuce

1. Cook potatoes 30 minutes, or just until tender in boiling salted water in a large kettle or saucepan; drain. Peel potatoes and cut into thin slices; place in a large glass bowl.
2. Combine oil, vinegar, onion, salt and pepper in a jar with a screwtop; cover jar and shake to mix. Pour dressing over potatoes; toss to blend. Cover bowl; chill.
3. Just before serving, mix mayonnaise with cream in a small bowl until smooth; pour over potatoes; toss. Add diced eggs and celery and toss lightly. Line a salad bowl with lettuce; fill with salad; garnish with red pepper.

ORANGE-RADISH SALAD

This unusual combination of flavors and textures adds color, as well as punch, to a curry barbecue.

Makes 6 servings.

- 6 medium-size California oranges
- 1 bunch or package radishes
- ⅓ cup lemon juice
- 2 tablespoons honey
- ¼ teaspoon salt
- ⅛ teaspoon ground ginger

1. Pare and section oranges; save orange peel for fruit drinks, or toss over hot coals to add a distinctive flavor to barbecued meat or fish. Trim and cut radishes into thin slices.
2. Combine lemon juice, honey, salt and ginger in a large ceramic or glass bowl until well blended. Add orange sections and radish slices. Toss to coat evenly. Cover bowl with plastic wrap. Chill at least 4 hours to blend flavors. Serve with curry-glazed lamb or chicken kabobs.

SPICY SPINACH SALAD

A pungent mushroom dressing tops spinach, lettuce and ripe olives.

Makes 6 servings.

- ½ cup vegetable oil
- ¼ cup wine vinegar
- 1½ teaspoons lemon juice
- ¼ teaspoon salt
  Few drops bottled red pepper seasoning
- 1 small clove garlic, minced
- 1 tablespoon chopped chives
  OR: 1 teaspoon freeze-dried chives
- 1 can (3 ounces) chopped mushrooms, drained
  OR: 6 large mushrooms, chopped
- 6 cups bite-sized iceberg lettuce
- 2 cups spinach leaves
- ⅓ cup sliced ripe olives

1. Combine oil, vinegar, lemon juice, salt, red pepper seasoning, garlic, chives and mushrooms in a jar with a screw top; shake to mix well.
2. Combine lettuce, spinach and olives in a large bowl. Pour dressing over and toss lightly to mix well.

BLENDER PÂTÉ

Fresh mushrooms add extra flavor to this quick-to-make hors d'oeuvre.

Makes 2 cups.

- 1 envelope unflavored gelatin
- ¼ cup dry white wine
- ¼ cup water
- 1 envelope or teaspoon instant chicken broth
- ½ cup sliced mushrooms
- 1 small onion, chopped (¼ cup)
- 1 tablespoon butter or margarine
- 1 package (8 ounces) liverwurst
- 1 tablespoon sharp mustard
  Few drops gravy coloring (optional)
- 1 hard-cooked egg
  Assorted raw vegetables
  Melba toast

1. Sprinkle gelatin over white wine in a small saucepan; stir to soften. Add water and instant chicken broth. Cook over low heat, just until gelatin dissolves. Remove from heat; cool.
2. Meanwhile, sauté mushrooms and onion in butter or margarine until soft in a small skillet.
3. Place cooled gelatin mixture, then sautéed vegetables, in container of electric blender. Dice liverwurst into container, then add mustard. Cover and process on high 30 seconds, or until smooth; add gravy coloring.
4. Pour mixture into a 2 cup bowl, preferably a metal one. Chill 3 hours.

5. To unmold, run a sharp-tipped thin-bladed knife around top of bowl, then dip bowl *very quickly* in and out of a pan of hot water. Cover mold with a large serving plate; turn upside down, then carefully lift off mold. Chop egg white and sprinkle around pâté; sieve egg yolk on top of pâté. Serve with assorted raw vegetables and Melba toast.

BEANS HAWAIIAN

These beans are sure to make a hit.

Grill for 40 minutes.
Makes 4 servings.

- 2 cans (about 1 pound each) beans in tomato sauce
- 1 small onion, grated
- ¼ cup light molasses
- 2 tablespoons prepared mustard
- 1 package (1 pound) frankfurters, cut in half crosswise
- 1 can (about 9 ounces) sliced pineapple, drained

1. Build a medium fire, or set gas or electric grill to medium.
2. Combine beans, grated onion, molasses and mustard in an 8-cup metal casserole; top with frankfurters and pineapple slices; cover casserole.
3. Cook on grill, 8 inches from heat, 40 minutes, or until bubbly-hot.

SALAD STRATA

Layer crunchy iceberg lettuce, red kidney beans and an unusual cheese dressing for a flavorful salad that's high in protein.

Makes 8 servings.

    1 medium-size head iceberg lettuce
       Cheddar Dressing (recipe follows)
    1 can (1 pound) red kidney beans,
       rinsed and drained
    1 small green pepper, halved,
       seeded and cut into thin strips
    ¼ cup sliced green onion

1. Core, rinse and thoroughly drain lettuce; refrigerate in plastic bag or crisper. Prepare CHEDDAR DRESSING and refrigerate.
2. Combine beans, green pepper and onion in a small bowl until well blended; cover with plastic wrap and refrigerate.
3. At serving time, cut lettuce into bite-sized pieces; place in large salad bowl or on individual plates. Top lettuce with bean mixture, then with CHEDDAR DRESSING. Garnish with sliced pimiento, if you wish.

CHEDDAR DRESSING: Makes 1½ cups. Combine ¾ cup mayonnaise or salad dressing, ¼ cup dairy sour cream, 1 tablespoon vinegar, 1 teaspoon chopped chives, ¾ teaspoon seasoned salt, ½ teaspoon onion powder, dash garlic powder, dash white pepper and 2 drops bottled red pepper seasoning in a small bowl until well blended. Fold in ½ cup shredded Cheddar cheese and ⅓ cup chopped pimiento-stuffed green olives.

TUNISIAN RELISH

Lime juice adds distinctive flavor to cucumber and green pepper in this classic salad from Morocco.

Makes 8 servings.

    2 medium-size cucumbers
    2 large green peppers
       Juice of 1 lime
    1 teaspoon salt
    ¼ teaspoon freshly ground pepper

1. Pare cucumbers; quarter lengthwise and remove seeds. Cut cucumbers into thin slices.
2. Halve, seed and dice green peppers. (Or, you may use one red and one green pepper for a more colorful relish.)
3. Combine lime juice, salt and pepper in a large glass or ceramic bowl and stir until salt dissolves. Add cucumber and green peppers. Toss until vegetables are evenly coated.
4. Cover bowl with plastic wrap and allow to stand at least 8 hours at room temperature. Serve with barbecued lamb or chicken.

GORGONZOLA SALAD

The tender heart of romaine and ripe beefeater tomato slices are crowned with crumbled cheese. Shown with T-bone Steak for Two on page 49.

Makes 2 servings.

    1 small head romaine
    1 large ripe tomato
    ¼ cup crumbled Gorgonzola cheese
       Salt and freshly ground pepper
       Italian Dressing (recipe follows)

1. Wash romaine and drain well on paper towels; place in a plastic bag and tie securely; chill overnight. Keep tomato at room temperature.
2. Arrange the tender center romaine leaves on 2 chilled salad plates. Cut tomato into thin slices; place on romaine and top with crumbled cheese. Season with salt and freshly ground pepper. Serve with ITALIAN DRESSING.

ITALIAN DRESSING: Makes 1 cup. Combine ⅓ cup olive oil, ⅓ cup vegetable oil, ⅓ cup red wine vinegar, 1 teaspoon salt, ¼ teaspoon freshly ground pepper and 1 bay leaf in a 1-cup jar with a screw top. Shake and chill.

COOL AS A CUCUMBER MOLD

It's light and refreshing, but packed with high-quality egg protein.

Makes 6 servings.

    1 package (3 ounces) lime-flavored
       gelatin
    1 cup boiling water
    1 package (3 ounces) cream
       cheese, cubed
    ½ cup bottled green goddess
       dressing
       Rind of 1 lime, grated
    1 to 2 tablespoons lime juice
    5 hard-cooked eggs
    1 medium-size cucumber, peeled,
       chopped and drained
       Lime wedges
       Cucumber slices

1. Dissolve gelatin in water in a large bowl. Add cream cheese, stirring until well blended; stir in dressing, lime rind and juice. Refrigerate 30 minutes, or until as thick as unbeaten egg white.
2. Chop eggs; fold into gelatin mixture along with cucumber. Pour into a 4-cup mold. Refrigerate at least 3 hours, or until firm.
3. To unmold, run a sharp-tipped thin-bladed knife around top of mold, then dip mold *very quickly* in and out of a pan of hot water. Cover mold with a large serving plate; turn upside down, then carefully lift off mold. Garnish with lime wedges, cucumber slices and egg wedges, if you wish.
CHEF'S TIP: To center a molded salad, moisten serving plate with cold water before unmolding.

RUSSIAN POTATO SALAD

Chunks of chicken and tangy capers mingle in a sour cream and mayonnaise dressing.

Makes 6 servings.

    4 medium-size boiling potatoes,
       cooked and peeled (1½ pounds)
    1 cup diced cooked chicken
    ½ cup chopped dill pickles
    1 small onion, chopped (¼ cup)
    ⅓ cup dairy sour cream
    ⅓ cup mayonnaise or salad dressing
    2 tablespoons drained capers
    1 teaspoon salt
       Salad greens
    2 medium-size tomatoes, sliced
    2 hard-cooked eggs, peeled and
       sliced
       Stuffed green olives

1. Combine potatoes, chicken, dill pickles and onion in a large glass or ceramic bowl until well blended. Combine sour cream, mayonnaise or salad dressing, capers and salt in a small bowl.
2. Pour dressing over potato salad and toss *gently* just until well blended. Cover bowl with plastic wrap and chill at least 4 hours to blend flavors.
4. Line salad bowl with greens; mound potato salad in center; alternate tomato and egg slices around side of salad and garnish top with olives. This salad is almost a meal in itself, but it teams beautifully with grilled sausages or hearty hamburgers.

FRENCH POTATO SALAD

Parmesan cheese and garlic combine in an oil and vinegar dressing for a Continental-style salad.

Makes 6 servings.

    6 large boiling potatoes
    ⅓ cup olive or vegetable oil
    ⅓ cup tarragon vinegar
    1 small onion, chopped (¼ cup)
    2 cloves garlic, crushed
    2 teaspoons salt
    ¼ teaspoon pepper
    ⅓ cup grated Parmesan cheese
    1 red or green pepper, halved,
       seeded and diced
       Romaine lettuce

1. Cook potatoes 30 minutes, or just until tender, in boiling salted water in a large kettle or saucepan; drain. Peel potatoes and slice into a large glass or ceramic bowl.
2. Combine oil, vinegar, onion, garlic, salt and pepper in a jar and shake well. Pour over potatoes and toss to coat. Cover bowl with plastic wrap and chill at least 3 hours.
3. Just before serving, toss potatoes with cheese and chopped peppers.
4. Line a serving platter with romaine; spoon potato salad on lettuce. Serve with sliced salami and marinated green beans.

BAGNA CAUDA

Crisp vegetable sticks are served with an anchovy-flavored dip for salad, Italian-style.

Makes 6 servings.

- 1 bunch green onions
- 2 medium-size zucchini
- 1 large cucumber
- 8 stalks celery
- ½ pound green beans
- 1 pint cherry tomatoes
- 1 bunch radishes
- 2 cups heavy cream
- ¼ cup (½ stick) butter or margarine
- 1 can (2 ounces) flat anchovy fillets, drained and chopped
- 1 clove garlic, minced
  Italian bread sticks

1. Trim green onions and cut into 3-inch pieces; cut zucchini into long diagonal slices; cut cucumber into long diagonal slices; trim celery and cut into 3-inch pieces; tip green beans; remove stems from cherry tomatoes; trim radishes.
2. Place vegetables in individual plastic bags and refrigerate at least 4 hours. Arrange vegetables on chilled serving tray.
3. Heat cream to boiling in a small saucepan; boil gently 15 minutes, or until cream thickens.
4. Heat butter or margarine in a large metal skillet with a flameproof handle on barbecue grill or on kitchen range; add anchovies and garlic. Cook 3 minutes. Stir in thickened cream and cook, stirring constantly, until dip simmers; do *not* allow to boil.
5. Dip chilled vegetables and Italian bread sticks into hot dip.

CUCUMBERS IN SOUR CREAM

Here's the perfect choice to star your home-grown cucumbers.

Makes 8 servings.

- 4 large or 8 medium-size cucumbers
- 2 large onions, thinly sliced
- 2 tablespoons white vinegar
- 2 tablespoons salt
- ¾ cup dairy sour cream
- 1 tablespoon prepared sharp mustard
- 1 tablespoon chopped fresh dill
  OR: 1 teaspoon dillweed, crumbled

1. Pare cucumbers; quarter, lengthwise; remove seeds; cut cucumbers into thin slices.
2. Combine cucumbers and onion slices in a large glass or ceramic bowl; sprinkle with vinegar and salt; toss to coat evenly. Allow to stand at room temperature at least 30 minutes; drain well in strainer.
3. Add sour cream, mustard and dill or dillweed; toss to coat evenly; cover bowl with plastic wrap. Chill 2 hours.

CRESS-TOMATO PLATTER

Creative cook Lisa Simon serves this salad when the watercress is tender and the tomatoes are ripe.

Makes 4 servings.

- 1 large bunch watercress
- 4 ripe tomatoes
- ¼ pound blue cheese, crumbled
  OR: ¼ pound sharp Cheddar cheese, diced
  Lemon Dressing (recipe follows)

1. Wash and trim watercress; drain thoroughly and refrigerate in a plastic bag or crisper.
2. At serving time, line chilled large platter with watercress. Slice tomatoes and arrange in rows over watercress. Sprinkle blue cheese or Cheddar cheese over tomatoes. Pour LEMON DRESSING over all.

LEMON DRESSING: Makes 1 cup. Combine ¾ cup olive or vegetable oil, ¼ cup lemon juice, ½ teaspoon celery salt and dash ground pepper in a jar with a screw top; cover jar and shake until well blended.

MARINATED ITALIAN SALAD

Elbow macaroni and a medley of vegetables combine to make this tasty salad.

Makes 8 servings.

- 1 package (7 or 8 ounces) elbow macaroni
- ¼ cup bottled Italian dressing
- 1 tablespoon salt
- 1 can (16 ounces) cut Italian green beans, drained
- 1 can (14 ounces) artichoke hearts, drained and halved
- 1½ cups sliced carrots
- 1 cup chopped green pepper
- ¾ cup ripe olives, sliced
- ½ cup sliced radishes
- ¼ cup chopped green onion
- ¾ cup bottled Italian dressing
- ⅓ cup mayonnaise or salad dressing
  Anchovies
  Tomato wedges
  Ripe olives

1. Cook macaroni in 4 quarts boiling water, the ¼ cup Italian dressing and salt 10 minutes, or until tender, yet firm; drain.
2. Combine cooked macaroni, green beans, artichoke hearts, carrots, green pepper, sliced olives, radishes, green onion and the ¾ cup Italian dressing in a large glass or ceramic bowl until well blended. Let stand at room temperature, at least 2 hours, turning frequently to blend flavors.
3. Add mayonnaise or salad dressing and toss until well blended. Refrigerate until serving time. Spoon onto pretty platter. Garnish with anchovies, tomato wedges and ripe olives.

CONFETTI MACARONI SALAD

A hearty and colorful alternative to potato salad, perfect with grilled chicken.

Makes 8 servings.

- 1 package (7 or 8 ounces) elbow macaroni
- ¾ cup mayonnaise or salad dressing
- ¼ cup sliced green onion
- 1 green pepper, halved, seeded and chopped (½ cup)
- 1 carrot, pared and shredded (½ cup)
- 2 tablespoons sweet pickle relish
- ¾ teaspoon salt
- ¼ teaspoon dry mustard
- ¼ to ½ teaspoon bottled red pepper seasoning
- 2 hard-cooked eggs, diced

1. Cook elbow macaroni and drain, following label directions; cool.
2. Mix macaroni with mayonnaise or salad dressing, green onion, green pepper, carrot, pickle relish, salt, dry mustard and red pepper seasoning in a large glass or ceramic bowl until well blended; carefully mix in hard-cooked eggs. Cover with plastic wrap and refrigerate at least 2 hours to blend flavors. Garnish with pimiento slices, if you wish.

CHEF'S TIP: You can make an assortment of hearty salads, using this one as the base. Diced cooked ham, chicken, beef or hot dogs can be added along with 1 cup diced raw zucchini or 1 pound garden-fresh peas, shelled. Be sure to add the vegetables, just before serving, to keep crisp.

SALSA FRIA

This tomato relish with a Spanish flavor has been a part of Californian outdoor cooking for many years.

Makes 8 cups.

- 8 medium-size very ripe tomatoes
- 1 large onion, chopped (1 cup)
- 1 to 4 canned green chilies or Jalapeno peppers (from a 4-ounce can), seeded and finely chopped
- 2 tablespoons cider vinegar
- 2 tablespoons vegetable oil
- 1 tablespoon chopped fresh coriander
  OR: 1 teaspoon leaf oregano, crumbled
- 1 teaspoon salt
- ¼ teaspoon freshly ground pepper

1. Dip tomatoes in boiling water in a large saucepan for 15 seconds; slip off skins.
2. Chop tomatoes; combine with onion, chilies, vinegar, oil, coriander or oregano, salt and pepper in a large glass bowl. Cover with plastic wrap; season in the refrigerator for at least 2 hours. Serve chilled, with pork, lamb or beef.

ZIPPY POTATO SALAD

Mustard, vinegar and red pepper seasoning give this salad its tangy flavor.

Makes 12 servings.

- 8 medium-size boiling potatoes (3 pounds)
- 1 small onion, chopped (¼ cup)
- 2 cups diced celery
- 1 green pepper, halved, seeded and chopped
- 8 radishes, sliced
- 2 teaspoons salt
- 1 cup mayonnaise or salad dressing
- 2 tablespoons prepared mustard
- 2 tablespoons vinegar
- ½ teaspoon bottled red pepper seasoning

1. Pare and dice potatoes; cook in salted boiling water in a large saucepan 10 minutes, or just until tender. Drain, reserving water for soups or sauces.
2. Return potatoes to saucepan and toss over low heat 5 minutes, or until potatoes are fluffy-dry; place in large glass or ceramic bowl.
3. Add onion, celery, green pepper and radishes to dish; sprinkle with salt and toss to blend.
4. Mix together mayonnaise or salad dressing, mustard, vinegar and red pepper seasoning in a small bowl; add to potato mixture. Toss gently with a fork until well blended, being careful not to break potatoes. Cover with plastic wrap; refrigerate at least 2 hours to blend flavors.
5. At serving time, garnish salad with watercress and tomato wedges in a pretty pattern around edge.

BLUE CHEESE SPINACH MOLD

Sparkling and green, the perfect choice for a hot summer evening.

Makes 8 servings.

- ½ cup cold water
- 2 envelopes unflavored gelatin
- 1 can beef broth
- ½ cup bottled chunky blue cheese dressing
- 1 small onion, quartered
- ¼ teaspoon salt
- 2 tablespoons lemon juice
- 1 package (10 ounces) frozen chopped spinach, thawed and drained
- 1 large cucumber, pared, quartered, seeded and finely chopped
- ½ cup chopped celery

1. Sprinkle gelatin over cold water in container of an electric blender.
2. Heat beef broth to boiling in a small saucepan; pour over gelatin in container. Cover and process on low speed 30 seconds, or until gelatin dissolves. Add blue cheese dressing and onion; cover and process on low until smooth. Add salt, lemon juice

and spinach; cover and process on low just until smooth.
3. Turn into bowl and chill, stirring occasionally, 30 minutes, or until mixture mounds slightly when dropped from a spoon.
4. Fold in cucumber and celery. Turn mixture into a 4-cup mold. Chill at least 4 hours, or overnight, until set.
5. To unmold, run a sharp-tipped thin-bladed knife around top of mold, then dip mold *very quickly* in and out of a pan of hot water. Cover mold with a large serving plate; turn upside down, then carefully lift off mold. Garnish with tomato wedges and parsley, if you wish.

SPRING SALAD BOWL

An unusual dill and caper dressing gives this salad its piquancy.

Makes 6 servings.

- 1 head iceberg lettuce
- 1 large cucumber
- ½ cup mayonnaise or salad dressing
- 2 tablespoons diced dill pickle
- 1 tablespoon tarragon or wine vinegar
- 1 tablespoon capers
- 1 tablespoon chopped pimiento
- ½ teaspoon seasoned salt
- ½ teaspoon dillweed
- ½ teaspoon onion powder
- ¼ teaspoon leaf tarragon, crumbled

1. Core, rinse and thoroughly drain lettuce; refrigerate in plastic bag or crisper. Rinse and chill cucumber.
2. Combine mayonnaise or salad dressing, diced pickle, vinegar, capers, pimiento, seasoned salt, dillweed, onion powder and tarragon in a small bowl until well blended. Cover with plastic wrap and refrigerate at least 2 hours to blend flavors.
3. At serving time, tear lettuce into bite-sized pieces. Thinly slice cucumber and arrange with lettuce in chilled salad bowl. Toss with dressing and serve immediately.

CARROT SLAW

This mixture of carrots, toasted almonds, golden raisins and candied ginger goes particularly well with grilled chicken; an orange cream dressing makes it refreshing.

Makes 8 servings.

- 6 cups coarsely shredded carrots
- ½ cup toasted slivered almonds
- ¼ cup golden raisins
- 2 tablespoons chopped candied ginger
- ¾ cup heavy cream
- ¾ cup orange juice
- 2 teaspoons lemon juice
- 1½ teaspoons sugar

Mix carrots, almonds, raisins and candied ginger in a large glass or

ceramic bowl. Combine cream, orange juice, lemon juice and sugar in a jar with a screw top; cover and shake until well blended. Pour dressing over carrot mixture; toss to coat evenly. Cover dish with plastic wrap and refrigerate until serving time. Garnish with orange slices and watercress.
CHEF'S TIP: If you have a food processor, be sure to use it for shredding the carrots. They'll be done very quickly, with no mess.

HOT BACON DRESSING

Gourmets will welcome this dressing for a salad with a difference.

Makes 1 cup.

- 4 slices bacon
- ¼ cup chopped green onion
- ¼ cup cider vinegar
- 2 tablespoons water
- 2 tablespoons sugar
- ½ teaspoon salt
- Pinch of pepper
- ½ teaspoon dry mustard
- 1 hard-cooked egg, chopped

1. Fry bacon until crisp in a small skillet; drain bacon on paper towels. Sauté green onions in bacon drippings in same skillet.
2. Add vinegar, water, sugar, salt, pepper and dry mustard; bring to boiling. Crumble bacon and add to mixture with chopped egg. Serve immediately on spinach leaves.

Suggested Variations:
WILTED LETTUCE—Toss hot mixture with 6 cups torn or shredded western iceberg lettuce. Serve at once.

CREAMY DRESSING—Add ¼ cup cream to HOT BACON DRESSING.

COOKED SALAD DRESSING

This old-fashioned favorite will make a hit with most guests.

Makes 1¼ cups.

- 2 tablespoons sugar
- 2 tablespoons all purpose flour
- ¾ teaspoon dry mustard
- ½ teaspoon salt
- ¼ teaspoon paprika
- ⅛ teaspoon white pepper
- ½ cup cold water
- 1 egg
- ¼ cup cider vinegar
- 2 tablespoons butter or margarine

1. Mix sugar, flour, mustard, salt, paprika, pepper and water in a small bowl until well blended.
2. Beat egg and vinegar in top of double boiler; add flour mixture. Cook and stir over boiling water until thick and creamy. Stir in butter or margarine until melted. Chill. Thin with milk or cream, if needed.

GERMAN POTATO SALAD

Frozen hash brown potatoes and a hot bacon dressing make short work of salad making.

Makes 4 servings.

4 cups boiling salted water
4 cups frozen chopped hash brown potatoes (from a 2-pound bag)
1 cup chopped celery
6 slices bacon
1 cup frozen chopped onion (from a 12-ounce bag)
¼ cup cider vinegar
2 tablespoons light brown sugar
2 tablespoons water
1 teaspoon salt
Dash pepper

1. Pour frozen potatoes into boiling salted water in a large saucepan; return to boiling and boil 1 minute. Drain potatoes; put in large bowl with celery.
2. Fry bacon until crisp in a large skillet; remove and drain on paper towels. Pour off all but ¼ cup of drippings from skillet.
3. Sauté onion in drippings until soft. Stir in vinegar, brown sugar, water, salt and pepper and bring to boiling; pour over potatoes in a medium-size glass bowl and toss to coat. Top with crumbled bacon. Serve warm.

COLD CASSOULET SALAD

The classic French dish becomes a hearty salad. Perfect with Steak Au Poivre.

Makes 12 servings.

1 can (16 ounces) chick peas, drained
2 cans (16 ounces each) red kidney beans, drained
1 can (16 ounces) pinto beans, drained
½ cup thinly sliced green onion
½ cup chopped pimiento
¾ cup vegetable oil
⅓ cup wine vinegar
1 tablespoon lemon juice
1 teaspoon leaf oregano, crumbled
½ teaspoon leaf basil, crumbled
½ teaspoon dillweed
½ teaspoon salt
½ teaspoon pepper
Few drops bottled red pepper seasoning
1 pound sliced hot dogs
½ pound thinly sliced salami
Fresh parsley

1. Combine chick peas, kidney beans, pinto beans, green onion and pimiento in a large glass or ceramic bowl until well blended.
2. Combine oil, vinegar, lemon juice, oregano, basil, dillweed, salt, pepper and red pepper seasoning in a jar with a screw top; shake well and pour over vegetable mixture. Cover with plastic wrap and refrigerate at least 3 hours.
3. At serving time, toss hot dogs with

bean mixture. Drain and place in a large salad bowl. Garnish with salami rosettes placed around edge of bowl. To make rosettes: Fold salami slices in half, roll loosely and secure with a wooden food pick; insert sprig of parsley in center of each.

LIMA-TUNA ANTIPASTO

A variation of the popular Italian hors d'oeuvre, starring fish and cheese.

Makes 8 servings.

1 package (10 ounces) frozen Fordhook lima beans
1 can (7 ounces) tuna fish, drained and flaked
1 cup chopped Provolone or Swiss cheese (4 ounces)
1 medium-size red onion, diced (½ cup)
½ cup bottled Italian dressing
¼ cup chopped parsley
6 anchovy fillets, chopped
2 cloves garlic, crushed
1 teaspoon lemon juice
Salt and black pepper

Cook lima beans in boiling salted water, following package directions; drain. Mix lima beans with tuna, cheese, onion, Italian dressing, parsley, anchovies, garlic and lemon juice in a large bowl until well blended. Taste and season with salt and pepper, if necessary. Cover with plastic wrap and refrigerate 1 hour. CHEF'S TIP: This salad can be prepared and refrigerated several hours before serving.

CARAWAY POTATO SALAD

Oil and lemon juice, plus a dash of caraway, give new character to the ever popular potato salad.

Makes 6 servings.

6 medium-size boiling potatoes (2 pounds)
½ cup vegetable or peanut oil
¼ cup lemon juice
1½ teaspoons salt
1 teaspoon caraway seeds, crushed
Dash cayenne pepper
Dash ground cumin

1. Pare and dice potatoes; cook in salted boiling water in a large saucepan 10 minutes, or just until tender. Drain; reserve water for soup.
2. Return potatoes to saucepan and toss over low heat 5 minutes, or until potatoes are fluffy-dry.
3. Heat oil, lemon juice, salt, caraway seeds, cayenne pepper and cumin in a small saucepan until bubbly.
4. Place potatoes in a glass or ceramic salad bowl; pour dressing over. Toss gently to coat evenly. Cool to room temperature; serve with beef.

SALAD BAR
(Continued from page 128.)

cooked; marinated artichokes; beets and pickled beets; peas and Chinese snow pea pods; tomatoes; cherry tomatoes; radish, slices or roses; sauerkraut; turnips; zucchini, raw or marinated; green pepper, chopped, strips or rings; water chestnuts; bamboo shoots; watercress; parsley.
Protein Foods—Meat: roast beef strips; meatballs; beef taco filling; salami, bologna, liverwurst and other cold cuts; frankfurters; ham; bacon; roast lamb strips; roast veal strips. **Fish:** lobster; shrimp and prawns; crab, Alaska King crab; smoked oysters; anchovies; tuna; salmon, fresh, smoked or canned; pickled herring; sardines. **Poultry and Poultry Products:** chicken strips; turkey strips; eggs, hard-cooked, deviled, egg salad. **Nuts, toasted:** almonds; macadamia; peanuts; pecans; pistachios; pine nuts; walnuts; sesame seeds; coconut; poppy seeds; roasted soy beans. **Miscellaneous:** tomato aspic; gelatin dessert cubes; jellied cranberry sauce; pimiento; chilies; capers; olives; pickles; lemon slices, wedges; mint; herbs and seeds; seasoned salts; croutons; crumbled cheese-flavored crackers; chutney; crystallized ginger; miniature marshmallows; rice; macaroni, macaroni salad. ■

SALAD TANGIERS

Roasted tomatoes and sweet peppers add a Middle Eastern flavor to any patio party, especially one featuring grilled fish.

Makes 8 servings.

4 large firm tomatoes
2 large red peppers
2 large green peppers
1 medium-size onion, chopped (½ cup)
OR: ½ cup sliced green onion
Juice of 1 lemon
1½ teaspoons salt
¼ teaspoon freshly ground pepper
¼ cup olive or peanut oil
½ cup sliced ripe olives

1. Grill tomatoes and red and green peppers, 4 inches from heat, turning often, 15 minutes for the tomatoes and 30 minutes for the peppers, or until skins turn brown.
2. Cool tomatoes; halve and remove seeds and juice. Chop tomatoes and place in a large glass or ceramic bowl.
3. Cool peppers for 5 minutes, then rub with paper towels to remove skin; halve, seed and thinly slice peppers; add to tomatoes in bowl.
4. Add onion, lemon juice, salt and pepper to salad; toss gently to coat evenly. Drizzle oil over and toss gently a second time. Top with ripe olives and chopped parsley, if you wish.

TOSSED GARDEN SALAD

A large clear bowl will display layers of colorful vegetables to perfection.

Makes 10 servings.

- 1 medium-size head iceberg lettuce, shredded
- 1 cup shredded carrots
- 2 small zucchini, thinly sliced (2 ½ cups)
- 1 can (16 ounces) cut wax beans, drained
- 1 package (10 ounces) frozen peas, cooked and drained
- 1 small onion, chopped (¼ cup)
- 1½ cups mayonnaise or salad dressing
- ⅓ cup pickle liquid (drained from dill pickles)
- 1 cup chopped dill pickles
- 1½ cups cheese croutons

1. Line bottom of large clear salad bowl or punch bowl with shredded lettuce. Top with layers of carrots, zucchini, wax beans, peas and chopped onion.
2. Mix mayonnaise or salad dressing and dill pickle liquid in a small bowl until well blended; spread over salad.
3. Mound chopped pickles in center of salad; sprinkle croutons around edge of bowl. Toss before serving.

MISSION BAY FRUIT BASKET

Summer's best fruits are bathed in a brandy and spice syrup and piled in a handsome cranshaw melon. Photographed in a San Diego garden and shown on page 95.

Makes 8 servings.

- 1 cranshaw, honeydew, casaba, muskmelon or cantaloupe
- 1 ripe papaya
- 1 small pineapple
- 1 pint strawberries
- 2 ripe kiwis
- 4 fresh kumquats (optional)
- 1 cup apple juice
- ½ cup sugar
- 1 three-inch piece stick cinnamon
- 4 whole cloves
- ½ cup apricot or peach brandy
  Rind of 1 lemon, cut into very thin strips

1. Buy fruits the day before or early in the morning; chill for at least 4 hours.
2. Combine apple juice, sugar, cinnamon stick and cloves in a small saucepan; simmer 5 minutes; remove from heat; pour into a glass bowl; add brandy and lemon rind strips. Let stand at room temperature.
3. Make basket handle by leaving a 1-inch section in top center of melon, cutting down to center of melon with a sharp French knife; cut a wedge in from either side of melon and remove melon wedges. Seed melon and cut a thin slice from bottom of melon if

basket doesn't stand evenly. Cover melon basket with plastic wrap and return to refrigerator.
4. Pare and dice melon wedges into a large bowl; halve, seed and pit papaya; dice into bowl; slice, pare, core and dice pineapple into bowl; wash, hull and halve strawberries; peel and slice kiwis; wash and slice fresh kumquats, if used. Pour brandy syrup over fruits, removing spices. Chill at least 1 hour.
5. To serve, place melon basket on a glass serving plate and pile fruit into the basket. Spoon remaining fruit and syrup into a glass serving bowl and pass after basket empties out.
CHEF'S TIP: As summer passes, change the fruit combinations to feature the ripest, most delicious fruits in your market.

IMPERIAL SALAD BOWL

The world's crispest, freshest salad greens combine to create the best of all barbecue salad bowls. Photographed at Moceri Produce in San Diego on page 86.

Makes 8 servings.

- 4 cups shredded red cabbage
- 1 pound small white onions
- 8 cups bite-sized pieces Western iceberg lettuce
  Limestone or red-tipped leaf lettuce
- ½ pound thinly sliced salami, quartered
- ½ pound Provolone cheese, cut into thin sticks
  Ripe olives
  Pimiento
  Creamy Italian Dressing (recipe follows)

1. Layer cabbage in the bottom of a very large salad bowl. Peel and halve onions and press against edge of bowl; pack iceberg lettuce behind and on top of onions; arrange leaf lettuce leaves around edge of salad bowl.
2. Pile salami pieces in center of bowl; arrange Provolone cheese, spoke-style, around salami. Garnish with ripe olives and pimiento. Cover bowl with plastic wrap and chill until serving time.
3. Add CREAMY ITALIAN DRESSING and toss to coat evenly; sprinkle with freshly ground pepper just before serving in chilled salad plates or soup bowls. Serve with bread sticks.

CREAMY ITALIAN DRESSING: Makes about 2 cups. Combine 1 container (8 ounces) dairy sour cream, ½ cup mayonnaise or salad dressing, and ½ cup bottled Italian dressing in a medium-size bowl. Wrap bowl with plastic wrap; chill until serving time. CHEF'S TIP: You can add ½ cup crumbled Gorgonzola, Roquefort or blue cheese to the above recipe.

RAINBOW SALAD

Curry-flavored vinaigrette seasons this salad —a mound of rice topped with rows of colorful vegetables.

Makes 6 servings.

- 2 cups water
- 1 cup uncooked long grain rice
- 1 tablespoon vegetable oil
- 1 teaspoon salt
  Curry Vinaigrette (recipe follows)
- ¼ cup mayonnaise or salad dressing
- 1 package (10 ounces) frozen peas
- 1 can (8½ ounces) whole-kernel corn, drained
- 2 tablespoons chopped pimiento
- 1 can (6 ounces) ripe olives, drained
- 1 red pepper, halved, seeded and cut into thin strips

1. Combine water, rice, oil and salt in a medium-size saucepan; cook over medium heat until mixture starts to bubble. Stir carefully with a fork; lower heat and cover saucepan.
2. Simmer 20 minutes, or until water is absorbed and rice is just tender.
3. Fluff rice with a fork; place in large glass or ceramic bowl. Pour ⅔ cup CURRY VINAIGRETTE over warm cooked rice; toss lightly with fork, just until all rice is moistened; let cool. Gently fold in mayonnaise or salad dressing; cover bowl with plastic wrap and refrigerate.
4. Rap unopened package of peas on countertop to separate peas; place peas in a small bowl. Pour over ¼ cup CURRY VINAIGRETTE; toss with fork; place in a pile in a shallow dish.
5. Mix corn and pimiento with ¼ cup CURRY VINAIGRETTE in same small bowl; toss with fork and place next to peas in dish. Pour ¼ cup CURRY VINAIGRETTE over olives in bowl; toss with fork and place next to corn in dish. Toss red pepper strips with remaining CURRY VINAIGRETTE and place next to olives. Cover dish with plastic wrap and refrigerate.
6. At serving time, mound rice onto large serving dish. Top with rows of peas, corn, olives and pepper strips.

CURRY VINAIGRETTE: Makes 1⅔ cups. Combine 1 cup olive or vegetable oil, ⅔ cup white wine vinegar, 2 tablespoons lemon juice, 2 tablespoons sugar, 1 large clove garlic, halved, 1 teaspoon curry powder, 1 teaspoon salt and ⅛ teaspoon freshly ground pepper in a jar with a screw top, cover jar and shake.

(Recipes continued on page 121.)

Filled with tropical fruits in a spiced brandy syrup, Mission Bay Fruit Basket reigns supreme as a salad or a light dessert. Recipe, this page.

PHOTOGRAPHED IN LA JOLLA, CALIFORNIA

MARINADES & GLAZES

BROWN SUGAR GLAZE

Brush on spareribs, lamb riblets or chicken wings for the last 10 minutes of grilling.

Makes 1½ cups.

- ¼ cup firmly packed dark brown sugar
- 2 tablespoons cornstarch
- 1 teaspoon salt
- ½ cup lemon juice
- ½ cup water
- 2 tablespoons catsup
- 1 clove garlic, minced
- ½ teaspoon ground ginger

1. Combine brown sugar, cornstarch and salt in a medium-size saucepan with a flameproof handle; stir in lemon juice, water, catsup, garlic and ginger until well blended.
2. Cook on grill, stirring often, until sauce thickens and bubbles 3 minutes; push to side of grill and keep warm.

CHUTNEY TOPPING

Give your burger a British touch.

Makes 1½ cups.

- 1 container (8 ounces) dairy sour cream
- ½ cup finely chopped chutney
- 1½ teaspoons curry powder

Combine sour cream, chutney and curry powder in a small glass bowl; cover with plastic wrap. Refrigerate at least 2 hours to blend flavors.

CALIFORNIA BARBECUE SAUCE

Lemon juice and molasses give distinction to this sauce. Just right with spareribs.

Makes 3 cups.

- 2 cans (8 ounces each) tomato sauce
- ½ cup lemon juice
- ¼ cup light molasses
- 3 tablespoons prepared mustard
- 2 tablespoons vegetable oil
- 2 teaspoons salt
- ⅛ teaspoon bottled red pepper seasoning

Combine tomato sauce, lemon juice, molasses, mustard, oil, salt and red pepper seasoning in a large bowl; stir until well blended. Store in a 4-cup glass jar with a screw top. Brush on pork spareribs, lamb riblets or beef.

A bevy of drinks for summertime entertaining: (left to right) Polynesian Cocktail, Coconut Sipper, Lime Rickey, Claret Lemonade and Pink Cooler. Recipes begin on page 98.

MANDARIN MARINADE

Use first to marinate, then to baste, chicken, pork or lamb.

Makes 3 cups.

- 1 cup lemon juice
- 1 cup vegetable oil
- ½ cup honey
- ½ cup soy sauce
- 1 tablespoon ground ginger
- 1 clove garlic, minced
- 1 teaspoon salt
- 1 teaspoon leaf basil, crumbled
- ½ teaspoon leaf marjoram, crumbled

Combine lemon juice, oil, honey, soy sauce, ginger, garlic, salt, basil and marjoram in a large jar with a screw top. Cover and shake to blend well. Refrigerate 2 hours to blend flavors.

SPICY BARBECUE SAUCE

Make up a batch and keep on hand for spur of the moment barbecues.

Makes 1 cup.

- ½ cup catsup
- ¼ cup water
- 2 tablespoons light brown sugar
- 2 tablespoons grated onion
- 2 tablespoons Worcestershire sauce
- 2 tablespoons cider vinegar
- ½ teaspoon salt
- ¼ teaspoon chili powder
- ⅛ teaspoon garlic powder
- ⅛ teaspoon pepper
- Dash bottled red pepper seasoning

Combine catsup, water, brown sugar, onion, Worcestershire sauce, cider vinegar, salt, chili powder, garlic powder, pepper and red pepper seasoning in a small saucepan. Simmer 15 minutes.

ORANGE-MUSTARD SAUCE

Just tart and spicy enough for ham steak or spareribs.

Makes 1½ cups.

- 1 can (6 ounces) frozen concentrate for orange juice, thawed
- 1¼ cups water
- 1 cup firmly packed light brown sugar
- ¼ cup cider vinegar
- 2 tablespoons prepared mustard

Combine thawed orange juice, water, brown sugar, vinegar and prepared mustard in a medium-size saucepan with a flameproof handle. Heat to boiling over grill, stirring several times; push to side of grill and simmer 20 minutes, or until sauce thickens. Brush over ham steak or spareribs for the last 15 minutes of grilling.

HORSERADISH SAUCE

Toasted almonds add a distinctive touch to this zippy sauce for grilled chicken or fish.

Makes 1¼ cups.

- ¼ cup sliced almonds
- 2 tablespoons butter or margarine
- 2 tablespoons all purpose flour
- ¼ teaspoon salt
- 1 small can evaporated milk (⅔ cup)
- ⅓ cup milk
- 2 tablespoons prepared horseradish

1. Sauté almonds in butter or margarine until golden brown in a small saucepan; remove almonds with slotted spoon and reserve.
2. Stir in flour and salt; cook, stirring constantly, just until bubbly. Stir in evaporated milk and milk; continue cooking and stirring until sauce thickens and bubbles 3 minutes.
3. Stir in horseradish and toasted almonds; serve warm.

LEMON-BUTTER BASTE

Here's a baste to make over the coals.

Makes 1¾ cups.

- 1 cup (2 sticks) butter or margarine
- 1 medium-size onion, chopped (½ cup)
- ⅔ cup lemon juice
- 2 tablespoons Worcestershire sauce
- 2 teaspoons salt
- 1 teaspoon paprika

1. Melt butter or margarine in a medium-size saucepan with a flameproof handle over grill; stir in onion and sauté until soft.
2. Stir in lemon juice, Worcestershire sauce, salt and paprika; simmer 10 minutes. Brush on fish.

LEMON-HERB MARINADE

Rosemary and lemon juice—so good with chicken, beef or lamb.

Makes ¾ cup.

- ⅓ cup vegetable oil
- ⅓ cup lemon juice
- 1 teaspoon grated lemon rind
- 3 tablespoons Worcestershire sauce
- 1 clove garlic, minced
- 1 teaspoon salt
- 1 teaspoon leaf rosemary, crumbled
- ¼ teaspoon freshly ground pepper

Combine oil, lemon juice and rind, Worcestershire sauce, garlic, salt, rosemary and pepper in a 1-cup jar with a screw top. Cover jar and shake to blend well; chill at least 1 hour to blend flavors.

(Recipes continued on page 114.)

LIME RICKEY

Tall, cool glasses of limeade and rum make the perfect ending to a hot summer's day. Shown with the Pacific Ocean as a background on page 96.

Makes 4 servings.

- 1 can (6 ounces) frozen concentrate for limeade
- 1 bottle (28 ounces) tonic water, chilled
- ¾ cup rum
  Ice cubes

1. Thaw limeade and pour into a tall pitcher; add tonic water and rum; stir to blend.
2. Fill tall stemmed glasses with ice cubes; pour rum mixture over and garnish with kumquat, lime and orange swizzle sticks, if you wish.

WATERMELON IN WINE

So cool and refreshing on a hot summer's day! Any melon can be substituted for the watermelon in this recipe. The photograph, taken in San Diego, is on page 84.

Makes 8 servings.

- 1 large lemon
- 3 envelopes unflavored gelatin
- 1½ cups water
- ⅔ cup sugar
- 1 three-inch piece stick cinnamon
- 6 whole allspice
- 3 cups sweet white wine
  Green food coloring
- 3 cups watermelon balls (directions follow)

1. Grate lemon and squeeze. Combine gelatin, lemon rind and juice in a large bowl and stir until gelatin softens.
2. Combine water, sugar, cinnamon and allspice in a small saucepan; bring to boiling; lower heat. Simmer 5 minutes; remove spices with slotted spoon and stir hot liquid into gelatin mixture until gelatin dissolves. Stir in wine and tint a light green with a few drops green food coloring.
3. Place an 8-cup mold in a pan of ice and water. Measure ½ cup gelatin into mold; chill until gelatin is as thick as unbeaten egg white. Refrigerate remaining gelatin.
4. Arrange enough melon balls in gelatin in mold to make a pretty pattern; chill until sticky-firm. Add remaining melon balls to gelatin in bowl and chill until mixture is syrupy.
5. Pour syrupy gelatin over firm layer in mold and refrigerate 6 hours, or overnight.
6. To unmold, run a thin-bladed knife around edge of mold; dip mold into a pan of hot water for 30 seconds; unmold onto a chilled serving plate. Chill until serving time.
To make melon balls: Cut a quarter of a watermelon, or halve other melon, and remove seeds. Form melon into balls with a melon-ball scoop or the ½ teaspoon of a measuring spoon set.

CHAMPAGNE STRAWBERRIES

Sun-ripened berries taste even better when topped with California champagne. Shown with T-bone Steak for Two on page 49.

Makes 2 servings.

- 1 pint strawberries
- 1 split bottle California champagne
- 1 tablespoon chopped candied orange peel

1. Wash unhulled strawberries in a strainer and drain well. Refrigerate at least 2 hours.
2. Serve berries in a chilled glass container to hull; pile in champagne glasses; top with champagne and sprinkle with candied orange peel.

COFFEE ITALIANO

Espresso, flavored with Amaretto liqueur and topped with a puff of whipped cream, makes the perfect ending to a memorable meal. Photographed with T-bone Steak for Two on page 49.

Makes 2 servings.

- Espresso coffee
- Sugar to taste
- Amaretto liqueur
- Softly whipped cream

1. Prepare espresso coffee for two servings and pour into a coffee server; place over candle warmer.
2. Pour espresso to within 2 inches of top of continental champagne glasses. Sweeten with sugar to taste; add Amaretto liqueur to glass and float whipped cream on top.

POLYNESIAN COCKTAIL

Pineapple and apricot blend perfectly with vodka in this cooler from the Islands. Shown near San Diego, on page 96.

Makes 6 servings.

- 1 can (6 ounces) concentrate for pineapple juice, thawed
- ½ cup apricot syrup
  OR: 1 can (6 ounces) apricot nectar
- 1 cup vodka
- 1 bottle (28 ounces) ginger ale, chilled

1. Combine concentrate for pineapple juice, apricot syrup or nectar and vodka in a tall pitcher; stir in ginger ale until well blended.
2. Fill 6 tall glasses with ice cubes; add pineapple mixture. Garnish each glass with a kabob of pineapple wedges and maraschino cherries.

MARY JOE'S APPLE CAKE

Teenage cook, Mary Joe Wilong, shares her favorite way to serve apples at a barbecue.

Bake a 350° for 1 hour.
Makes one 13x9x2-inch cake.

- 3 cups all purpose flour
- 2 cups sugar
- 1 tablespoon baking powder
- 2 teaspoons ground cinnamon
- 1 teaspoon salt
- 1 cup (2 sticks) butter or margarine, melted
- 4 eggs
- ½ cup milk
- 3 large apples
- ½ cup granulated sugar
- ½ cup firmly packed brown sugar
- 1 teaspoon ground allspice
- ½ cup (1 stick) butter or margarine, melted

1. Sift flour, the 2 cups sugar, baking powder, cinnamon and salt into the large bowl of an electric mixer.
2. Add the 1 cup melted butter or margarine, eggs and milk to bowl.
3. Beat at medium speed 2 minutes, scraping down side of bowl several times. Pour batter into a greased 13x9x2-inch baking pan.
4. Pare, quarter, core and slice apples and arrange in rows on top of batter. Combine the ½ cup granulated sugar, brown sugar and allspice in a small bowl; sprinkle over apples. Spoon the ½ cup melted butter over.
5. Bake in moderate oven (350°) 1 hour, or until a wooden food pick inserted into center comes out clean. Cool in pan on wire rack. Cut while still warm and serve with whipped cream or ice cream on top.

APRICOT PUNCH

Freeze a small bowl of water with slices of lemon, lime or orange for a decorative punch bowl ice block.

Makes 12 servings.

- 1 can sweetened condensed milk (not evaporated milk)
- 2 tablespoons lemon juice
- 1 can (48 ounces) apricot nectar
- ¼ cup apricot brandy
- 1 bottle (28 to 32 ounces) club soda, chilled

1. Combine sweetened condensed milk and lemon juice in a tall pitcher; stir in apricot nectar and brandy; cover pitcher with plastic wrap. Chill until serving time.
2. Fill small metal bowl with water, add maraschino cherries, fresh mint sprigs or halved lemon slices, if you wish. Freeze until solid.
3. Pour apricot mixture into punch bowl; stir in club soda. Dip bowl of ice in hot water; lower ice block into punch. Garnish punch bowl with fresh mint.

COCONUT SIPPER

Coconut milk and rum are a Caribbean contribution to cooling summer drinks. Shown among wild flowers, on page 96.

Makes 4 servings.

- 1 can (10 ounces) coconut milk, chilled
- ⅓ cup rum
- 1 bottle (28 ounces) club soda, chilled
  Chocolate Curles (directions follow)

1. Shake coconut milk several times; open can and divide among 4 tall glasses; stir in rum, then club soda, until foamy.
2. Sprinkle with CHOCOLATE CURLES, just before serving.

CHOCOLATE CURLES - Shave a square of semisweet chocolate or a thick chocolate bar with a vegetable parer, making long strokes.

PINK COOLER

Milk never tasted so good. Serve icy cold. Photographed in La Jolla, California, and shown on page 96.

Makes 4 servings.

- 2 cups milk
- 1 bottle (12 ounces) club soda, chilled
- ½ cup strawberry syrup
- ¼ cup apricot brandy

1. Combine milk, club soda, strawberry syrup and apricot brandy in a tall pitcher. Add ice cubes and stir until mixture is extra cold. Remove ice cubes with a slotted spoon.
2. Pour into tall stemmed glasses and garnish with fresh strawberries, if you wish.

MARASCHINO MOUSSE

We chose marashino syrup, but you can also use strawberry or raspberry syrups to create this party-perfect dessert. Shown overlooking Mission Bay, on page 84.

Makes 8 servings.

- 2 envelopes unflavored gelatin
- ¾ cup sugar
- 3 eggs, separated
- 2 cups water
- 1 cup maraschino, strawberry or raspberry syrup
  Red food coloring (optional)

1. Combine gelatin and ¼ cup of the sugar in a medium-size heavy saucepan; stir in egg yolks and water until well blended.
2. Cook, over low heat stirring constantly, until mixture coats a metal spoon; remove from heat and stir in maraschino, strawberry or raspberry syrup. Pour into a large metal bowl. Chill in a pan of ice and water 15 minutes, or until as thick as unbeaten egg white.
3. While gelatin thickens, beat egg whites with electric mixer at high speed in a deep bowl until foamy-white and double in volume; add remaining sugar, 1 tablespoon at a time, beating well after each addition, until meringue forms firm peaks.
4. Beat gelatin mixture with mixer until fluffy; fold in meringue mixture until no streaks of pink or white remain. Tint a deeper pink with red food coloring, if you wish.
5. Spoon mixture into 8 individual molds or sherbet dishes, or a 6-cup mold. Chill 4 hours, or overnight.
6. To serve, run a thin-bladed knife around molds; dip into a pan of hot water for 15 seconds; invert onto serving dishes. Serve with sliced berries and whipped cream, if you wish.

COFFEE PRALINE ICE CREAM

Fold a classic European confection into coffee ice cream for a rich and satisfying treat. Serve in crystal parfait glasses.

Makes 1 quart.

- ½ cup unblanched almonds
- ½ cup sugar
- 1 quart coffee ice cream, softened
- 2 tablespoons Amaretto or coffee liqueur

1. Combine almonds and sugar in a heavy-based saucepan. Cook over very low heat, stirring often with a metal spoon, until sugar melts and turns a deep golden color. (Watch for burning.) Immediately remove pan from heat to a heat-resistant surface.
2. Pour almond mixture onto a well-oiled cookie sheet, spreading as thinly as possible; let cool and harden completely. (Soak pan and spoon in very hot water for easier clean-up.)
3. Invert hardened praline onto a sheet of heavy-duty foil; crack into chunks with a hammer. Place a few chunks in container of electric blender or food processor; cover. With hand on cover, process on high until mixture is completely pulverized, stopping and starting machine several times and pushing down mixture with a rubber scraper. Repeat until all praline is pulverized, returning chunks to be reprocessed, if necessary.
4. Place softened ice cream in a large glass or ceramic bowl; fold in praline powder and Amaretto or coffee liqueur. Pack ice cream mixture into a small metal bowl; wrap in heavy-duty aluminum foil.
5. Freeze at least 8 hours, or overnight, until firm. Garnish scoops of ice cream with candy coffee beans, instant coffee powder or 2 teaspoons of Amaretto or coffee liqueur, if you wish.

CHEF'S TIP: The praline recipe can be doubled or tripled. Store unused powder in an airtight container; it may soften but the flavor will not be impaired. This powder is delicious as a topping for ice cream, or folded into whipped cream or butter cream frosting, or sprinkle over cake.

PAPAYA MOLD

Papaya, a native fruit of California, Hawaii and Texas, makes a delicious dessert. You can use peaches in this recipe, if you wish. Photographed at the dock of Vacation Village in San Diego, on page 84

Makes 8 servings.

- 1 package (6 ounces) lemon-flavored gelatin
- 2 cups boiling water
- 1 cup cold water
- 1 ripe papaya
  OR: 3 large ripe peaches
- 3 egg whites
- ⅓ cup sugar
- 1 tablespoon lemon juice

1. Dissolve gelatin in boiling water in a medium-size bowl; stir cold water into dissolved gelatin.
2. Place an 8-cup mold in a pan of ice and water; pour in ¼ cup of the gelatin mixture and chill until mixture is as thick as unbeaten egg white.
3. While gelatin thickens, halve, seed and peel papaya and cut enough thin slices to make a pretty pattern in mold. (Or pare, halve and pit peaches and slice one-half peach.) Arrange fruit slices in gelatin. (If gelatin seems to be setting too quickly while arranging fruit slices, remove mold from pan of ice and water.) Allow gelatin to become sticky-firm over ice and water; add an additional ½ cup gelatin to mold and allow to set.
4. Pour ½ cup of the remaining gelatin into the container of an electric blender; dice remaining papaya or peaches into container; cover. Process on high until mixture is smooth.
5. Beat egg whites until foamy-white and double in volume in a deep bowl; add sugar, one tablespoon at a time, beating well after each addition, until meringue forms firm peaks.
6. Place remaining gelatin in a large bowl in a pan of ice and water; chill until syrupy. Beat until foamy-light and triple in volume.
7. Fold in fruit purée, then meringue, with a wire whip until no streaks of white or orange remain; pour over clear layer in mold. Refrigerate mold 6 hours, or overnight.
8. To unmold, run a thin-bladed knife around edge of mold; dip mold into a pan of hot water for 30 seconds, then invert mold onto chilled serving plate. Refrigerate until serving time.

CLARET LEMONADE

Victorian hostesses liked to offer this cooling refresher to summer-weary guests. Photographed in a field of wild rosemary, on page 96.

Makes 6 servings.

- 3 lemons
- ¾ cup sugar
- 1 bottle (28 ounces) club soda, chilled
- 2 cups red Burgundy wine, chilled
- 6 tablespoons light corn syrup

1. Squeeze lemons into a tall pitcher; add sugar and stir to mix well; add club soda and stir until sugar dissolves. Chill at least 1 hour.
2. Divide wine among 6 glasses; stir 1 tablespoon corn syrup into wine in each glass. Carefully pour lemonade over the back of a spoon and down the side of glass, so it will layer, rather than mix with the wine.

BERRY SPRITZERS

Blueberries and grapes give wine spritzers a new dimension.

Makes 4 servings.

- 2 cups white wine
- ½ cup blueberries
- ½ cup seedless grapes
- 1 bottle (28 ounces) club soda, chilled

Pour ½ cup wine into each of four ice-filled tall glasses; divide blueberries and grapes among glasses. Fill each glass with club soda.

DOUBLE STRAWBERRY CUPS

Top fresh strawberries with an ice cream sauce for a pleasant variation of Strawberries Romanoff.

Makes 8 servings.

- 1 quart fresh strawberries
- ¼ cup superfine sugar
- 1 tablespoon orange liqueur
- 1 pint strawberry ice cream, softened
- 2 tablespoons orange liqueur

1. Wash strawberries; reserve 8 whole ones. Hull remaining berries and halve into a large glass or ceramic bowl. Sprinkle with sugar and the 1 tablespoon orange liqueur; stir carefully until well combined. Cover with plastic wrap and refrigerate at least 1 hour to blend flavors.
2. At serving time, combine softened ice cream and the 2 tablespoons orange liqueur in a medium-size bowl until soft and well blended. Divide sliced strawberries among 8 bowls. Spoon ice cream mixture over berries. Garnish with reserved whole berries and candied orange peel, if you wish.

CHILLED FRUIT SOUP

Light and refreshing, fruit soup is an elegant way to end an outdoor summer meal.

Makes 4 servings.

- 1 can (1 pound, 13 ounces) yellow cling peach halves
- 1 package (10 ounces) frozen quick-thaw strawberries
- 1 can (12 ounces) peach nectar
- ¼ cup sweet Sherry or port wine (optional)
- Sour cream or plain yogurt
- Crushed almond macaroons

1. Place peach halves and their syrup in the container of an electric blender; cover and process on high 30 seconds, or until smooth; pour purée into large glass or ceramic bowl.
2. Place strawberries and peach nectar in container of electric blender; cover and process on high 30 seconds, or until smooth. Pour into bowl with peach purée; stir until well blended. Cover bowl with plastic wrap and refrigerate at least 1 hour to blend flavors.
3. Add sweet Sherry or port wine and stir until well blended. Serve soup in bowls, topped with a dollop of sour cream or yogurt and crushed macaroons.

DARTMOUTH PUNCH

Kate Kanter serves this frosty drink whenever she gives a barbecue.

Makes 4 servings.

- 1 bottle (28 ounces) club soda, chilled
- 1 cup blended whiskey
- 1 can (6 ounces) frozen concentrate for limeade
- Crushed ice
- Lime slices

Combine club soda, whiskey and undiluted concentrate in a large bottle; seal and shake until well blended. Pour into tall glasses filled with crushed ice. Garnish with lime slices.

GEORGIA PEACH NOG

Rich and sweet enough to be a dessert, but refreshing as a drink, too.

Makes 3 servings.

- 1 pint vanilla ice cream
- 1 can (16 ounces) cling peach slices
- ¼ cup Amaretto or peach liqueur
- Ground nutmeg

Place ice cream, peach slices and their syrup and liqueur in container of electric blender; cover and process on high 30 seconds, or until smooth and frothy. Pour into three tall glasses; sprinkle with nutmeg and serve with crisp cookies, if you wish.

CRYSTAL CLEAR ICED TEA

For a sparkling beverage, use the cold water method.

Makes 10 servings.

- 20 tea bags
- 2 quarts cold tap water
- Sugar
- Lemon or orange slices

1. Remove tags from tea bags; place tea bags in 2½-quart tall pitcher; pour water over. Cover pitcher with plastic wrap. Let stand at room temperature, or refrigerate, at least 6 hours, or overnight.
2. Remove tea bags, squeezing each one against side of pitcher. Refrigerate, covered, until serving time. To serve, pour tea into ice-filled tall glasses. Sweeten to taste with sugar and garnish with lemon slices.

FRUIT FIZZ

Your blender whirls this magenta drink in seconds. Serve in long, tall glasses.

Makes 4 servings.

- 2 cups orange juice
- 1 package (10 ounces) frozen quick-thaw mixed fruits
- 1 cup club soda, chilled
- Crushed ice

Combine orange juice and frozen fruit in container of electric blender; cover and process on high 30 seconds, or until well blended. Pour mixture into a large bottle; add club soda; seal and shake until well blended. Pour into glasses filled with crushed ice.

AMBROSIA SALAD

Dessert or salad, it's up to you. Just be sure to make it the day before for best flavor.

Makes 8 servings.

- 1 can sweetened condensed milk (not evaporated milk)
- 1 container (8 ounces) plain yogurt
- 2 teaspoons grated lime rind
- ½ cup lime juice
- 1 can (1 pound, 5 ounces) pineapple tidbits or chunks, drained
- 1 can (11 ounces) mandarin oranges, drained
- 1 can (3½ ounces) flaked coconut
- 1 cup miniature marshmallows
- ½ cup chopped pecans

1. Combine condensed milk, plain yogurt, lime rind and juice in a large glass bowl; stir until well blended.
2. Fold in pineapple, mandarin oranges, coconut and marshmallows until well blended; cover with plastic wrap. Chill 3 hours, or overnight.
3. Spoon into dessert dishes or lettuce-lined dishes; sprinkle with chopped nuts.

GRAPE-PINEAPPLE DRINK

Combine two favorite juices to make a new drink that's so cooling and refreshing.

Makes 6 servings.

- 1 can (6 ounces) frozen concentrate for grape juice, thawed
- 1 can (6 ounces) frozen concentrate for pineapple juice, thawed
- 1 tablespoon lemon juice
- 1 can (12 ounces) ginger ale
- 1 can (12 ounces) club soda
  Fresh pineapple spear
  Fresh mint

1. Combine frozen concentrate for grape juice, frozen concentrate for pineapple juice, lemon juice and 3 juice-cans cold water in large bottle; seal and shake until well blended. Refrigerate until serving time.
2. At serving time, pour juice mixture into large pitcher; add ginger ale and club soda; stir until well blended. Garnish each serving with pineapple spears and mint.

CHEF'S TIP: For a special touch, make decorative ice cubes. Place pieces of lemon rind, fresh mint leaves or maraschino cherries in each compartment of an ice cube tray; fill with water or lemonade and freeze.

PEANUT BUTTER SUNDAES

Let everyone make his own creamy-rich sundae with this special topping.

Makes 8 servings.

- 2 tablespoons butter or margarine
- 1 can sweetened condensed milk (not evaporated milk)
- ¼ cup crunchy peanut butter
- 1 quart vanilla ice cream
  Whipped cream
  Chopped peanuts

1. Melt butter or margarine in a small metal saucepan with a flameproof handle over grill. Stir in condensed milk and peanut butter until smooth. Cook, stirring constantly, until sauce thickens and bubbles.
2. Spoon ice cream into dessert dishes; pour sauce over; top with whipped cream and chopped nuts.

INSTANT BANANA WHIP

Bring your blender out on the patio and whip up a delicious dessert in seconds.

Makes 4 servings.

- 2 large bananas
- ⅓ cup lemon juice
- 1 can sweetened condensed milk (not evaporated milk)
- 2 cups crushed ice
  Orange slices
  Fresh mint

1. Peel bananas and slice into con-

tainer of electric blender; add lemon juice, condensed milk and crushed ice; cover blender.
2. Process on high 30 seconds, or until smooth; pour into 4 dessert dishes. Garnish with orange slices and sprigs of fresh mint.

BASIC BLOODY MARY MIX

This drink became a favorite soon after its creation in New York in the 1930's.

Makes 6 servings.

- 4 cups tomato juice (from 48-ounce can)
- 4 teaspoons lime or lemon juice
- 1 tablespoon Worcestershire sauce
- 1 teaspoon salt
- ¼ teaspoon bottled red pepper seasoning
  Vodka or gin

Combine tomato juice, lime or lemon juice, Worcestershire sauce, salt and bottled red pepper seasoning in a tall pitcher; stir well. Cover pitcher with plastic wrap; chill until serving time. To prepare one drink: Place two or three ice cubes in a tall glass; pour in 1 to 1½ ounces vodka or gin. Fill glass with mix; stir well. Garnish with lime or lemon slice.

CHEF'S TIP: This delicious juice makes an excellent nonalcoholic drink, too. Pour over ice in glass; garnish with lime or lemon slice.

TROPICAL SANGRIA

Like fruit salad in a glass, this wine drink is refreshing and delicious.

Makes 12 servings.

- 1 cup orange juice
- ⅔ cup light corn syrup
- ½ cup Cointreau or Curaçao
- ¼ cup lime or lemon juice
- ½ gallon red or rosé wine
- 1 bottle (28 ounces) club soda, chilled
- 1 pint strawberries, washed and hulled
- 2 peaches or apricots
- 1 cup seedless grapes
- 1 cup melon balls
- 1 orange
- 1 lime or lemon
  Ice cubes

1. Combine orange juice, corn syrup, Cointreau or Curaçao and lime or lemon juice in a large pitcher; stir until well blended. Add wine. Cover pitcher with plastic wrap and refrigerate at least 2 hours to blend flavors.
2. Just before serving, pour wine mixture into a large punch bowl; add club soda. Slice strawberries and peaches or apricots into bowl; add grapes and melon balls. Halve orange and lime or lemon; thinly slice and add to bowl. Add ice. Serve with a spoon.

MANHATTAN SUNDAES

Ice cream tastes marvelous on pound cake that's been toasted over a slow fire.

Grill for 6 minutes
Makes 8 servings.

- 1 package (10 ounces) frozen pound cake, thawed
- 1 quart vanilla or butter almond ice cream
- ½ cup almond liqueur
- ¼ cup toasted slivered almonds

1. Cut pound cake into 8 slices, using a long-bladed sharp-tipped knife. Place on grill, 6 inches from heat.
2. Grill 3 minutes, or until lightly toasted; turn; grill 3 minutes more, or until lightly toasted.
3. Place pound cake slices on individual serving plates; top with scoops of ice cream. Drizzle 1 tablespoon liqueur over each serving, sprinkle with toasted almonds; serve immediately.

SUNSHINE COUPES

Apricots in orange liqueur top creamy vanilla ice cream.

Makes 4 servings.

- 1 can (1 pound, 14 ounces) apricots
- 2 tablespoons orange liqueur
- 1 pint vanilla ice cream
- ¼ cup toasted slivered almonds

1. Mix apricots and their syrup with orange liqueur in a large glass or ceramic bowl; cover bowl with plastic wrap and refrigerate at least 1 hour to blend flavors.
2. Divide ice cream among 4 serving bowls; top with apricots and syrup. Sprinkle toasted almonds over and serve immediately.

CHEF'S TIP: The apricot mixture is delicious served alone or topped with yogurt or sour cream.

SANTA CLARA FRUIT CUP

Sun-ripened apricots are coated with a creamy lime sauce.

Makes 8 servings.

- 1 can sweetened condensed milk (not evaporated milk)
- ½ cup water
- 2 teaspoons grated lime rind
- ¼ cup lime juice
- 2 pounds apricots, halved, pitted and sliced
  OR: 6 large peaches, halved, pitted and sliced

1. Combine condensed milk, water, lime rind and juice in a small bowl; mix until well blended. Cover with plastic wrap; chill at least 2 hours.
2. Slice apricots or peaches into a large glass bowl; pour lime sauce over; fold, to blend. Garnish with mint. ∎

CANYON BEEF RIBS

Man-pleasing short ribs are grilled to a crisp turn.

Grill for 1 hour, 30 minutes.
Makes 4 servings.

- **4 pounds beef short ribs**
- **½ cup vegetable oil**
- **1 medium-size onion, peeled and sliced**
- **2 teaspoons salt**
- **2 teaspoons leaf oregano, crumbled**
- **¼ teaspoon bottled red pepper seasoning**

1. Trim any excess fat from short ribs.
2. Build a medium fire, arranging coals around a drip pan, following directions on page 45, or set gas or electric grill to medium, following manufacturer's directions.
3. Grill ribs over drip pan, 6 inches from heat, turning several times, 1 hour, or until ribs are tender.
4. Heat oil in a small metal saucepan with a flameproof handle; sauté onion until soft; stir in salt, oregano and red pepper seasoning; brush part over meat.
5. Grill, 6 inches from heat, turning and brushing often with onion sauce, 30 minutes longer, or until meat is tender and crispy-brown.

BURGUNDY BEEF

Noted Detroit barbecue chef, Joe Walsh, has developed this method for making rotisserie beef even moister and more flavorful with a wine sauce.

Rotis for 50 to 60 minutes.
Makes 8 servings.

- **1 eye round (about 5 pounds)**
  Seasoned salt or hickory salt
- **1 can condensed beef broth**
- **4 cups red Burgundy wine**
- **½ pound fresh mushrooms, sliced**
  Grill-Roasted Potatoes (recipe follows)

1. Remove beef from refrigerator at least 1 hour before rotissing. Sprinkle with seasoned salt or hickory salt, just before attaching to rotisserie spit.
2. Build a medium fire in a grill with a rotisserie unit, arranging coals around a 9x5x3-inch metal loaf pan, or set electric or gas grill to medium, arranging ceramic chips around 9x5x3-inch loaf pan. Add broth and wine to pan.
3. Insert spit through center of meat, lengthwise, and testing for balance to be sure meat is directly over pan of broth and wine in grill. Fasten meat with holding forks, so it won't slip while roasting. Place rotisserie rod into position, following manufacturer's directions.
4. Rotis in covered grill, 50 minutes for rare and 60 minutes for medium. Check loaf pan, and if liquid is evaporating too quickly, add more wine. Add sliced mushrooms to wine mixture during last 10 minutes of rotissing. Allow meat to "rest" 15 minutes on a heated platter before slicing; serve with mushrooms in wine sauce and GRILL-ROASTED POTATOES.
CHEF'S TIP: This recipe can also be used for poultry. Substitute chicken broth for the beef broth and dry white wine for the red Burgundy. Chickens and Rock Cornish hens will rotis in 50 to 60 minutes. A 12-pound turkey will take 2 hours, 30 minutes. If you prefer a thicker sauce, combine 3 tablespoons softened butter or margarine and 3 tablespoons all purpose flour in a cup to make a smooth paste. Drop by tiny pieces into liquid in loaf pan and stir until well blended. Allow to simmer 5 minutes; taste and adjust salt and pepper.

GRILL-ROASTED POTATOES:
Makes 8 servings. Pare and parboil 8 large baking potatoes in boiling salted water 5 minutes; drain potatoes and cut into thin slices, keeping each potato's slices in order. Reshape potato slices in a large metal pan; brush with ½ cup (1 stick) melted butter or margarine. Season with salt and pepper. Place pan right on coals to side of rotissing meal. Grill, turning with a slotted spoon several times, 50 minutes, or until golden brown.

BARBECUED LEG OF LAMB

Sheep were first brought to Western America in 1519 by Cortez's soldiers.

Grill for 2 to 2 hours, 30 minutes.
Makes 8 servings.

- **1 leg of lamb (about 7 pounds)**
- **2 cloves garlic**
  Salt and pepper
  Tomato-Beer Baste (recipe, page 114)

1. Trim excess fat from lamb; cut garlic into slivers; make small cuts in lamb and insert garlic; sprinkle lamb with salt and pepper. Allow to stand at room temperature 1 hour.
2. Build a medium fire for kettle-roasting around aluminum foil pan, following directions on page 45, or set gas or electric grill to medium, following manufacturer's directions.
3. Roast with cover on grill 1 hour; baste with TOMATO-BEER BASTE. Cook 1 hour longer for rare, 1 hour, 15 minutes for medium and 1 hour, 30 minutes for well done, basting several times. Serve with a cracked wheat pilaf.

KEY WEST RIBS

Lime juice adds a distinctive flavor to barbecued spareribs—or try the glaze with lamb or veal ribs.

Grill for 1 hour, 30 minutes.
Makes 4 servings.

- **4 pounds fresh spareribs**
- **½ cup catsup**
- **¼ cup lime juice**
- **¼ cup soy sauce**
- **¼ cup honey**

1. Build a medium fire, arranging coals around a drip pan, following directions on page 45, or set gas or electric grill to medium, following manufacturer's directions.
2. Grill, 6 inches from heat, turning several times, 1 hour, or until meat is almost tender.
3. Mix catsup, lime juice and soy sauce in a small metal saucepan with flameproof handle; heat to bubbling over grill; brush part over ribs. Continue grilling, turning and brushing several times with sauce mixture, 20 minutes.
4. Blend honey into remaining sauce; brush over ribs. Grill, turning and brushing once or twice with remaining honey mixture, 10 minutes, or until mixture is tender and richly glazed.
5. Remove ribs to a carving board; cut into serving-size pieces. Serve with onion halves cooked in foil.

LAMB CUMBERLAND

Cumberland sauce is a classic made with currant jelly, lemon juice and ginger.

Grill for 2 to 2 hours, 30 minutes.
Makes 6 servings.

- **1 boned and rolled lamb shoulder (about 4 pounds)**
  Salt and pepper
- **1 jar (10 ounces) currant jelly**
- **¼ cup orange juice**
- **1 tablespoon lemon juice**
- **¾ teaspoon ground ginger**
- **½ teaspoon grated orange rind**

1. Trim excess fat from lamb; allow to stand at room temperature for 1 hour. Season with salt and pepper.
2. Build a fire for kettle-roasting around aluminum foil pan, following directions on page 45, or set electric or gas grill to low, following manufacturer's directions.
3. Roast in covered grill 1 hour, 30 minutes. Combine currant jelly, orange juice, lemon juice, ginger and orange rind in a small metal saucepan with a flameproof handle; heat over grill until mixture is smooth.
4. Baste lamb with sauce and grill 30 minutes longer for rare, 45 minutes for medium, and 60 minutes for well done. Serve with CUCUMBERS IN SOUR CREAM (recipe, page 91).

DAKOTA RIBS

Smoke-flavored barbecue sauce adds a touch of the Old West campfire.

Grill for 1 hour, 30 minutes.
Makes 4 servings.

 4 **pounds fresh spareribs**
 1 **can (12 ounces) beer**
 ⅔ **cup catsup**
 ½ **cup bottled smoke-flavored barbecue sauce**
 ¼ **cup light corn syrup**

1. Have butcher crack ribs in half lengthwise to form long strips. Thread strips, accordion-style, onto long skewers. Brush with part of the beer.
2. Build a medium fire, or set gas or electric grill to medium, following manufacturer's directions.
3. Grill skewers, 6 inches from heat, turning and basting with remaining beer, 1 hour.
4. Mix catsup, barbecue sauce and corn syrup in a small metal saucepan with a flameproof handle; heat on grill; brush part over ribs. Grill, turning and brushing often with remaining sauce, 30 minutes, or until richly glazed. Serve with baked sweet potatoes and corn.

ROSEMARY LAMB

This recipe could make your reputation as a barbecue chef. Try it rare—you'll love it!

Grill for 40 to 60 minutes.
Makes 8 servings.

 1 **leg of lamb (about 7 pounds)**
 ¼ **cup olive or vegetable oil**
 ¼ **cup tarragon vinegar**
 1 **medium-size onion, chopped (½ cup)**
 2 **cloves garlic, minced**
 1 **teaspoon leaf rosemary, crumbled**
 1 **teaspoon salt**
 ¼ **teaspoon freshly ground pepper**

1. Bone leg of lamb, following directions for butterflied leg of lamb, page 32, saving bones for a soup. Place lamb in a large plastic bag.
2. Add oil, vinegar, onion, garlic, rosemary, salt and pepper to bag; tie bag securely; rotate bag to coat lamb evenly; place in a large bowl.
3. Marinate in refrigerator, turning several times, 4 hours, or overnight. Allow to stand at room temperature at least 1 hour before grilling.
4. Build a medium fire, or set electric or gas grill to medium, following manufacturer's directions.
5. Grill, 4 inches from heat, turning and basting with marinade every 10 minutes, 40 minutes for rare, 50 minutes for medium, and 60 minutes for well done. Place on carving platter and allow to "rest" 10 minutes. Carve into diagonal slices. Serve with rice pilaf and minted peas.

FRONTIER LAMB RIBLETS

The French Buccaneers were the first to introduce barbecue cooking in America.

Grill for 20 minutes.
Makes 4 servings.

 3 **pounds lamb riblets**
 2 **cups water**
 1 **tablespoon mixed pickling spices**
 1 **teaspoon salt**
   Plum Chutney Glaze (recipe, page 114)

1. Place lamb riblets in a large skillet; add water, mixed pickling spices and salt; bring to boiling; lower heat and simmer 30 minutes; allow riblets to cool in liquid. (This much can be done the day before.)
2. Build a medium-hot fire, or set gas or electric grill to medium-high, following manufacturer's directions.
3. Cut riblets into individual ribs; brush generously with PLUM CHUTNEY GLAZE.
4. Grill, 4 inches from heat, basting and turning often, 20 minutes, or until well glazed. Serve with sliced tomatoes and Spanish onions.

CITRUS-GLAZED RIBS

Spareribs can be cooked completely over the barbecue, just be sure to baste and turn often to keep them moist and tender.

Grill for 1 hour, 30 minutes.
Makes 6 servings.

 6 **pounds fresh spareribs**
 1 **bottle (12 ounces) ginger ale**
 1 **cup bottled barbecue sauce**
 1 **tablespoon grated orange peel**
 1 **cup freshly squeezed orange juice**
 ⅓ **cup lemon juice**
 ⅓ **cup firmly packed brown sugar**
 2 **tablespoons instant minced onion**
 2 **tablespoons soy sauce**
 1 **teaspoon salt**

1. Build a slow fire, or set electric or gas grill to low, following manufacturer's directions.
2. Trim excess fat from spareribs; brush generously with ginger ale.
3. Grill, 6 to 8 inches from heat, turning and basting with ginger ale, 1 hour, or until ribs are tender when pierced with a two-tined fork.
4. While ribs grill, combine barbecue sauce, orange peel, orange juice, lemon juice, brown sugar, instant minced onion, soy sauce and salt in a medium-size saucepan with a flameproof handle.
5. Place on side of grill and cook, stirring often, 20 minutes, or until sauce thickens.
6. Brush ribs with sauce and continue cooking and basting 30 minutes, or until ribs are richly glazed. Cut into pieces, between ribs. Serve with an apple and cabbage coleslaw.

RIBS HONOLULU

Aromatic bitters and pineapple—two ingredients that are sure to add glamour to barbecued ribs.

Grill for 1 hour.
Makes 4 servings.

 4 **pounds breast of veal, lamb or fresh spareribs**
 1 **can (6 ounces) frozen concentrate for pineapple juice, thawed**
 1 **can (9 ounces) crushed pineapple**
 2 **teaspoons bottled aromatic bitters**
 2 **teaspoons garlic salt**
 ¼ **teaspoon lemon pepper**

1. Cut breast of veal, lamb or spareribs into pieces of 1 or 2 ribs each. Place in a single layer in a 15x10x1-inch metal baking pan.
2. Blend concentrate for pineapple juice with crushed pineapple and syrup, bitters, garlic salt and lemon pepper in a small bowl; spoon over meat.
3. Build a medium fire, or set electric or gas grill to medium, following manufacturer's directions.
4. Grill, 6 inches from heat, turning and spooning pan sauce over ribs several times, 1 hour, or until ribs are richly glazed. Serve with curried rice salad and Chinese cabbage coleslaw, if you wish.

RUMAKI

Polynesian restaurants often feature these kabobs of chicken livers, water chestnuts and bacon as an appetizer. They're perfect to grill on a hibachi.

Grill for 10 minutes.
Makes 24 appetizers.

 1 **pound chicken livers, halved**
 1 **can (5 ounces) water chestnuts, drained and sliced**
 ½ **pound bacon, halved**
 1½ **cups soy sauce**
 ½ **cup Sake or dry Sherry**
 1 **clove garlic, halved**
   Light brown sugar

1. Place a water chestnut slice on either side of chicken liver; wrap with a piece of bacon; thread on a small wooden kabob.
2. Combine soy sauce, Sake or dry Sherry and garlic in a large shallow glass dish; add kabobs, basting with marinade. Cover dish with plastic wrap. Refrigerate at least 2 hours.
3. Build a medium fire, or set gas or electric grill to medium, following manufacturer's directions.
4. Grill, 4 inches from heat, turning and basting with marinade several times, 8 minutes. Sprinkle brown sugar on a large metal pan. Dip kabobs in sugar.
5. Grill 2 minutes longer, or until glazed. Serve remaining marinade in tiny cups as a dipping sauce.

JAY'S BARBECUE FOR A CROWD

Have a crowd to feed and need an easy way to serve them all? Jay Hytone's special barbecue sauce and technique for ribs or chicken will make a delicious dinner for any number, even when they come back for seconds! Make the sauce indoors, start the fire and grill, turning the meat every 15 minutes, so it smokes and simmers to full, juicy perfection.

BARBECUE SAUCE

Makes about 2 cups.

- **1 cup catsup**
- **1 cup wine or beer or beef broth or water**
- **⅓ cup Worcestershire sauce**
- **1 teaspoon chili powder**
- **1 teaspoon garlic powder**
- **1 teaspoon salt**
- **½ teaspoon pepper**
  Dash red pepper seasoning
- **1 teaspoon liquid smoke (optional)**

Combine catsup, wine, Worcestershire sauce, chili powder, garlic powder, salt, pepper and red pepper seasoning in a large saucepan over a low flame. (If you are cooking the sauce indoors and do not have room to let some simmer on the grill with the meat, add liquid smoke to ingredients.) Simmer all ingredients in pan for 30 minutes. (This sauce recipe is enough for 6 servings. For 25 servings, make 4 times this recipe.)

Thirty minutes before starting fire, put a handful of hickory chips to soak in a pan of water. The chips will be added to the fire just before grilling to add a hickory smoke flavor to the meat.

Build a medium fire in any large, covered grill with enough surface area so all meat can cook at one time, or set gas or electric grill to medium. The fire must be large enough to last 2 hours for ribs, or 1 hour for chicken. After fire is well started (about 40 minutes), put fresh coals around it to insure long, even heat. (See page 46 for directions on how Jay Hytone built his grill.)

To prepare the meat for 25 servings, spread out a large area of wax paper on a countertop or comparable working space and lay 25 pounds of country spareribs or 13 broiler-fryers, split (about 2 pounds each), on it.

Pour 4 cups vegetable oil into large metal saucepan with flameproof handle. Using a large new paintbrush or similar brush, baste meat well with oil on all sides. When well coated with oil, liberally apply seasoned pepper and garlic salt to both sides of meat. Set meat aside until fire is hot.

If there will be room on the grill surface, add oil to pan to make at least 4 cups and add 4 cups of the sauce. (The sauce will sink to the bottom of the pan, and as the oil is used for basting during the grilling time, the sauce will absorb the smoke flavor as it simmers inside the grill.)

When the fire is ready, spread coals out evenly with long tongs; drain hickory chips and sprinkle them liberally over fire. After chips are smoking, place meat on grill, bone side down, leaving a small amount of room around each piece. Place flameproof saucepan containing oil and sauce on grill and close cover.

CHEF'S TIP: There will be a lot of smoke inside the grill; should a fat fire start, have water nearby in a cleaned liquid detergent bottle to sprinkle over coals, as necessary.

Every 15 minutes, open the grill cover, turn meat quickly with long tongs and baste the side now turned up with oil (just skim brush over oil in pan; do not baste with the sauce because it will burn and give the meat a bad flavor.) After basting top sides of meat with oil, close cover again for another 15 minutes. Repeat the turning and basting procedure through the cooking time: chicken, 1 hour, or ribs, 2 hours, or until done as you like. (To know when the ribs are done, the meat will shrink and pull away from the bones on ends.)

When meat is done, turn it with tongs one last time; dip basting brush into bottom of saucepan to cover well with sauce and smear sauce liberally over top of meat. Close cover and let meat cook 5 minutes longer.

Pile ribs or chicken on a large heated serving platter. Cut ribs into slabs of 4 or 5 ribs by running a large kitchen knife between 2 bones while the slab is held up with tongs.

Skim the remainder of oil from the saucepan on grill and pour sauce liberally over meat. Add any remaining sauce on grill to sauce kept warm indoors and put in a serving bowl on table with gravy ladle. Serve with mugs of frosty beer and have plenty of napkins on hand.

KALUA PORK

Soy and ginger give pork a delectable flavor.

Grill for 2 hours, 30 minutes.
Makes 8 servings.

- **1 fresh pork arm roast (about 5 pounds)**
- **¼ cup soy sauce**
- **1 tablespoon salt**
- **1 tablespoon Worcestershire sauce**
- **1 teaspoon monosodium glutamate (MSG)**
- **1 clove garlic, minced**
- **2 tablespoons chopped ginger root**
  Bottled liquid smoke

1. Trim excess fat from pork; score remaining fat in an attractive pattern; place meat in a large plastic bag.
2. Combine soy sauce, salt, Worcestershire sauce, monosodium glutamate, garlic and ginger in a small container of electric blender. Process on high until smooth; add a few drops liquid smoke.
3. Pour over pork; tie bag securely; turn bag to coat pork evenly with marinade; place bag in a bowl. Marinate in refrigerator, turning several times, 4 hours, or overnight. Allow to stand at room temperature at least 1 hour before grilling.
4. Build a fire for kettle-roasting around aluminum foil pan, following directions on page 45, or set gas or electric grill to low, following manufacturer's directions.
5. Grill, 5 inches from heat, basting often with marinade, 2 hours, 30 minutes, or until a meat thermometer inserted into center of meat registers 170°. Serve with baked sweet potatoes and spiced pineapple chunks.

BARBECUED POT ROAST

Long, slow, foil-covered cooking gives the tenderest, moistest pot roast you have ever served to guests.

Grill for 2 hours, 30 minutes.
Makes 6 servings.

- **1 beef blade pot roast (about 4 pounds)**
- **2 large onions, sliced**
- **1 cup catsup**
- **¼ cup all purpose flour**
- **1 tablespoon red cooking wine**
- **2 teaspoons salt**
- **¼ teaspoon freshly ground pepper**

1. Measure roast and tear a sheet of heavy-duty aluminum foil that is three times the circumference and 8 inches longer than the roast. Fold foil in half to make a double thickness.
2. Spread half the onion slices in center of foil. Combine catsup, flour, cooking wine, salt and pepper in a small bowl; spoon half the mixture over onions; center roast on onions; spoon remaining catsup mixture over roast; top with remaining onion slices. Wrap roast in foil, following directions on page 47.
3. Build a slow fire, or set gas or electric grill to low, following manufacturer's directions.
4. Grill, 4 inches from heat, turning with tongs every 30 minutes, 2 hours, 30 minutes, or until meat is tender when pierced with a two-tined fork.
5. Place roast on a heated serving platter and spoon gravy into a heated gravy boat. Serve with barbecued baked potatoes and corn on the cob, if you wish.
CHEF'S TIP: If foil packet leaks, set a drip pan of heavy-duty aluminum foil under pot roast.

NAPA VALLEY BEEF

Dry red wine, oregano and rosemary make a pungent marinade for beef.

Grill for 1 to 1 hour, 30 minutes.
Makes 8 servings.

- 1 bone-in chuck roast, cut 2-inches thick (about 5 pounds)
- 1 cup dry Burgundy or red wine
- ½ cup olive or vegetable oil
- 1 clove garlic, minced
- 2 teaspoons leaf oregano, crumbled
- 1 teaspoon leaf rosemary, crumbled
- 1 teaspoon salt
- ¼ teaspoon freshly ground pepper

1. Trim excess fat from beef; score remaining fat around edge at 1-inch intervals.
2. Combine wine, oil, garlic, oregano, rosemary, salt and pepper in a 2-cup measure; pour over beef; turn beef in marinade; cover dish.
3. Marinate at room temperature 2 hours, or refrigerate overnight; allow beef to stand at room temperature 1 hour before roasting.
4. Build a medium fire for kettle-roasting around aluminum foil pan, following directions on page 45, or set gas or electric grill to medium, following manufacturer's directions.
5.. Roast in covered grill, basting several times with marinade, 1 hour for rare, 1 hour, 15 minutes for medium and 1 hour, 30 minutes for well done, or until beef is done as you like it. Remove to heated serving platter and allow to "rest" 20 minutes. Serve with ratatouille.

PEKING PORK

It's even more delicious as cold sliced meat, if you can keep any for leftovers.

Grill for 1 hour, 30 minutes.
Makes 6 servings.

- 1 pork loin center cut (about 5 pounds)
  - OR: 1 boneless pork loin roast (about 3 pounds)
- 1 large onion, chopped (1 cup)
- 1 clove garlic, minced
- ⅓ cup peanut or vegetable oil
- ⅓ cup tarragon vinegar
- 1 tablespoon salad seasoning for oil and vinegar dressing (see Cook's Guide)

1. Remove meat from pork rib bones, following directions on page 31; trim excess fat from roast. Place in a large plastic bag in a utility dish.
2. Add onion, garlic, oil, vinegar and salad seasoning for oil and vinegar dressing to meat; tie bag securely; turn bag several times to coat meat evenly with marinade. Marinate at room temperature 2 hours, or refrigerate overnight; let meat stand at room temperature 1 hour before grilling.

3. Build a medium fire for kettle-roasting around an aluminum foil pan, following directions on page 47, or set gas or electric grill to medium, following manufacturer's directions.
4. Grill, 5 inches from heat, basting with marinade several times, 1 hour, 30 minutes, or until a meat thermometer inserted in center registers 170°. Place on heated platter and allow to "rest" 10 minutes.

GLAZED CORNED BEEF

This cut of beef is best cooked in water until tender, then covered with a glaze and finished on the grill.

Grill for 20 minutes.
Makes 8 servings.

- 1 corned beef brisket (about 4 pounds)
- Water
- 1 medium-size onion, sliced
- 1 tablespoon mixed pickling spices
- ½ cup firmly packed brown sugar
- 1 tablespoon Worcestershire sauce
- 1 teaspoon instant coffee powder

1. Place corned beef in a large kettle; cover with cold water; add onion slices and mixed pickling spices to the kettle, immersing in water.
2. Bring slowly to boiling; lower heat, just to simmer; cover kettle; simmer 2 hours, 30 minutes, or until meat is tender when pierced with a two-tined fork. Remove kettle from heat and allow meat to cool in liquid.
3. Build a medium fire, or set gas or electric grill to medium, following manufacturer's directions.
4. Combine brown sugar, Worcestershire sauce and instant coffee powder in a small bowl; add a few drops corned beef cooking liquid, if necessary, for a paste-like consistency.
5. Pat meat dry with a paper towel; spread brown sugar mixture on top of brisket to coat completely.
6. Grill, 4 inches from heat, 20 minutes, or until meat is heated through and well glazed. Serve with barbecued baked sweet potatoes and corn on the cob.

SANTA CLARA RIBS

Dry wine and apricot nectar are equally delicious on veal, lamb or spareribs.

Rotis for 1 hour.
Makes 4 servings.

- 4 pounds breast of veal
  - OR: 4 pounds lamb riblets or spareribs
- 4 teaspoons seasoned salt
- ½ cup dry vermouth or white wine
- ½ cup vegetable oil
- ½ cup apricot nectar

1. Build a medium fire in a grill with

a rotisserie, positioning coals around drip pan, following directions on page 45, or set electric or gas grill to medium, following manufacturer's directions.
2. Thread breast of veal, lamb or spareribs, accordion-style, onto rotisserie spit, testing for balance by rotating spit in hands. Fasten ribs with holding forks; sprinkle evenly with seasoned salt.
3. Mix vermouth or wine and oil in a small metal saucepan with a flameproof handle; brush over meat.
4. Place rotisserie rod into position.
5. Grill, checking rotisserie several times, 45 minutes.
6. Stir apricot nectar into remaining oil mixture; brush over meat. Continue cooking, brushing several times with apricot mixture, 15 minutes, or until meat is tender and golden brown. Remove to a carving board; take out spit. Cut ribs into serving-size pieces. Serve with a salad of iceberg lettuce, sliced peaches, strawberries and bananas and a blue-cheese dressing.

SAVORY VEAL ROAST

A boneless fresh pork shoulder would be equally delicious grilled this way.

Rotis for 2 hours, 30 minutes.
Makes 8 servings.

- 1 rolled boneless veal shoulder roast (about 5 pounds)
- ½ cup (1 stick) butter or margarine
- 1 cup catsup
- 2 tablespoons cider vinegar
- 1 tablespoon Worcestershire sauce
- 1 teaspoon salt
- 1 teaspoon leaf basil, crumbled
- 1 teaspoon leaf thyme, crumbled
- ¼ teaspoon freshly ground pepper

1. Build a hot fire on a grill with a rotisserie, or set gas or electric grill to high, following manufacturer's directions.
2. Place meat on spit of grill with a rotisserie, following manufacturer's directions. If using a meat thermometer, insert bulb in end of roast to center without touching spit.
3. Grill, checking roast several times, 1 hour, 30 minutes.
4. While meat roasts, place butter or margarine, catsup, vinegar, Worcestershire sauce, salt, basil, thyme and pepper in a small metal saucepan with a flameproof handle. Heat on grill until butter melts.
5. Brush roast with mixture; continue roasting and basting 1 hour, or until thermometer registers 170° and meat is richly glazed.
6. Remove to a cutting board; take out rod. Carve roast into ¼-inch-thick slices; serve with remaining sauce and buttered zucchini.

BUTTERFLY LAMB

A butterfly leg of lamb is one that has been boned and spread out flat like a thick steak.

Grill for 40 to 60 minutes.
Makes 8 servings.

1 leg of lamb (about 7 pounds)
½ cup olive or vegetable oil
½ cup wine vinegar
2 teaspoons grated orange peel
1 teaspoon dried mint flakes, crumbled
1 teaspoon salt
½ teaspoon garlic powder
¼ teaspoon pepper

1. Butterfly leg of lamb, following directions on page 32. Place in a large plastic bag. Add oil, vinegar, orange peel, mint, salt, garlic powder and pepper to bag; seal bag and turn lamb in marinade to coat evenly.
2. Place plastic bag in a large bowl; refrigerate to marinate overnight; let stand at room temperature 1 hour before grilling.
3. Build a medium-hot fire, or set gas or electric grill to medium-high, following manufacturer's directions.
4. Grill, 4 inches from heat, basting with marinade and turning several times, 40 minutes for rare, 50 minutes for medium and 60 minutes for well done. Serve with a watercress and blue-cheese salad.

ORANGE-GLAZED SPARERIBS

Orange marmalade and soy sauce make a quick and easy barbecue glaze.

Grill for 1 hour, 30 minutes.
Makes 6 servings.

6 pounds fresh spareribs
1 small onion, chopped (¼ cup)
½ cup cider vinegar
¼ cup vegetable oil
1 tablespoon mixed Italian herbs, crumbled
½ cup orange marmalade
¼ cup soy sauce
1 tablespoon prepared mustard

1. Place spareribs in a large plastic bag. Add onion, vinegar, oil and Italian herbs to meat; tie bag securely. Turn bag several times to coat meat evenly. Marinate at room temperature 2 hours.
2. Build a slow fire for kettle-roasting around aluminum foil pan, following directions on page 45, or set electric or gas grill to low, following manufacturer's directions.
3. Grill, 5 inches from heat, basting with marinade and turning several times, 1 hour, 15 minutes, or until meat is tender when pierced with a two-tined fork.
4. Combine orange marmalade, soy sauce and mustard in a small bowl; brush over ribs.

5. Grill, basting with glaze and turning several times, 15 minutes, or until richly glazed. Cut between ribs and serve with cold beer.

VAN NUYS PORK RIBS

The secret's in the sauce—tangy with freshly squeezed orange juice.

Grill for 30 minutes.
Makes 6 servings.

6 pounds fresh spareribs
1 large carrot, pared and chopped
1 cup chopped celery
1 medium-size onion, sliced
1 bay leaf
1 teaspoon salt
4 peppercorns
Orange-Soy Sauce (recipe, page 114)

1. Place spareribs in a large shallow metal baking pan; add carrot, celery, onion, bay leaf, salt and peppercorns; cover with water.
2. Bring slowly to boiling; lower heat to simmer; cover pan with foil; simmer 1 hour, or until ribs are tender when pierced with a two-tined fork.
3. Drain water and vegetables from pan; pour ORANGE-SOY SAUCE over ribs; allow to marinate at least 1 hour at room temperature, or cover pan with plastic wrap and refrigerate overnight. Reserve marinade.
4. Build a medium fire, or set electric or gas grill to medium, following manufacturer's directions.
5. Grill, 6 inches from heat, turning and basting often with sauce, 30 minutes, or until ribs are richly glazed. Cut between ribs; serve with plenty of paper napkins and end with hot towels scented with a lemony cologne.

TERIYAKI BEEF ROAST

Soy and sesame seeds give beef a definite Oriental flavor.

Grill for 2 to 3 hours.
Makes 8 servings.

1 eye round roast (about 5 pounds)
Instant unseasoned meat tenderizer
1 large onion, chopped (1 cup)
2 cloves garlic, minced
1 cup soy sauce
1 teaspoon seasoned salt
¼ teaspoon lemon pepper

1. Sprinkle meat with meat tenderizer, following label directions. Place beef in a large plastic bag in a shallow utility dish.
2. Add onion, garlic, soy sauce, seasoned salt and lemon pepper to meat; tie bag securely; turn bag several times to cover meat evenly. Marinate 2 hours at room temperature or overnight in refrigerator; allow meat to

stand at room temperature 1 hour before grilling. Reserve marinade.
3. Build a fire for kettle-roasting around aluminum foil pan, following directions on page 45, or set gas or electric grill to low, following manufacturer's directions.
4. Grill, 5 inches from heat, basting often with marinade, 2 hours for rare, 2 hours, 30 minutes for medium and 3 hours for well done, or until beef is done as you like it. Place meat on carving board and allow to "rest" 15 minutes before carving. Serve with pita bread and dilled cucumber slices.

GRILLED FILLET OF BEEF

Not for everyday—but for a special occasion when only the king of beef will do.

Grill for 30 to 60 minutes.
Makes 12 servings.

1 fillet of beef (about 5 pounds)
¾ cup olive or peanut oil
⅓ cup wine vinegar
1 tablespoon leaf rosemary, crushed
Freshly ground pepper
Salt
Béarnaise Sauce (recipe, page 115)

1. Remove fillet of beef from refrigerator and brush generously with a mixture of oil, vinegar and rosemary. Allow to stand at room temperature for 2 hours; sprinkle generously with freshly ground pepper.
2. Build a medium fire, or set gas or electric grill to medium, following manufacturer's directions.
3. Grill, 4 inches from heat, turning and basting often with oil mixture, 30 minutes for rare, 45 minutes for medium and 60 minutes for well done, or until beef is done as you like it.
4. Remove beef to a heated serving platter and season with salt. Allow to "rest" 15 minutes. Garnish platter with watercress and serve with BÉARNAISE SAUCE.

COUNTRY-STYLE RIBS

Choose the thicker, chunkier pork ribs for this dish.

Rotis for 1 hour, 30 minutes.
Makes 4 servings.

4 pounds country-style spareribs
Garlic salt
Plum Sauce (recipe follows)

1. Build a medium fire in a grill with a rotisserie, positioning coals around drip pan, following directions on page 45, or set gas or electric grill to medium, following manufacturer's directions.
2. Thread ribs on rotisserie spit, and test for balance by rotating spit on

hands. Fasten ribs with holding forks; sprinkle with garlic salt. Set rod in position on grill; start rotisserie.

3. Rotis, checking rotisserie several times, 1 hour, 30 minutes, or until meat is tender and richly browned.

4. Remove to a carving board; take out spit. Serve with PLUM SAUCE and an apple and sliced celery salad.

PLUM SAUCE: Makes 1 cup. Combine 1 cup plum jam, 1 tablespoon cider vinegar, 1 teaspoon grated onion, ½ teaspoon ground allspice and ¼ teaspoon ground ginger in a small saucepan. Heat slowly to boiling, stirring constantly. Serve warm or cold.

ORANGE-GLAZED SHORT RIBS

No need to precook ribs on the range if you follow our simple cooking directions, then add a glaze for the finishing touch.

Grill for 2 hours.
Makes 4 servings.

    3 pounds beef short ribs, cut into
          serving-size pieces
    2 teaspoons salt
    ¼ teaspoon pepper
    ½ cup water
    ¾ cup orange marmalade
    ½ cup dry red wine
    1 teaspoon dry mustard

1. Build a slow fire, or set electric or gas grill to low, following manufacturer's directions.

2. Place short ribs in a single layer in a large shallow metal pan; sprinkle with salt and pepper; add water; cover pan with heavy-duty aluminum foil.

3. Cook on grill, 5 inches from heat, turning ribs several times, 1 hour, 30 minutes, or until ribs are tender when pierced with a two-tined fork.

4. While ribs cook, combine orange marmalade, wine and mustard in a small metal saucepan with a flame-proof handle; place on grill and heat, stirring several times, until bubbly.

5. Remove ribs from baking pan; brush generously with orange glaze.

6. Grill, turning often and brushing with glaze, 30 minutes, or until richly glazed. Serve with cucumbers in sour cream and garlic bread.

BARBECUED CORNED BEEF

Richly glazed corned beef makes a deliciously different barbecue treat.

Grill for 50 minutes.
Makes 12 servings.

    5 pounds corned beef brisket
    1 medium-size onion, sliced
    1 tablespoon mixed pickling spices
    ¼ cup prepared mustard
    2 tablespoons brown sugar
    ¼ teaspoon ground nutmeg
    ¼ teaspoon freshly ground pepper

1. Simmer corned beef with onion and pickling spices in water to cover in a large kettle 3 hours, or until meat is tender when pierced with a two-tined fork. Let stand in broth until ready to glaze.

2. Build a medium fire, or set electric or gas grill to medium, following manufacturer's directions.

3. Brush meat all over with half of the mustard. Mix remaining mustard with brown sugar, nutmeg and pepper in a cup.

4. Grill meat, 6 inches from heat, 15 minutes; turn; grill 15 minutes longer. Brush half of mustard mixture over meat; turn again and grill 10 minutes. Brush with remaining mustard mixture; turn again and grill 10 minutes longer, or until meat is crusty-brown and coated with mustard mixture.

5. Remove meat to cutting board; slice across grain and serve on thick slices of rye or pumpernickel bread with an assortment of your favorite mustards and dill pickles.

BUTTERFLY PORK LEG

The shank portion of a fresh pork leg is butterflied, marinated and grilled to perfection. Pork never tasted better.

Grill for 1 hour.
Makes 8 servings.

    1 pork leg shank portion (about 6
          pounds)
    1 cup pineapple juice
    ½ cup peanut or vegetable oil
    2 cloves garlic, minced
    1 tablespoon grated ginger root
          OR: 1 teaspoon ground ginger
    1 teaspoon salt
    ¼ teaspoon pepper

1. Butterfly leg of pork, following directions for lamb on page 32; trim all excess fat; place meat in a large plastic bag. Add pineapple juice, oil, garlic, ginger, salt and pepper; seal bag tightly and turn meat in marinade several times to coat evenly.

2. Place plastic bag in a large bowl; refrigerate to marinate overnight; let stand at room temperature 1 hour before grilling.

3. Build a medium-hot fire, or set electric or gas grill to medium-high, following manufacturer's directions.

4. Grill, 6 inches from heat, basting with marinade and turning several times, 1 hour, or until meat thermometer inserted in thickest part registers 170°. Place meat on heated platter and allow to "rest" 20 minutes before slicing. Serve with toasted garlic bread, apple salad and mugs of frosty beer.

CHEF'S TIP: Any leftover BUTTERFLY PORK LEG is delicious served cold. Try it on rye bread with mustard, or in a salad with sliced oranges.

LAMB IN SOUR CREAM

Herb-seasoned sour cream coats a boned leg of lamb. Try it, it's superb!

Grill for 40 to 60 minutes.
Makes 8 servings.

    1 leg of lamb (about 7 pounds)
    1 container (8 ounces) dairy sour
          cream
    ¼ cup chopped shallots
          OR: 1 small onion, chopped
          (¼ cup)
    1 clove garlic, minced
    1 teaspoon leaf rosemary, crumbled
    1 teaspoon salt
    ¼ teaspoon freshly ground pepper

1. Butterfly leg of lamb, following directions on page 32. Place in a large shallow utility dish.

2. Combine sour cream, shallots or onion, garlic, rosemary, salt and pepper in a small bowl; spread half the mixture over lamb, turn lamb; coat second side with remaining sour cream mixture; cover with plastic wrap.

3. Marinate in refrigerator 4 hours, or overnight. Remove from refrigerator 1 hour before grilling.

4. Build a medium-hot fire, or set electric or gas grill to medium-high, following manufacturer's directions.

5. Grill, 4 inches from heat, basting with marinade and turning several times, 40 minutes for rare, 50 minutes for medium and 60 minutes for well done, or until lamb is done as you like it. Serve with rice pilaf and marinated cucumber slices.

CALIFORNIA GLAZED HAM

Keep a canned ham in the refrigerator for unexpected summer company.

Grill for 1 hour, 30 minutes.
Makes 10 servings.

    1 canned ham (about 5 pounds)
          Whole cloves
    1 bottle (12 ounces) beer
    ½ cup orange marmalade
    ¼ cup soy sauce
    2 tablespoons prepared mustard

1. Place ham in a shallow metal baking pan; score top in a diamond pattern. Insert a whole clove in center of each diamond. Pour beer over ham.

2. Build a slow fire in a grill with a cover, or set gas or electric grill to low, following manufacturer's directions.

3. Grill, 4 inches from heat, basting with beer several times, 45 minutes.

4. Combine orange marmalade, soy sauce and mustard in a small bowl. Brush on ham to coat evenly.

5. Grill, basting several times with pan drippings, 45 minutes, or until richly glazed. Place on carving board and cut into ¼-inch slices. Serve with kabobs of fresh pineapple. ■

HAMBURGERS & HOT DOGS
(Continued from page 25.)

MAC KING BURGERS

It's like setting up a fast-food restaurant in your own backyard.

Grill for 8 to 16 minutes.
Makes 4 servings.

1½ pounds ground beef
1 teaspoon salt
⅛ teaspoon pepper

1. Build a medium fire, or set gas or electric grill to medium, following manufacturer's directions.
2. Mix ground beef lightly with salt and pepper in a medium-size bowl. Mix in one of the special seasonings below before shaping into four 1-inch-thick patties.
3. Grill, 4 inches from heat, 4 to 8 minutes per side, or until beef is done as you like. Serve on toasted sesame seed buns with catsup.

Suggested Variations:
WASHINGTON BURGERS—¼ cup bottled hickory smoke barbecue sauce and 2 thinly sliced green onions.

NEBRASKA BURGERS—1 can (2¼ or 3 ounces) deviled ham, 1 tablespoon prepared mustard and 1 tablespoon sweet pickle relish.

WISCONSIN BURGERS—½ cup grated Cheddar cheese and ¼ cup catsup.

GEORGIA BURGERS—⅓ cup chopped walnuts, peanuts or toasted almonds.

OHIO BURGERS—¼ cup dairy sour cream, 1 tablespoon chopped parsley, 1 teaspoon each leaf thyme and leaf oregano, crumbled.

MONTANA BURGERS—½ cup chopped fresh mushrooms or drained canned mushroom pieces.

VERMONT BURGERS—¼ cup chopped stuffed green olives or 2 tablespoons each chopped pimiento and chopped ripe olives.

FLORIDA BURGERS—½ cup grated pared carrot, 2 tablespoons grated radishes and 1 teaspoon grated onion.

RHODE ISLAND BURGERS—¼ cup grated Parmesan cheese, ¼ cup canned tomato sauce and ¼ teaspoon leaf oregano, crumbled.

ALABAMA BURGERS—1 cup cooked rice, 2 tablespoons soy sauce and 1 green onion, sliced.

NEW HAMPSHIRE BURGERS—3 slices crumbled crisp bacon and ½ cup canned applesauce.

ARIZONA BURGERS—½ cup crushed cheese crackers, or other flavored crackers, or plain or seasoned potato chips or corn chips.

ARKANSAS BURGERS:—Add ¼ cup chopped parsley and 2 tablespoons horseradish mustard to meat mixture.

NORTH CAROLINA BURGERS:—Add ½ cup chopped stuffed olives and 2 teaspoons curry powder to meat mixture.

TENNESSEE BURGERS:—Add 1 small green pepper, halved, seeded and chopped, and ¼ cup chopped walnuts to meat mixture.

WEST VIRGINIA BURGERS:—Add 1 cup plain wheat germ and ½ cup raisins to meat mixture.

HAWAIIAN BURGERS:—Add 1 can (8½ ounces) crushed pineapple, drained, and ½ cup flaked coconut to meat mixture.

SMOKY LINKS

Grill for 10 minutes.
Makes 8 servings.

2 packages (12 ounces each) smoky links
Orange-Soy Sauce (recipe, page 114)
Peachy Barbecue Sauce (recipe, page 115)
2 packages (8 buns each) hot dog buns, toasted

1. Build a hot fire, or set gas or electric grill to high, following manufacturer's directions.
2. Score smoky links with cuts ½-inch deep. Brush with ORANGE-SOY SAUCE or PEACHY BARBECUE SAUCE.
3. Grill, 6 inches from heat, turning and brushing once or twice with more sauce, 10 minutes, or until glazed.
Suggested Variations:
CALIFORNIA DOGS:—Prepare 1 package fresh or frozen vegetables for chop suey, following package directions. Spoon into toasted hot dog buns; top with grilled smoky links.

WISCONSIN DOGS:—Line toasted hot dog buns with sauerkraut; center smoky links in buns and tuck grilled apple slices around.

SOUTH CAROLINA DOGS:—Top grilled smoky links in buns with peach-apricot ham glaze and toasted coconut.

TENNESSEE DOGS:—Spoon heated pork and beans into toasted hot dog buns; add grilled smoky links; top with shredded American cheese.

KANSAS DOGS:—Spread toasted hot dog buns with applesauce and place grilled smoky links over; top with coconut chips.

ALABAMA DOGS:—Line toasted hot dog buns with shredded lettuce tossed with creamy French dressing, and place grilled smoky links over.

LOUISIANA DOGS:—Top grilled smoky links with bottled steak sauce and marinated artichoke hearts.

NEW JERSEY DOGS:—Brush toasted hot dog buns with bottled barbecue sauce and center smoky links in buns; top with marinated cucumber slices.

FAST FOOD BURGERS

Layer thin beef patties with an assortment of goodies.

Grill for 8 to 16 minutes.
Makes 8 servings.

3 pounds ground beef
1 medium-size onion, grated
2 teaspoons salt
¼ teaspoon freshly ground pepper

1. Build a medium fire, or set gas or electric grill to medium, following manufacturer's directions.
2. Mix beef with onion, salt and pepper in a large bowl; divide into 16 portions; shape each into a thin patty. Put two patties together with any of the fillings below.
3. Grill, 4 inches from heat, 4 to 8 minutes per side, or until beef is done as you like. Serve on toasted buns.

Suggested Variations:
NEW JERSEY BURGERS—thinly sliced tomatoes sprinkled lightly with seasoned salt and grated parmesan cheese.

MASSACHUSETTS BURGERS—canned baked beans seasoned with crumbled crisp bacon and a dash catsup.

TEXAS BURGERS—chili con carne spooned right from the can.

INDIANA BURGERS—canned French fried onions, coarsely crushed.

DELAWARE BURGERS—drained canned, chopped or sliced mushrooms.

ALASKA BURGERS—dill, sweet or crisp cucumber pickle slices.

MINNESOTA BURGERS—assorted sliced cheeses: American, Swiss, pimiento, or sharp Cheddar.

CONNECTICUT BURGERS—crumbled or mashed blue cheese mixed with an equal amount of cream cheese.

WYOMING BURGERS—grated Parmesan cheese or sharp cheese spread mixed with a little chili sauce.

MISSOURI BURGERS—thinly sliced frankfurters with mustard.

SOUTH CAROLINA BURGERS—
pickle relish blended with chopped celery, grated carrot and a little mayonnaise or salad dressing.

CONEY ISLAND HOT DOGS

Molasses and mustard bubble on plump frankfurters.

Grill for 10 minutes.
Makes 8 servings.

- 2 packages (1 pound each) frankfurters
- ¼ cup prepared mustard
- ¼ cup molasses
- 2 tablespoons cider vinegar
- 1 tablespoon Worcestershire sauce
- 1 tablespoon vegetable oil
- 16 split frankfurter rolls, toasted

1. Build a hot fire, or set gas or electric grill to high, following manufacturer's directions.
2. Score frankfurters in crisscross cuts about ¼-inch deep.
3. Mix mustard, molasses, vinegar, Worcestershire sauce and oil in a small metal saucepan with a flameproof handle; brush part over frankfurters.
4. Grill, 6 inches from heat, turning and brushing once or twice with more sauce, 10 minutes, or until richly glazed and puffed.
5. Serve in toasted rolls with French fried onion rings and QUICK CORN RELISH (recipe, page 29).

POLISH SAUSAGES

Grill for 15 minutes.
Makes 8 servings.

- 2 packages (12 or 16 ounces each) Polish sausages or knackwurst
  Brown Sugar Glaze (recipe, page 97)
  Orange-Mustard Sauce (recipe, page 97)
- 1 package (8 buns) hot dog buns, toasted

1. Build a medium fire, or set gas or electric grill to high, following manufacturer's directions.
2. Score Polish sausages or knackwurst with cuts about 1-inch deep. Brush with BROWN SUGAR GLAZE or ORANGE-MUSTARD SAUCE.
3. Grill, 6 inches from heat, turning and brushing once or twice with more sauce, 15 minutes, or until richly glazed. Serve in buns.

Suggested Variations:
WEST VIRGINIA DOGS:—Line toasted hot dog buns with pickled red cabbage from a jar; place grilled sausages on and top with sharp mustard.
ALASKA DOGS:—Line toasted hot dog buns with potato salad; place grilled sausages on and top with mustard pickles.

NORTH CAROLINA DOGS:—Line toasted hot dog buns with grilled apple slices; add grilled sausages and top with sauerkraut.

MICHIGAN DOGS:—Spread toasted hot dog buns with sharp mustard; center sausages in buns and top with dill pickle slices.

NEBRASKA DOGS:—Melt longhorn Cheddar cheese on toasted hot dog buns; center sausages on buns and top with sautéed onion rings.

PENNSYLVANIA DOGS:—Center grilled sausages on toasted hot dog buns; top with mashed potatoes and sautéed mushroom slices.

OREGON DOGS:—Line toasted hot dog buns with a slaw of shredded red cabbage, sour cream, raisins and peanuts. Center sausages on top.

BURGER SMÖRGÅSBORD

Here is a burger-bar assortment of toppings for your next cook-out.

Grill for 8 to 16 minutes.
Makes 12 servings.

- 4 pounds ground beef
- 1 large onion, grated
- 1 egg
- 1 cup canned applesauce
- 2 teaspoons salt
- ¼ teaspoon pepper
  Chili Topping (recipe follows)
  Walnut Topping (recipe follows)
  Rarebit Topping (recipe follows)
  Spaghetti Topping (recipe follows)

1. Mix ground beef lightly with onion, egg, applesauce, salt and pepper in a large bowl until well blended; shape into 12 patties about 1-inch thick. Chill while grill heats.
2. Build a medium fire, or set electric or gas grill to medium, following manufacturer's directions.
3. Grill, 4 inches from heat, 4 to 8 minutes on each side, or until beef is done as you like.
4. Serve with an assortment of rolls, breads and toppings.

CHILI TOPPING

Give burgers a Mexican flavor.

Makes about 4 cups.

- 1 medium-size onion, chopped (½ cup)
- 2 teaspoons chili powder
- 2 tablespoons olive or vegetable oil
- 1 can (1 pound) red kidney beans
- 1 can (1 pound) stewed tomatoes
- ½ teaspoon salt
- ¼ teaspoon pepper
- 1 cup sliced pitted ripe olives

1. Sauté onion with chili powder in oil just until onion is soft in a large saucepan; stir in kidney beans, tomatoes, salt and pepper; cover.
2. Simmer over low heat, stirring often, 30 minutes to blend flavors. Stir in olives.

WALNUT TOPPING

A crunchy treat for a different burger taste.

Makes about 1½ cups.

- ½ cup (1 stick) butter or margarine
- 1 package (8 ounces) walnuts, chopped
- 1 teaspoon seasoned salt

1. Melt butter or margarine in a small saucepan; stir in walnuts and seasoned salt.
2. Sauté, stirring often, 5 minutes, or until sauce is bubbly-hot.

RAREBIT TOPPING

Welsh rarebit makes a great sauce for burgers. Serve on English muffins.

Makes about 3 cups.

- 2 tablespoons butter or margarine
- 2 tablespoons all purpose flour
- 1 teaspoon salt
- ¼ teaspoon dry mustard
- 1 tablespoon Worcestershire sauce
- 2 cups milk
- 1 pound process American cheese, cut into small chunks

1. Melt butter or margarine in a medium-size saucepan; blend in flour, salt, mustard and Worcestershire sauce; cook just until bubbly. Stir in milk; continue cooking, stirring constantly, until sauce thickens and bubbles 3 minutes.
2. Stir in cheese; cook, stirring constantly, just until cheese melts. Do *not* overcook.

SPAGHETTI TOPPING

This makes a knife-and-fork topper for burgers. Serve on crusty rolls.

Makes about 7 cups.

- 2 envelopes (1½ ounces each) spaghetti sauce mix
- 1 can (6 ounces) tomato paste
- 1 can (8 ounces) tomato sauce
- ¼ cup vegetable oil
- 3 cups water
- 1 package (8 ounces) thin spaghetti
- ½ cup grated Parmesan cheese

1. Blend spaghetti sauce mix with tomato paste and tomato sauce in a large saucepan; stir in oil and water.
2. Heat to boiling; simmer, stirring once or twice, 25 to 30 minutes to blend flavors.
3. While sauce simmers, cook spaghetti, following label directions; drain. Spoon sauce over; sprinkle with cheese. Toss to mix well.

HAMBURGERS FOR A CROWD

Every May, students at the University of Montana at Missoula pitch in for a day of volunteer campus clean-up. The tradition, known as Aber Day, culminates in a special barbecue for all participants.

The Lodge Food Service makes barbecue pits from 50-gallon drums cut in half and mounted on legs. A wire mesh screen is laid on top of each pit after two 20-pound bags of charcoal are placed in the bottom of each barrel. The pits are ready in about an hour.

MISSOULA HAMBURGER STEAKS: Makes 220 servings. Place 80 pounds ground beef, 1 gallon finely ground onions and 2 quarts water in a very large bowl or pot. Combine 1 pound old fashioned oatmeal, 1 cup salt and 1 tablespoon freshly ground pepper in a small bowl; add to meat mixture and mix lightly just until blended. Divide into 220 patties, using a #10 scoop or weighing out 6-ounce portions. Pat each into a 5-inch round. Arrange a single layer on grill. Grill 7 to 10 minutes on each side; or until done as you like beef.

BASIC BURGERS

This is our favorite just-plain-good recipe for barbecued burgers.

Grill for 8 to 16 minutes.
Makes 4 servings.

- 2 pounds ground beef
- 1 small onion, grated
- 2 teaspoons salt
- ½ teaspoon monosodium glutamate (MSG)
- ¼ teaspoon pepper
- 4 split hamburger buns, toasted

1. Build a medium-hot fire, or set gas or electric grill to medium-high, following manufacturer's directions.
2. Combine ground beef with onion, salt, MSG and pepper in a medium-size bowl; mix lightly until well blended; shape into 4 patties about 1-inch thick.
3. Grill, 4 inches from heat, 4 to 8 minutes on each side, or until beef is done as you like. Place on toasted buns and top with sliced tomato.

Suggested Variations:

TIVOLI BURGERS—Prepare mixture for BASIC BURGERS; grill, following directions above. Mix ¼ cup mashed blue cheese, 1 tablespoon mayonnaise or salad dressing, and ½ teaspoon soy sauce in a small bowl; spread on patties. Grill until cheese is bubbly.

HERBED BURGERS—Prepare mixture for BASIC BURGERS, adding 1 teaspoon mixed Italian herbs, crumbled. Grill, following directions above. Cream 2 tablespoons butter or margarine with 2 teaspoons finely cut chives; spread over hot patties.

CHILI-CHEESE BURGERS—Prepare mixture for BASIC BURGERS, adding ½ cup diced Monterey Jack cheese and 1 teaspoon chili powder. Grill, following directions above.

ORIENTAL BURGERS

Soy sauce and molasses give beef patties a deep, rich flavor.

Grill for 8 to 16 minutes.
Makes 6 servings.

- 3 pounds ground beef
- 1 small onion, grated
- ½ cup soy sauce
- ½ cup chili sauce
- 1 tablespoon molasses
  Few drops bottled red pepper seasoning

1. Mix ground beef lightly with onion in a medium-size bowl; shape into twelve 1-inch-thick patties. Place in a shallow glass casserole.
2. Combine soy sauce, chili sauce, molasses and red pepper seasoning in a small bowl; pour over meat; turn to coat well. Cover dish with plastic wrap; chill at least one hour to season.
3. Build a medium fire, or set gas or electric grill to medium, following manufacturer's directions.
4. Grill, 4 inches from heat, basting with remaining sauce, 4 to 8 minutes on each side, or until beef is done as you like. Serve with Chinese noodles and stir-fried green beans and water chestnuts, if you wish.

PARISIAN BURGERS

So elegant, you'll want to serve this to your favorite gourmets.

Grill for 10 to 20 minutes.
Makes 4 servings.

Béarnaise Sauce
- ¼ cup white wine
- ¼ cup water
- 1 tablespoon finely chopped shallots or green onions
- ½ teaspoon dried tarragon, crumbled
- ½ cup (1 stick) butter or margarine
- 2 egg yolks
- 1 teaspoon chopped parsley
  Burgers
- 2 pounds ground beef
- ⅓ cup dry red wine
- 1 tablespoon finely cut chives
- 1 teaspoon salt
- 1 teaspoon pepper

1. Make Béarnaise Sauce: Combine wine, water, shallots or green onions and tarragon in a small saucepan.

Heat to boiling, then simmer 8 to 10 minutes, or until mixture is reduced to ¼ cup. Strain into top of double boiler. Cut butter or margarine into 8 pieces. Add egg yolks to double boiler; beat with wire whip until foamy. Set over simmering, *not boiling,* water. Add butter or margarine, 1 piece at a time, stirring constantly and letting each piece melt before adding the next. When sauce is fluffy-thick, season with salt and pepper, if needed. Stir in parsley. Remove top saucepan from water immediately.
2. Build a medium fire, or set gas or electric grill to medium, following manufacturer's directions.
3. Make Burgers: Mix beef with wine, chives, salt and pepper in a medium-size bowl. Shape into 4 patties, about 1-inch thick.
4. Grill, 4 inches from heat, 5 to 10 minutes on each side, or until beef is done as you like. Place on toasted English muffins on heated serving platter. Spoon Béarnaise Sauce over. Garnish with watercress, mushrooms and tomato halves.

JUMBO JIMS

Here are hero sandwiches a big appetite will appreciate—two burgers and beans.

Grill for 8 to 16 minutes.
Makes 8 servings.

- 3 pounds ground beef
- 2 eggs
- 2 teaspoons salt
- ¼ teaspoon pepper
- 1 to 3 teaspoons chili powder
- 1 medium-size onion, peeled and sliced
- 2 tablespoons vegetable oil
- 2 cans (about 1 pound each) barbecue beans
- 1 package (8 ounces) sliced sharp Cheddar cheese
- 16 slices white bread, toasted

1. Build a medium fire, or set gas or electric grill to medium, following manufacturer's directions.
2. Combine ground beef with eggs, salt, pepper and half of the chili powder in a large bowl; mix lightly until well-blended; shape into 16 large patties the size of the bread slices.
3. Sauté onion in oil just until soft in a medium-size metal saucepan with flameproof handle on grill, 4 inches from heat; stir in beans and remaining chili powder; simmer on grill, 6 inches from heat, until thick.
4. Grill patties, 4 inches from heat, 4 to 8 minutes on each side, or until beef is done as you like. Top half the patties with cheese for the last 2 minutes of grilling.
5. Place plain patties on 8 slices of toasted bread on serving plates; spoon beans over; top with cheeseburgers and second bread slice.

KUN KOKI BURGERS

Marinate beef patties in a soy sauce marinade for burgers with an Oriental flavor.

Grill for 8 to 16 minutes.
Makes 8 servings.

- ¼ cup vegetable oil
- ¼ cup soy sauce
- 2 tablespoons corn syrup
- 1 tablespoon lemon juice
- ½ teaspoon ground ginger
- ¼ teaspoon garlic powder
- 2 green onions, thinly sliced
- 3 pounds ground beef
- 8 split sesame seed buns

1. Mix oil, soy sauce, corn syrup, lemon juice, ginger, garlic powder and green onions in a large shallow glass casserole.
2. Shape ground beef into 8 patties about ¾-inch thick. Dip in sauce mixture to coat both sides, then place in a single layer in same casserole. Chill 3 to 4 hours or overnight to season. Remove from marinade.
3. Build a medium fire, or set gas or electric grill to medium, following manufacturer's directions.
4. Grill, 4 inches from heat, basting with marinade, 4 to 8 minutes on each side, or until beef is done as you like. Serve on toasted buns.

BARBECUED CABBAGE

Try this Hungarian favorite for a change of pace barbecue.

Grill for 2 hours.
Makes 6 servings.

- 1 large head cabbage
- 2 pounds ground round
- ¾ cup uncooked rice
- 1 medium-size onion, grated
- 2 eggs
- 1 tablespoon paprika
- 1 teaspoon salt
- ¼ teaspoon pepper
- 1 large onion, sliced
- 2 cups tomato juice
- ½ cup catsup
- ½ cup firmly packed brown sugar
- ¼ cup dry white wine

1. Build a slow fire in a grill with a cover, or set gas or electric grill to low, following manufacturer's directions.
2. Fill a metal Dutch oven with flameproof handle with water; bring to boiling. Core cabbage; plunge into water and boil for 3 minutes to soften. Remove cabbage and peel off about 12 leaves. Shred rest of cabbage.
3. Combine ground round, rice, grated onion, eggs, paprika, salt and pepper in a medium-size bowl, mixing lightly, just until blended. Place a small mound of mixture on each cabbage leaf. Fold over the sides and roll. Place rolls, seam-sides down, in Dutch oven. Add onion slices and shredded cabbage. Combine tomato juice, catsup, brown sugar and wine; pour over cabbage rolls; cover Dutch oven.
4. Grill, 6 inches from heat with cover on grill, 2 hours, or until cabbage rolls are tender when pierced with a two-tined fork. Serve with buttered noodles sprinkled with caraway.

HOBO SUPPER

Out in the wilderness? Try cooking in cans. It's fun and there's no clean-up.

Grill for 1 hour.
Makes 6 servings.

- 2 pounds ground beef
- 3 tablespoons all purpose flour
- 1 teaspoon salt
- 1 teaspoon leaf thyme, crumbled
- ¼ teaspoon pepper
- 6 medium-size carrots, pared
- 6 medium-size potatoes, pared
- 2 cups tomato juice

1. Collect and wash out six 1-pound metal cans.
2. Shape ground beef into 6 patties the size of the cans; coat with a mixture of flour, salt, thyme and pepper and place in bottom of cans.
3. Slice carrots and potatoes into cans over meat; add ⅓ cup tomato juice to each can. Cover top of cans with a double thickness of heavy-duty aluminum foil.
4. Build a medium fire, or set electric or gas grill to medium, following manufacturer's directions.
5. Cook on grill, 4 inches from heat, 1 hour, or until vegetables are tender when pierced with a two-tined fork. Serve with crisp celery and cucumber sticks.

SOUR CREAM BURGERS

Thick beef patties simmer in a wine and sour cream sauce after grilling—perfect with piles of mashed potatoes.

Grill for 8 to 16 minutes.
Makes 4 servings.

- 2 pounds ground beef
- 1 egg
- ½ cup soft bread crumbs (1 slice)
- ⅓ cup evaporated milk (not sweetened condensed milk)
- 2 tablespoons minced onion
- 2 teaspoons salt
- ¼ teaspoon seasoned pepper
- 1 can condensed cream of chicken soup
- ½ cup dry white wine
- 2 teaspoons paprika
- ½ cup dairy sour cream
- 2 teaspoons all purpose flour

1. Build a medium fire, or set gas or electric grill to medium, following manufacturer's directions.
2. Combine ground beef with egg, bread crumbs, evaporated milk, onion, salt and pepper in a medium-size bowl; mix lightly until well blended; shape into 4 patties about 1-inch thick.
3. Grill, 4 inches from heat, 4 to 8 minutes per side, or until beef is done as you like.
4. While patties grill, combine soup, wine and paprika in a large metal skillet with flameproof handle; heat, stirring constantly, until bubbling. Combine sour cream and flour in a small bowl; stir in part of hot sauce; stir into skillet; add patties; simmer 1 minute. Serve with mashed potatoes and buttered wax beans.

CHILIBURGERS

So quick to mix; so great to serve.

Grill for 15 minutes.
Makes 4 servings.

- 1 pound ground beef
- 1 can condensed chili-beef soup
- 1 can (about 9 ounces) cream-style corn
- 8 split hamburger buns, toasted

1. Build a medium fire, or set gas or electric grill to medium, following manufacturer's directions.
2. Shape ground beef into a large patty in a large metal skillet with flameproof handle; brown on grill, 4 inches from heat, 5 minutes on each side; break into chunks.
3. Stir in soup and corn; simmer on grill, 6 inches from heat, stirring often, 5 minutes.
4. Spoon into toasted buns. Serve with small sweet pickles.

MEXICAN FRANKS

Tortillas make a different "bun" for hot dogs.

Grill for 10 minutes.
Makes 8 servings.

- 2 packages (1 pound each) frankfurters
- 16 tortillas
- 1 can (1 pound) refried beans, heated
- 1 cup shredded Cheddar cheese (4 ounces)
- Sliced green onions
- Shredded iceberg lettuce

1. Build a medium fire, or set gas or electric grill to medium, following manufacturer's directions.
2. Grill frankfurters, 4 inches from heat, 10 minutes, or until bubbly-hot.
3. While frankfurters cook, heat tortillas on grill, turning with tongs.
4. Place frankfurters in tortillas and top with refried beans, shredded cheese, green onions and lettuce; roll up and serve hot. ■

111

STEAKS, CHOPS & BUTTERS
(Continued from page 57.)

CHARCOAL STEAK

Here is a show-stopper. You actually cook your steak right on the coals. This is only for those who like rare or medium-rare steaks.

Grill for 15 to 20 minutes.
Makes 4 servings.

> 1 sirloin steak, cut 2-inches thick
>   (about 3 pounds)
>   Salt
>   Freshly ground pepper
>   Blue-Cheese Butter (recipe,
>   page 57)

1. Trim excess fat from steak; score remaining fat at 1-inch intervals. Let stand at room temperature 2 hours.
2. Build a hot fire at least 3 inches deep and wider than twice the width of the steak. Brush excess ash off coals with a wire brush.
3. Grill steak on coals 8 to 10 minutes, or until meat juices show on top; turn steak, placing steak on unused coals. Grill 7 minutes longer for rare and 10 minutes for medium rare.
4. Remove steak to heated serving platter and allow to "rest" 10 minutes; season with salt and pepper; top with BLUE-CHEESE BUTTER and cut into thin slices. Serve with French fries.

SAN ANTONIO STEAK

Here's the choice for those who like their beef spicy-hot.

Grill for 25 to 35 minutes.
Makes 6 servings.

> 1 round steak, cut 2-inches thick
>   (about 3 pounds)
> 1 cup vegetable oil
> ½ cup cider vinegar
> 2 to 4 teaspoons chili powder
> 1 teaspoon leaf oregano, crumbled
> 1 teaspoon garlic powder
> ¼ teaspoon bottled red pepper
>   seasoning
>   Instant unseasoned meat
>   tenderizer

1. Remove steak from refrigerator 1 hour before grilling. Trim off any excess fat, then score remaining fat at 1-inch intervals so that meat will lie flat on grill. Place steak in a shallow glass utility dish.
2. Mix oil, vinegar, chili powder, oregano, garlic powder and bottled red pepper seasoning in a small bowl; pour over steak. Let stand at room temperature, 2 hours, turning several times.
3. Build a medium fire, or set electric or gas grill to medium, following manufacturer's directions.
4. Remove steak from marinade; sprinkle with tenderizer, following label directions.
5. Grill, 5 inches from heat, 12 minutes on each side for rare, 15 minutes on each side for medium, and 18 minutes on each side for well done, or until steak is done as you like it.
6. Remove to a cutting board or large platter; carve into ¼-inch-thick slices and serve with tacos and an avocado and orange salad.

GARLIC-GRILLED PORK CHOPS

Thick pork blade or arm steaks are perfect to grill, especially this way.

Grill for 35 to 45 minutes.
Makes 6 servings

> 6 pork blade or arm steaks, cut
>   1-inch thick (about 3 pounds)
> ¼ cup peanut or vegetable oil
> 2 tablespoons red wine vinegar
> 2 cloves garlic, minced
> 1 teaspoon leaf sage, crumbled
> 1 teaspoon salt
> ¼ teaspoon freshly ground pepper

1. Trim excess fat from pork steaks; place in a large shallow utility dish.
2. Combine oil, wine vinegar, garlic, sage, salt and pepper in a cup; pour over pork; turn to coat second side; cover dish with plastic wrap.
3. Marinate 2 hours at room temperature or 4 to 6 hours in refrigerator, allowing to stand 1 hour at room temperature before grilling.
4. Build a medium fire, or set electric or gas grill to medium, following manufacturer's directions.
5. Grill, 5 inches from heat, basting with marinade several times and turning once, 35 to 45 minutes, or until well done.

LONDON BROIL

This steak house favorite was first prepared with flank steak, then round steak, and today chuck is the popular cut of beef. Just remember to carve steak into thin, diagonal slices before serving.

Grill for 30 to 50 minutes.
Makes 6 servings.

> 1 chuck steak, cut 2 inches thick
>   (about 3 pounds)
>   Instant unseasoned meat
>   tenderizer
> ¼ cup vegetable oil
> 1 clove garlic, halved
> ¼ cup (½ stick) butter or margarine
>   Salt and pepper

1. Trim excess fat from steak and score remaining fat at 1-inch intervals; sprinkle with meat tenderizer, following label directions. Allow to stand at room temperature at least 1 hour before grilling.
2. Combine oil and garlic in a cup and allow to stand with steak.
3. Build a medium fire, or set gas or electric grill to medium, following manufacturer's directions.
4. Coat steak generously with garlic oil on both sides.
5. Grill, 6 inches from heat, 15 minutes per side for rare, 20 minutes per side for medium, and 25 minutes per side for well done, or until steak is done as you like it.
6. Remove steak to sizzle platter; spread with butter or margarine to coat evenly; sprinkle with salt and pepper. Carve into thin, diagonal slices and serve, spooning part of the platter juices over steak, with sautéed sliced mushrooms and onions.

FREEZER STEAKS

We've tested and tasted and believe it's better to grill steak right from the freezer —no need to thaw first.

Grill for 15 to 50 minutes.
Makes 4 to 8 servings.

> 1 sirloin steak, ¾-inch to 2-inches
>   thick (2½ to 5 pounds)
>   Seasoned salt
>   Freshly ground pepper
>   Butter or margarine
>   Fresh chives, chopped

1. Prepare steak for freezer by trimming excess fat; score remaining fat at 1-inch intervals around edge. Wrap steak tightly in heavy-duty aluminum foil, pressing out as much air as possible from package. Label, date and freeze steak.
2. Build a medium fire, or set gas or electric grill to medium, following manufacturer's directions.
3. Grill, following distance, time and temperature in chart on page 53. Remove steak to heated sizzle-platter; season with salt and pepper; top with a generous pat of butter or margarine; rub over surface of steak until butter melts. Sprinkle with chopped chives. Serve with a crisp romaine and watercress salad and a hearty red wine.

DIPPING STEAK

Flank steak is the classic choice for this dish, but you can substitute chuck or round and follow grilling time on page 53.

Grill for 10 to 18 minutes.
Makes 6 servings.

> 1 flank steak (about 2 pounds)
>   Instant unseasoned meat
>   tenderizer
>   Soy Dip (recipe follows)
>   Zippy Horseradish Dip (recipe
>   follows)

1. Remove steak from refrigerator 1 hour before grilling. Moisten steak and sprinkle with tenderizer, following label directions.
2. Build a medium fire, or set gas or

electric grill to medium, following manufacturer's directions.

3. Grill, 4 inches from heat, 5 minutes per side for rare, 7 minutes per side for medium, and 9 minutes per side for well done, or until steak is done as you like it.

4. Remove steak to a cutting board or large platter; carve diagonally into ¼-inch-thick slices. Serve with SOY DIP and ZIPPY HORSERADISH DIP.

SOY DIP: Makes ¾ cup. Blend ½ cup soy sauce, ¼ cup wine vinegar or cider vinegar, 1 teaspoon garlic powder and ½ teaspoon ground ginger in a small bowl. Chill at least 1 hour to blend flavors.

ZIPPY HORSERADISH DIP: Makes ¾ cup. Blend ½ cup bottled chili sauce, 2 tablespoons prepared horseradish, 1 tablespoon lemon juice and 1 teaspoon Worcestershire sauce in a small bowl. Chill at least 1 hour to blend flavors.

HERB 'N' LEMON STEAK

Adventurous chefs might like to try this tangy combination of thyme and lemon for their next steak marinade.

Grill for 8 to 15 minutes.
Makes 6 servings.

  1 **blade chuck steak, cut 1-inch thick (about 3 pounds)**
⅔ **cup lemon juice**
½ **cup beef broth**
  1 **tablespoon vegetable oil**
  1 **tablespoon sugar**
  2 **teaspoons garlic salt**
  1 **teaspoon leaf thyme, crumbled**

1. Trim excess fat from steak; score remaining fat around edge at 1-inch intervals; place in a large plastic bag or a shallow glass baking dish.

2. Combine lemon juice, beef broth, oil, sugar, garlic salt and thyme in a small saucepan; bring to boiling; simmer 5 minutes; cool to lukewarm.

3. Pour over steak, coating evenly; seal plastic bag or cover dish with plastic wrap. Refrigerate at least 4 hours, or overnight. Let stand 1 hour at room temperature. Remove from marinade and reserve.

4. Build a medium-hot fire or set gas or electric grill to medium-high, following manufacturer's directions.

5. Grill steak, 3 inches from heat, 4 minutes for rare, 6 minutes for medium, and 8 minutes for well done; brush with reserved marinade; turn with tongs.

6. Grill 4 minutes for rare, 5 minutes for medium, and 7 minutes for well done, or until steak is done as you like it. Serve with kabobs of plum and orange wedges, basted with part of the marinade.

TERIYAKI STRIP STEAKS

Individual steaks grill in a soy-wine sauce.

Grill for 10 to 30 minutes.
Makes 4 servings.

  4 **top loin or strip steaks, cut 1-inch thick (about 3 pounds)**
½ **cup soy sauce**
½ **cup dry Sherry**
  2 **tablespoons sugar**
½ **teaspoon powdered ginger**
¼ **teaspoon dry mustard**
⅛ **teaspoon garlic powder**

1. Place steaks in plastic bag or shallow glass dish. Combine soy sauce, Sherry, sugar, ginger, dry mustard and garlic powder in a 2-cup measure; pour marinade over steaks. Turn steaks to coat all sides and seal bag or cover dish with plastic wrap.

2. Marinate in refrigerator (or insulated container after chilling) 4 to 6 hours. Let stand at room temperature 1 hour. Remove from marinade and reserve marinade.

3. Build a medium-hot fire, or set gas or electric grill to medium-high, following manufacturer's directions.

4. Grill, 4 inches from heat, 5 minutes for rare, 7 minutes for medium and 10 minutes for well done; brush with remaining marinade; turn with tongs.

5. Grill 5 minutes for rare, 7 minutes for medium and 10 minutes for well done, or until done as you like.

GRILLED LONDON BROIL

Flank steak is a lean, flavorful cut of beef.

Grill for 8 to 16 minutes.
Makes 4 servings.

  1 **beef flank steak (1¼ to 1¾ pounds)**
¼ **cup vegetable oil**
  1 **tablespoon lemon juice**
  1 **clove garlic, minced**
½ **teaspoon salt**
¼ **teaspoon pepper**

1. Place steak in plastic bag or flat glass dish.

2. Combine oil, lemon juice, garlic, salt and pepper in a cup; pour over flank steak. Close bag securely, or cover pan with plastic wrap, and refrigerate 4 to 6 hours or overnight, turning occasionally. Let steak stand at room temperature 1 hour before grilling. Pour off and reserve marinade.

3. Build a medium-hot fire, or set electric or gas grill to medium-high, following manufacturer's directions.

4. Grill, 3 inches from heat, 4 minutes for rare, 6 minutes for medium and 8 minutes for well done; brush with marinade; turn; grill 4 minutes for rare, 6 minutes for medium and 8 minutes for well done.

5. Place on wooden carving board

and cut into diagonal slices, across the grain; serve over shredded lettuce and top with heated remaining marinade.

GOURMET BEEF TENDERLOIN

Save this recipe for when tenderloin is on special, or choose an eye round and treat it with tenderizer.

Grill for 30 to 60 minutes.
Makes 8 servings.

  1 **beef tenderloin (about 4 pounds)**
    Vegetable or olive oil
    Salt and freshly ground pepper
  1 **package (4 ounces) blue cheese**
  1 **tablespoon Worcestershire sauce**
  1 **tablespoon chopped chives**

1. Let tenderloin stand at room temperature for 1 hour.

2. Build a medium fire, or set electric or gas grill to medium, following manufacturer's directions.

3. Rub beef with oil to coat well; season with salt and pepper.

4. Grill, 6 inches from heat, turning and basting with oil, 30 minutes for rare, 45 minutes for medium and 60 minutes for well done.

5. Combine blue cheese, Worcestershire sauce and chives in a small bowl.

6. Ten minutes before beef is done, spread cheese mixture over top and continue grilling until cheese melts and beef is done.

STEAK ITALIANO

Cubed steaks make a quick and delicious barbecue meat.

Grill for 6 to 10 minutes.
Makes 6 servings.

  6 **cubed beef steaks (about 1½ pounds)**
  1 **can (8 ounces) tomato sauce**
¼ **cup grated Parmesan cheese**
  1 **teaspoon instant minced onion**
½ **teaspoon leaf oregano, crumbled**
½ **teaspoon leaf basil, crumbled**
½ **teaspoon garlic powder**
  6 **English muffins, split and toasted**
    Small stuffed green olives, sliced
  6 **slices mozzarella cheese**

1. Build a medium fire, or set gas or electric grill to medium, following manufacturer's directions.

2. Let steaks stand at room temperature for 1 hour.

3. Combine tomato sauce, Parmesan cheese, onion, oregano, basil and garlic powder in a small metal saucepan with a flameproof handle. Cook on grill 5 minutes, stirring to blend.

4. Grill steaks 3 to 5 minutes on each side. Place steaks on bottoms of English muffins. Spread steaks with sauce and top with olives. Cut slices of cheese in half; place on each steak.

5. Grill 3 minutes, or until cheese melts. Serve with muffin tops. ■

MARINADES & GLAZES
(Continued from page 97.)

PLUM CHUTNEY GLAZE

Pungent and spicy, this baste makes lamb riblets, spareribs or pork chops taste extra-special. Shown in a decanter sold at Simi Winery, in photo on page 26.

Makes 4 cups.

    1 large red onion, chopped (1 cup)
    1 large green pepper, halved,
        seeded and chopped
    1 California orange, peeled,
        sectioned and chopped
    1 large tomato, cored and chopped
    1 clove garlic, minced
    ½ cup lime juice
    1 jar (1 pound) plum jam
    1 tablespoon pumpkin pie spice

1. Combine chopped onion, green pepper, orange and tomato in a large heavy saucepan. Add garlic and lime juice; stir with wooden spoon.
2. Bring slowly to boiling, stirring often; lower heat; simmer 45 minutes; stir in plum jam and pumpkin pie spice; simmer 15 minutes longer, stirring often.
3. Pour into a glass bowl to cool completely. Store in a glass decanter or a 4-cup glass jar with a screw top.

LEMON-PINEAPPLE GLAZE

Sweet and tangy—just great for chicken, fish or hot dogs. Shown on an old wooden cart, in photo on page 26.

Makes 3 cups.

    1 jar (1 pound) pineapple jam
    1 can (6 ounces) apricot nectar
    ½ cup lemon juice
    2 teaspoons ground ginger

Combine pineapple jam, apricot nectar, lemon juice and ginger in a medium-size bowl until smooth. Pour into a decanter or 4-cup glass jar with a screw top. Chill at least 2 days.

TOMATO-BEER BASTE

Deep and tangy enough to give character to any cut of beef or sausages. Photographed at the Simi Winery, Healdsburry, California, and shown on page 26.

Makes 3½ cups.

    1 bottle (16 ounces) barbecue sauce
    1 can (12 ounces) beer
    2 tablespoons Worcestershire sauce
        Few drops bottled red pepper
        seasoning

Combine barbecue sauce, beer, Worcestershire sauce and red pepper seasoning in a 4-cup glass jar with a screw top. Store at least 1 day to develop flavors. Brush on meat, for the last 15 minutes of grilling.

MORGANVILLE SAUCE

The Wilfong family of Morganville, New Jersey, chose this sauce for their super-special franks and burgers.

Makes 2 cups.

    2 cups catsup
    2 teaspoons dry mustard
    2 teaspoons garlic powder
    2 teaspoons light corn syrup
    2 teaspoons Worcestershire sauce

Combine catsup, dry mustard, garlic powder, corn syrup and Worcestershire sauce in a small bowl. Brush over frankfurters or hamburgers during the last 10 minutes of grilling.

ROSÉ SAUCE

Great with sliced steak.

Makes 2 cups.

    2 tablespoons cornstarch
    2 envelopes or teaspoons instant
        beef broth
    ½ cup water
    ¼ cup (½ stick) butter or margarine
    1 cup Rosé wine
    2 tablespoons catsup
    ¼ teaspoon leaf thyme, crumbled
    1 clove garlic, minced
    ½ cup thinly sliced green onions

1. Combine cornstarch and instant beef broth in a small metal saucepan with a flameproof handle; stir in water until smooth.
2. Add butter or margarine, wine, catsup, thyme and garlic.
3. Cook over grill, stirring constantly, until sauce thickens and bubbles; push to one side of grill; simmer 10 minutes. Add green onions and simmer 5 minutes longer.

BASIC BURGER GLAZE

So quick to mix—just three pantry-shelf items.

Makes ¾ cup.

    ½ cup catsup
    ¼ cup prepared mustard
    ¼ teaspoon bottled red pepper
        seasoning

Combine catsup, mustard and red pepper seasoning in a small bowl. Brush over burgers or hot dogs for the last 10 minutes of grilling.

MOLASSES BARBECUE SAUCE

This is an all purpose baste—goes just as well with poultry as with beef.

Makes 3 cups.

    1 cup light molasses
    1 cup prepared mustard
    1 cup cider vinegar

Combine molasses, mustard and vinegar in a large jar with a screw top; shake well. Store in refrigerator.

Suggested Variations:
GINGER SAUCE: Makes 1½ cups. Mix 1 cup MOLASSES BARBECUE SAUCE with ½ cup ginger marmalade and 1 teaspoon ground ginger.

ZIPPY SAUCE: Makes 1½ cups. Mix 1 cup MOLASSES BARBECUE SAUCE with ¼ cup catsup, ¼ cup vegetable oil and 2 tablespoons Worcestershire sauce.

ITALIAN HERB SAUCE: Makes 1½ cups. Mix 1 cup MOLASSES BARBECUE SAUCE with ½ cup chili sauce and ½ teaspoon oregano.

ZESTY TOMATO SAUCE: Makes 1½ cups. Mix 1 cup MOLASSES BARBECUE SAUCE with ½ cup tomato juice and ½ teaspoon ground pepper.

SAUTERNE SAUCE

Try this wine-sparkled white sauce over grilled trout or salmon steaks.

Makes 2 cups.

    ¼ cup (½ stick) butter or margarine
    ¼ cup chopped green onion
    ¼ cup all purpose flour
    1½ cups milk
    ½ cup Sauterne wine
    1 teaspoon salt
    1 teaspoon leaf thyme, crumbled
    ¼ teaspoon white pepper

1. Melt butter or margarine in a small metal saucepan with a flameproof handle over grill; sauté green onion until soft.
2. Stir in flour and cook, stirring constantly, until mixture bubbles; stir in milk, wine, salt, thyme and pepper.
3. Cook, stirring constantly, until sauce thickens and bubbles 3 minutes; push to side of grill and simmer 10 minutes. Serve warm over fish.

ORANGE-SOY SAUCE

Florida orange juice gives tang to grilled chicken or pork kabobs.

Makes 2 cups.

    1 cup orange marmalade
    1 cup orange juice
    ½ cup sliced green onions
    ½ cup soy sauce
    1 teaspoon salt
    1 teaspoon ground ginger

Combine marmalade, orange juice, green onions, soy sauce, salt and ginger in a small metal saucepan with flameproof handle. Heat over grill, stirring often, until bubbly hot. Push to side of grill. Brush over chicken or pork during the last 15 minutes of grilling for best glazing.

MEDITERRANEAN MARINADE

Great with lamb kabobs, beef or pork.

Makes 2½ cups.

- 1 cup lemon juice
- 1 cup vegetable or peanut oil
- ⅔ cup dry red wine
- 2 teaspoons salt
- 1 clove garlic, minced
- 2 teaspoons mixed Italian herbs, crumbled
- ½ teaspoon freshly ground pepper

Combine lemon juice, oil, red wine, salt, garlic, Italian herbs and pepper in a large jar with a screw top. Cover and shake to blend well. Refrigerate at least 2 hours to blend flavors.

SPECIAL MARINADE

Make a batch to keep on hand and season roasts, steaks or even hamburgers.

Makes 2½ cups.

- 2 large onions, coarsely chopped
- 2 cloves garlic, peeled
- 1 cup soy sauce
- 2 teaspoons mixed Italian herbs
- ¼ cup bottled gravy coloring

Combine onions, garlic, soy sauce and Italian herbs in container of an electric blender; cover; process at high speed 1 minute, or until mixture is very smooth. Stir in gravy coloring. Store in a large jar with a screw top.

SPICY HORSERADISH SAUCE

Here's a topping for grilled shrimp or a thick, juicy burger.

Makes ¾ cup.

- ½ cup chili sauce
- 3 tablespoons lemon juice
- 1 tablespoon prepared horseradish
- 2 teaspoons Worcestershire sauce
- 1 small clove garlic, minced
  Few drops bottled red pepper seasoning

Combine chili sauce, lemon juice, horseradish, Worcestershire sauce, garlic and red pepper seasoning in a small glass or ceramic bowl. Cover bowl with plastic wrap and chill at least 1 hour to blend flavors. Spoon over hot shrimp or hamburgers.

PEACHY BARBECUE SAUCE

Baste on your next roast pork loin.

Makes ¾ cup.

- ½ cup peach preserves
- 2 tablespoons cider vinegar
- 1 tablespoon bottled steak sauce

Combine peach preserves, cider vinegar and steak sauce in a small metal saucepan with a flameproof handle. Heat on grill, stirring often, until sauce bubbles; push to side of grill and keep warm. Brush on pork loin, to coat evenly, for last 30 minutes of cooking.

BÉARNAISE SAUCE

A classic French sauce—the perfect topping for grilled T-bone or sirloin steak.

Makes 1 cup.

- ½ cup dry white wine
- 1 tablespoon tarragon vinegar
- 1 tablespoon finely chopped shallots or onions
- ⅛ teaspoon freshly ground pepper
- 1 sprig parsley
- ½ teaspoon leaf tarragon, crumbled
- 2 egg yolks
- ½ cup (1 stick) butter or margarine, melted
  Dash cayenne
- 1 teaspoon chopped parsley

1. Combine wine, vinegar, shallots or onion, pepper, parsley sprig and tarragon in a small saucepan. Bring to boiling, then simmer, uncovered, 8 to 10 minutes, or until liquid measures about ⅓ cup; strain into a cup.
2. Beat egg yolks slightly in the top of a double boiler; stir in ⅓ of the melted butter or margarine. Place top over simmering, not boiling, water.
3. Beat in wine liquid, alternately with remaining melted butter or margarine, with electric hand mixer on medium; continue beating, keeping top over simmering water, until mixture is fluffy-thick. Remove from heat at once.
4. Stir in cayenne and chopped parsley. Serve warm and *never* bring to boiling.

SWEET-SOUR SAUCE

Ribs never had a better taste.

Makes 1¾ cups.

- 1 can (8 ounces) tomato sauce
- ¼ cup honey
- ¼ cup lemon juice
- 1 tablespoon soy sauce
- 1 tablespoon Worcestershire sauce
- 1 clove garlic, minced
- 2 teaspoons salt
- 1 teaspoon leaf basil, crumbled
- 1 teaspoon dry mustard
- ¼ teaspoon bottled red pepper seasoning

Combine tomato sauce, honey, lemon juice, soy sauce, Worcestershire sauce, garlic, salt, basil, mustard and red pepper seasoning in a large jar with a screw top. Cover and shake to blend well. Refrigerate for at least 2 hours to blend flavors. Brush on short ribs, chops or chicken breasts for the last 20 minutes of grilling.

TOMATO-SOY SAUCE

Tasty and tangy, this is the perfect baste for chicken legs or chuck steaks.

Makes 2½ cups.

- 1 can (15 ounces) tomato sauce with tomato bits
- 1 medium-size onion, chopped (½ cup)
- 1 clove garlic, minced
- ¼ cup soy sauce
- 2 tablespoons sugar
- 1 teaspoon dry mustard
- ⅛ teaspoon cayenne pepper

Combine tomato sauce with tomato bits, onion, garlic, soy sauce, sugar, dry mustard and cayenne in a large jar with a screw top; shake to blend.

LOUISIANA SAUCE

Just made for grilled crayfish or shrimp!

Makes ⅔ cup.

- ½ cup (1 stick) butter or margarine
- 2 tablespoons lime or lemon juice
  Few drops bottled red pepper seasoning

Melt butter or margarine in a small metal pan with a flameproof handle over grill; stir in lime or lemon juice and red pepper seasoning. Push to side of grill and keep warm.

CHUTNEY BARBECUE GLAZE

Your blender does all the work in seconds.

Makes about 2 cups.

- 1 cup mango chutney
- ½ cup catsup
- ½ cup lemon juice
- 1 tablespoon Worcestershire sauce

Combine chutney, catsup, lemon juice and Worcestershire sauce in container of electric blender. Process on high 30 seconds, or until smooth. Store in a 2-cup glass jar with screw top. Brush on chicken, burgers or pork chops.

MOLASSES SAUCE

Split chicken and grill it with this Southern-style barbecue sauce.

Makes 1½ cups.

- ½ cup light molasses
- ½ cup cider vinegar
- ½ cup prepared mustard
- ¼ cup Worcestershire sauce
- 1 teaspoon bottled red pepper seasoning

Combine molasses, vinegar, mustard, Worcestershire sauce and red pepper seasoning in a small bowl; stir to blend. Spoon into a 2-cup jar with a screw top. ■

VEGETABLES & BAKE-ALONGS

CHEERY CHERRY TOMATOES

They add a festive touch to any meat platter. Photographed with Meatloaf Wellington and shown on page 19.

Makes 8 servings.

- 1 pint cherry tomatoes
- 2 tablespoons butter or margarine
- 1 teaspoon seasoned salt
- ¼ teaspoon seasoned pepper
- ½ teaspoon leaf basil, crumbled

1. Stem and wash tomatoes.
2. Heat butter or margarine in a medium-size saucepan; add tomatoes and stir, just until skin begins to break.
3. Sprinkle with seasoned salt, seasoned pepper and basil. Spoon around MEATLOAF WELLINGTON.

CARROT PENNIES

Even kids will ask for seconds when you cook carrots this way. Photographed with Crown Roast of Hot Dogs, shown on page 19.

Makes 8 servings.

- 1 package (1 pound) carrots
- 1 teaspoon sugar
- ½ cup water
- 1 teaspoon or envelope instant chicken broth
- 2 tablespoons butter or margarine
- 2 tablespoons chopped parsley

1. Pare carrots and cut into long diagonal slices.
2. Place in a large skillet; sprinkle with sugar; add water and instant chicken broth; bring to boiling; lower heat; cover pan.
3. Steam carrots 15 minutes, or just until tender; pour off cooking liquid and reserve for soup. Add butter or margarine and chopped parsley and toss to coat evenly.

PILAF AMANDINE

Tangy chunks of orange and sliced almonds simmer in fluffy rice. Shown on page 74, served with Smoked Turkey Orientale.

Makes 12 servings.

- 2 cups long grain rice
- ¼ cup (½ stick) butter or margarine
- 1 large onion, chopped (1 cup)
- 5 envelopes or teaspoons instant chicken broth
- 5 cups boiling water
- 4 large California oranges
- 1 package (3½ ounces) naturally sliced almonds
- Chopped parsley

1. Brown rice in butter or margarine in a large heavy saucepan; push to one side; sauté onion in same pan until soft.
2. Add instant chicken broth and boiling water; bring to boiling; lower heat to simmer; cover saucepan.
3. Cook 30 minutes, or until rice is tender and liquid is absorbed.
4. While pilaf cooks, trace a scallop pattern around side of oranges; cut out with a small sharp paring knife; scoop out orange pulp and dice; reserve orange shells.
5. Just before serving, stir orange pieces, almonds and parsley into pilaf with a fork, just until lightly blended. Spoon part of the rice mixture into orange shells. Spoon remaining rice onto heated serving platter around turkey and garnish platter with orange cups.

ZUCCHINI CORONADO

Long slender slices of zucchini are layered with a zesty tomato sauce. Shown from the tower at Vacation Village in San Diego, page 83.

Grill for 30 minutes.
Makes 8 servings.

- 6 large zucchini (3 pounds)
- 1 cup water
- 2 envelopes or teaspoons instant chicken broth
- 3 tablespoons olive or vegetable oil
- 1 large onion, chopped
- ½ pound mushrooms, sliced
  OR: 1 can (6 ounces) sliced mushrooms
- 1 jar (about 2 pounds) meatless spaghetti sauce
- ¼ cup chopped parsley

1. Trim zucchini; cut lengthwise into very thin slices with a very sharp French knife.
2. Heat water and instant chicken broth to boiling in a large skillet; lower to simmering; cook zucchini slices, part at a time, in liquid 5 minutes, or just until soft; remove with pancake turner and slotted spoon to large cookie sheet.
3. Pour remaining cooking liquid into a cup and reserve. Heat oil in skillet; sauté onion until soft; add sliced mushrooms and sauté 3 minutes; pour in spaghetti sauce and reserved cooking liquid.
4. Simmer, stirring several times, 15 minutes, stir in chopped parsley. Layer zucchini and sauce in a 13x9x2-inch flameproof casserole; cover with aluminum foil.
5. Cook on grill 30 minutes, or until bubbly-hot.
CHEF'S TIP: This dish can be made up early in the day and refrigerated until 1 hour before serving time. Cook on grill 50 minutes, or until bubbly-hot. If you don't have a flameproof casserole, bake in moderate oven (350°) 30 minutes, then bring out and place to side of grill with foil on top until serving time.

BASQUE VEGETABLE BOWL

A subtle flavor of garlic and thyme gives zucchini, broccoli and tomatoes a Spanish touch. Shown in photograph with Smoked Turkey Orientale, page 74.

Makes 12 servings.

- 2 bunches broccoli (about 2 pounds each)
- 4 large zucchini (about 2 pounds)
- 4 large ripe tomatoes
- ¼ cup olive or peanut oil
- 1 large onion, chopped (1 cup)
- 1 clove garlic, minced
- 2 teaspoons seasoned salt
- ¼ teaspoon seasoned pepper
- 1 teaspoon leaf thyme, crumbled
- ½ cup chicken broth

1. Trim broccoli and separate into flowerets; soak in warm salted water; trim zucchini and cut into long diagonal slices; core tomatoes and cut into wedges. Drain broccoli well.
2. Heat oil in a large skillet; sauté onion and garlic until soft; stir in seasoned salt and pepper, thyme and chicken broth.
3. Arrange vegetables in separate piles in skillet; spoon part of onion mixture over; cover pan.
4. Simmer 15 minutes, or until crisply tender. Arrange in separate rows in a heated serving plate.
CHEF'S TIP: You can prepare the vegetables and onion mixture ahead of time, and cook the dish while the turkey is "resting."

CHINATOWN VEGETABLE BOWL

Stir-fry garden-fresh vegetables for a dish with a definite difference. Photographed in San Diego and shown on page 83.

Grill for 15 minutes.
Makes 6 servings.

- 3 tablespoons vegetable oil
- 1 large onion, thinly sliced and separated into rings
- 1 clove garlic, minced
- 2 large yellow squash, thinly sliced
- 2 large green peppers, halved, seeded and diced
- ½ pound Chinese snow peas
  OR: 1 package (6 ounces) frozen Chinese snow peas, thawed
- ½ cup chicken broth
- 1 teaspoon leaf rosemary, crumbled
- 1 teaspoon salt
- ¼ teaspoon pepper

1. Heat oil in a wok or flameproof skillet on grill, 4 inches from heat; sauté onion and garlic in oil; push to one side.
2. Stir-fry yellow squash, green peppers and snow peas 3 minutes, or until vegetables are shiny-bright; add chicken broth, rosemary, salt and pepper. Toss to coat evenly; cover.
3. Cook on grill 5 minutes, or until vegetables are crisply tender.

GRILLED ONION & MUSHROOMS

Here's a new twist to an old favorite. Shown with Balboa Beef Roast on our cover and on page 6.

Makes 12 servings.

    6 large white or yellow onions
    ¼ cup (½ stick) butter or margarine
    2 pounds fresh mushrooms
    2 teaspoons salt
    ¼ teaspoons freshly ground pepper
    ½ cup chicken broth

1. Peel onions and halve, crosswise.
2. Heat butter or margarine in a large skillet; brown cut surfaces of onions, part at a time, in butter; remove and reserve.
3. Wipe mushrooms with damp paper towels; halve and sauté in same pan; until soft; remove and reserve.
4. Return onion halves, cut-side up, to pan; sprinkle with salt and pepper; pour chicken broth over; cover pan; simmer 10 minutes; add mushrooms, simmer 5 minutes longer, or until vegetables are crisply tender. Arrange on heated serving platter around roast, spooning liquid over onions.

LA MESA PEPPER CUPS

Kidney beans and chick peas were the mainstay of hearty "49ers" in Gold Rush Days. Now they make a tangy filling for green peppers. Photographed in Mission Bay, and shown on page 83.

Grill for 30 minutes.
Makes 8 servings.

    8 medium-size green peppers
    1 can (1 pound) red kidney beans, drained
    1 can (1 pound) chick peas, drained
    1 can (1 pound) cut green beans, drained
    ½ cup bottled Italian-style dressing
    ½ cup frozen chopped onion
    ¼ cup chopped parsley
    2 cans (8 ounces each) tomato sauce with herbs
    2 slices mozzarella cheese (from an 8-ounce package)

1. Cut a thin slice from top of each pepper; scoop out seeds and membrane. Parboil peppers in a small amount of boiling salted water 10 minutes; drain well on paper towels. Place, cut side up, in a shallow 10-cup flameproof casserole.
2. Combine kidney beans, chick peas, green beans, Italian dressing, onion and parsley in a large bowl; spoon mixture into pepper cups, dividing evenly; pour tomato sauce into casserole; cover.
3. Grill 25 minutes, or until bubbly-hot; cut cheese into thin strips; lay over peppers. Grill 5 minutes longer, or until cheese melts.
CHEF'S TIP: This dish can be pre-pared early in the day and refrigerated. Remove from refrigerator 1 hour before serving time. Grill 45 minutes, or until bubbly-hot. If you don't have a flameproof casserole, bake, uncovered, in moderate oven (350°) 30 minutes for freshly prepared and 45 minutes for refrigerated peppers, or until bubbly-hot. Place casserole on side of grill to keep warm until ready to serve.

GARLIC BREAD

Flavorful crusty bread adds a finishing touch to barbecued meats.

Grill for 15 minutes
Makes 8 servings.

    1 loaf French, Italian or sourdough bread
    ¼ cup (½ stick) butter or margarine
    1 clove garlic, mashed

1. Cut bread into ½-inch-thick slices and keep slices in order.
2. Melt butter or margarine and garlic in a small metal saucepan with a flameproof handle; brush generously over each slice of bread. Reshape loaf on heavy-duty aluminum foil; wrap.
3. Cook, at side of grill and turning foil packet several times, 15 minutes. Loosen foil from around bread and serve from foil packet.

Suggested Variations:
PARSLEY BREAD: Add ¼ cup chopped parsley to melted butter.

PARMESAN BREAD: Sprinkle grated Parmesan cheese over each brushed bread slice.

CURRY BREAD: Add 1 teaspoon curry powder to melted butter and cook 3 minutes before brushing on bread.

FABULOUS FRIED ONION RINGS

Our favorite recipe for crisp and delicate results; the perfect accompaniment to grilled steak, burgers or chops.

Makes 6 servings.

    1½ cups all purpose flour
    1 can (12 ounces) beer
    1 teaspoon leaf sage, crumbled
    3 very large yellow onions
    3 to 4 cups vegetable shortening
       Salt and pepper

1. Combine flour, beer and sage in a large glass or ceramic bowl with a wire whip until well blended. Cover with plastic wrap; allow batter to rest at room temperature at least 3 hours. (This makes the batter extra light.)
2. Cut onions into ¼-inch-thick slices; separate slices into rings and remove skin rings.
3. Melt enough shortening in a 10-inch heavy skillet over low heat to a depth of 2″; heat to 375°, using a deep-fat thermometer.
4. Dip a few onion rings into batter, using metal tongs; carefully place them in hot fat.
5. Fry rings, turning once or twice, 3 minutes, or until golden; transfer to paper towel-lined cookie sheet and keep warm in preheated very slow (250°) oven. Continue until all onion rings are fried.

CHEF'S TIP: To Freeze—Fry rings and drain on paper towels at room temperature. Arrange on cookie sheet and freeze. When frozen, pack in plastic bags and return to freezer. To reheat—Arrange onion rings on cookie sheet. Heat in a preheated 400° oven 4 to 6 minutes, or until hot.

HERBED CLUB ROLLS

Brown 'n' serve rolls make quick and easy hot breads.

Bake at 375° for 15 minutes.
Makes 8 rolls.

    1 package (8 to a package) brown 'n' serve club rolls
    ¼ cup (½ stick) butter or margarine, softened
    3 tablespoons chopped parsley
    2 teaspoons leaf basil, crumbled

1. Cut 3 or 4 diagonal cuts into each roll with a sharp knife. Combine butter or margarine, parsley and basil in a small bowl.
2. Spread butter mixture into cuts in rolls. Place on a small cookie sheet.
3. Bake in moderate oven (375°) 15 minutes, or until golden brown. Transfer rolls to a napkin-lined basket and keep warm at edge of grill.

BARBECUED LIMA BEANS

Grated Parmesan cheese adds a new touch to lima beans.

Makes 4 servings.

    2 packages (10 ounces each) frozen Fordhook lima beans
    ¼ cup (½ stick) butter or margarine
    ¼ cup grated Parmesan cheese
    1 teaspoon salt

1. Place lima bean block on a large sheet of heavy-duty aluminum foil, or on a double thickness of regular aluminum foil; dot with butter or margarine and sprinkle with cheese and salt.
2. Bring long edges of foil together, up and over beans, and fold over twice to seal. Make a double fold at each end of package.
3. Cook on grill 20 minutes, turning package carefully after 10 minutes.

CORN PAPRIKASH

Chopped green pepper and paprika give color and zesty flavor to cream-style corn.

Grill for 30 minutes.
Makes 4 servings.

> 2 packages (10 ounces each) frozen cream-style corn
> ¼ cup chopped green pepper
> Paprika
> Salt and pepper

1. Remove frozen corn from pouches; place blocks side by side on a large piece of heavy-duty aluminum foil, or on a double thickness of regular aluminum foil. Top with green pepper and sprinkle liberally with paprika; season with salt and pepper.
2. Bring edges of foil together over center of vegetables. Fold over with a double fold, leaving a little space for steam expansion. Seal ends securely. (See directions on page 47.)
3. Cook on grill, turning occasionally, 30 minutes, or until pepper is tender and sauce is hot. Stir to mix.

BUTTERED BEANS ITALIANO

Garden-fresh green beans are shown to their best advantage when served whole. Shown with Tiburon Chicken on page 61.

Makes 6 servings.

> 1½ pounds green beans
> ½ cup water
> 1 envelope or teaspoon instant beef broth
> 1 teaspoon mixed Italian herbs, crumbled
> 3 tablespoons butter or margarine

1. Tip green beans; wash well. Place in a large skillet. Add water, instant beef broth and Italian herbs.
2. Bring to boiling; lower heat; cover skillet; steam 10 minutes, or until crisply-tender. Pour off cooking liquid and reserve for soup. Add butter or margarine and toss to coat evenly.

PARMESAN PARTY ROLLS

Freshly baked rolls always add a touch of elegance to patio parties.

Bake at 400° for 15 minutes.
Makes 16 rolls.

> 1 package (13¾ ounces) hot roll mix
> Water
> 1 egg
> ⅓ cup butter or margarine, melted
> 1 teaspoon mixed Italian herbs, crumbled
> ¾ cup grated Parmesan cheese

1. Prepare hot roll mix with water and egg, following label directions. Cover bowl with plastic wrap and let rise, away from drafts, 45 minutes, or until double in bulk.

2. Turn dough out onto a lightly floured board and knead 30 seconds; divide into 16 parts. Shape into balls.
3. Dip balls into a mixture of butter or margarine and Italian herbs in a small bowl. Divide balls between 2 greased 8-inch layer-cake pans. Sprinkle with cheese to coat evenly.
4. Cover cake pans and allow to rise 30 minutes, or until double in bulk.
5. Bake in hot oven (400°) 15 minutes, or until golden. Transfer to a napkin-lined basket and keep warm at edge of grill until serving time.

DILL-CHEDDAR BREAD

Quick breads are the perfect choice for the summertime baker.

Bake at 350° for 55 minutes.
Makes one 9x5-inch loaf.

> 3½ cups buttermilk biscuit mix
> 2 cups shredded Cheddar cheese (8 ounces)
> 2 teaspoons dillweed
> 2 eggs
> 1⅓ cups milk

1. Combine biscuit mix, cheese and dillweed in a large bowl until well blended. Beat eggs in a small bowl with a wire whip; gradually beat in milk until blended.
2. Pour egg mixture over dry ingredients and mix with a wooden spoon, just until blended. Spoon into a well-greased 9x5x3-inch loaf pan.
3. Bake in moderate oven (350°) 55 minutes, or until crust is golden; cool in pan on wire rack; loosen around edges with a sharp knife; invert onto wire rack and cool 30 minutes. Slice with a serrated knife.
CHEF'S TIP: This bread is even more delicious when toasted over the grill, several minutes to a side, just before serving.

RYE THINS

Extra thin slices of toast are the perfect accompaniment to a crisp salad.

Bake at 325° for 10 minutes.
Makes 8 to 10 servings.

> 1 loaf (about 12 ounces) unsliced rye bread
> ⅓ cup butter or margarine, melted
> 1 teaspoon savory, crumbled

1. Slice bread into the thinnest pieces possible with a serrated knife, or use your electric knife.
2. Brush each slice lightly with a mixture of melted butter or margarine and savory. Arrange in a single layer on large cookie sheets.
3. Bake in slow oven (325°) 10 minutes, or until slices crisp and curl. Serve warm or store in a glass jar with a screw top. Reheat before serving.

CHEESE BREAD

Husky chunks of rye or crusty white bread filled with marvelous melted cheese—what a complement to steak!

Grill for 15 minutes.
Makes 8 servings.

> 1 round loaf rye, Italian or sourdough bread
> ¼ cup (½ stick) butter or margarine, softened
> 2 tablespoons prepared sharp mustard
> 2 cups shredded Cheddar cheese (8 ounces)

1. Cut bread into quarters, then cut each quarter into ½-inch slices and keep in order.
2. Combine softened butter or margarine, and mustard in a small bowl; spread butter mixture on slices, then sprinkle cheese over.
3. Reshape loaf on heavy-duty aluminum foil; wrap tightly.
4. Cook at side of grill, 15 minutes, or until cheese melts. Loosen foil from around bread and serve from foil.

Suggested Variations:
BLUE-CHEESE BREAD: Omit mustard and add 1 tablespoon Worcestershire sauce to butter; sprinkle 1 cup crumbled blue cheese over bread slices.

SANTA FE BREAD: Combine 2 cups shredded Monterey Jack cheese with 1 cup chopped ripe or stuffed green olives and sprinkle over bread slices.

POTATO FLAKE BISCUITS

Instant potato flakes give a crunchy coating to quick-to-serve refrigerated biscuits.

Bake at 400° for 10 minutes.
Makes 10 biscuits.

> 1 package (8 ounces) refrigerated buttermilk biscuits
> 2 tablespoons butter or margarine
> ¼ cup instant mashed potato flakes
> 2 tablespoons grated Romano cheese
> 1 teaspoon mixed Italian herbs, crumbled

1. Open refrigerated biscuits, following label directions; separate into 10 biscuits.
2. Melt butter or margarine in a small skillet; combine potato flakes, Romano cheese and Italian herbs on a square of wax paper.
3. Dip biscuits, first into butter, then in seasoned potato flakes. Arrange biscuits, topping-side up, on a small cookie sheet.
4. Bake in hot oven (400°) 10 minutes, or until biscuits are golden. Cool on cookie sheet on wire rack 10 minutes; keep warm at side of grill.

ZUCCHINI-CORN SKILLET

Green and gold vegetables are colorful, as well as delicious.

Grill for 30 minutes.
Makes 8 servings.

¼ cup (½ stick) butter or margarine
4 medium-size zucchini, sliced
1 large onion, chopped (1 cup)
1 teaspoon salt
¼ teaspoon pepper
2 teaspoons leaf oregano, crumbled
2 cans (12 ounces each) Mexican-style whole kernel corn

1. Melt butter or margarine in a large metal skillet with a flameproof handle on grill over hot coals. Stir in zucchini and onion; sprinkle with salt, pepper and oregano.
2. Sauté, stirring several times, 15 minutes; push to one side.
3. Add corn to pan. Simmer 15 minutes, or until flavors blend.

HOT DOG ONIONS

Try your next hot dog New York-style, with a topping of braised onion rings.

Grill for 20 minutes.
Makes 2 cups.

2 large onions
¼ cup vegetable oil
2 tablespoons paprika
1 teaspoon salt
¼ teaspoon pepper
¾ cup chicken broth

1. Cut onions into thin slices; separate into rings.
2. Heat oil in a medium-size metal saucepan with a flameproof handle on grill; add onions to saucepan and toss in oil to coat evenly. Season with paprika, salt and pepper; cover saucepan; push pan to side of grill.
3. Cook, stirring several times, 10 minutes; add chicken broth to saucepan. Cook 10 minutes longer.

BAKED POTATOES

Here's the best way to grill potatoes. Change topping to suit the rest of menu.

Grill for 1 hour.
Makes 8 servings.

8 medium-size baking potatoes, scrubbed and dried
Vegetable oil
⅓ cup butter or margarine
3 tablespoons grated Parmesan cheese
2 teaspoons garlic salt
Freshly ground pepper

1. Rub each potato with vegetable oil; wrap in a square of heavy-duty aluminum foil.
2. Grill directly on the coals or on top of the grill, turning several times, 1 hour, or until soft when pierced with a two-tined fork. (Protect fingers with a potholder.)
3. While potatoes bake, blend butter or margarine with Parmesan cheese, garlic salt and pepper in a small bowl; cover bowl with plastic wrap; chill.
4. Unwrap each potato and fold foil back to form a serving dish. Make a crisscross cut in top of each potato, then squeeze firmly at both ends to fluff up. Top with butter mixture.

CORN BREAD

Some form of this recipe has been cooked in open fires on the range or the cottage hearth since Colonial days.

Bake at 425° for 25 minutes.
Makes one 8-inch square.

2 cups all purpose flour
1½ cups yellow cornmeal
2 tablespoons sugar
4 teaspoons baking powder
1 teaspoon salt
2 eggs, slightly beaten
2 cups milk
¼ cup vegetable oil

1. Combine flour, cornmeal, sugar, baking powder and salt in a medium-size bowl with a wire whip.
2. Stir in eggs, milk and vegetable oil, just until blended. Pour into a well-greased 8x8x2-inch baking pan.
3. Bake in hot oven (425°) 25 minutes, or until crust is golden brown; cool in pan on wire rack 10 minutes; keep warm in pan on grill.

FRENCH FRIED POTATOES

This classic accompaniment to steaks or burgers should never be made on or near the grill. Here is a method that saves on oil and gives you super-crisp potatoes.

Makes 6 servings.

Vegetable oil
1 package (1 pound) frozen French fries or crinkle cut potatoes
Salt
Pepper

1. Pour vegetable oil to the depth of ¾-inch in a large electric frypan or large skillet.
2. Spread frozen potatoes in oil in pan.
3. Turn frypan to 375° or place skillet over medium heat.
4. Cook, stirring often, 10 minutes, or until potatoes turn golden brown. Remove with slotted spoon to paper-towel-lined cookie sheet; season with salt and pepper. Keep hot in oven until ready to serve.
CHEF'S TIP: Allow oil in pan to cool completely, then strain through cheesecloth into a glass jar with a screw top. Store in refrigerator until ready to fry again.

PEAS COLIFLOR

Sweet green peas and cauliflower mingle in a butter-cheese sauce.

Grill for 30 minutes.
Makes 6 servings.

1 package (10 ounces) frozen peas in butter sauce
1 package (10 ounces) frozen cauliflower in cheese sauce
2 tablespoons diced pimiento

1. Remove frozen peas and cauliflower from pouches; place blocks side by side on a large piece of heavy-duty aluminum foil, or on a double-thickness of regular aluminum foil. Top with pimiento.
2. Bring edges of foil together over center of vegetables; fold over with a double fold, leaving a little space for steam expansion. Seal ends securely. (See directions on page 47.)
3. Cook on grill, turning occasionally, 30 minutes, or until vegetables are tender and sauce is hot; stir.

MARINATED VEGETABLE MEDLEY

Six kinds of vegetables combine with shrimp in an herb vinaigrette dressing.

Makes 8 servings.

1 package (10 ounces) frozen cauliflower
1 package (10 ounces) frozen baby lima beans
1 package (10 ounces) frozen Brussels sprouts
1 package (10 ounces) frozen broccoli spears
1 pound shrimp, shelled, deveined and cooked
1 cup pitted ripe olives
¼ cup chopped pimiento
Herb Vinaigrette (recipe follows)

1. Place vegetables in separate piles in two skillets or a skillet and saucepan; fill each pan with boiling water to a depth of ½ inch. Cook over medium heat until crisply tender. Cut cauliflower into small flowerets; cut Brussels sprouts in half.
2. Combine cauliflower, lima beans, Brussels sprouts, broccoli, shrimp, ripe olives and pimiento in a large glass or ceramic bowl until well blended; pour HERB VINAIGRETTE over and toss to coat all vegetables evenly. Cover with plastic wrap and refrigerate at least 4 hours.

HERB VINAIGRETTE: Makes 1½ cups. Combine 1 cup lemon juice, ½ cup vegetable oil, 2 teaspoons salt, 1 teaspoon leaf basil, crumbled, 2 tablespoons chopped parsley and 1 teaspoon monosodium glutamate (optional) in a jar with a screw top; cover and shake well. Refrigerate.

SESAME BREAD STICKS

Refrigerated biscuits turn into tangy sticks with a twist of the wrist.

Bake at 400° for 15 minutes.
Makes 20 sticks.

- 2 packages (8 ounces each) refrigerated buttermilk biscuits
- 1 egg white
  Toasted Sesame Seeds (recipe follows)

1. Open refrigerated biscuits, following label directions; separate each package into 10 biscuits.
2. Cut each biscuit into thirds; stretch and pull each piece into a rope. Braid 3 ropes together, pinching ends to seal. Place on a large cookie sheet.
3. Brush sticks with egg white, then sprinkle with TOASTED SESAME SEEDS to coat evenly.
4. Bake in hot oven (400°) 15 minutes, or until sticks are golden. Remove from cookie sheet immediately with a long spatula and keep warm in a napkin-lined basket at edge of grill.

TOASTED SESAME SEEDS: Makes ¼ cup. Sprinkle ¼ cup sesame seeds in a small skillet. Brown over low heat, stirring often, 5 minutes, or until seeds are golden.

ZUCCHINI ALLA PIEDMONT

Eggplant, tomatoes and green peppers bubble with tender zucchini slices in this Italian vegetable casserole.

Grill for 1 hour.
Makes 6 servings.

- 2 large onions, sliced
- 1 clove garlic, minced
- ¼ cup olive or vegetable oil
- 6 medium-size zucchini, sliced (2 pounds)
- 1 small eggplant, diced (about 1 pound)
- 2 green peppers, halved, seeded and diced
- 2 teaspoons salt
- 1 teaspoon sugar
- 1 teaspoon leaf basil, crumbled
- ½ teaspoon freshly ground pepper
- ½ teaspoon leaf thyme, crumbled
- 1 can (2 pounds, 3 ounces) Italian tomatoes

1. Sauté onion and garlic in oil in a large metal kettle on grill, 4 inches from heat, until soft; push to one side. Sauté zucchini, eggplant and green peppers 3 minutes, or until soft, but not brown.
2. Sprinkle salt, sugar, basil, pepper and thyme over vegetables and stir to blend; add tomatoes.
3. Simmer on grill, stirring several times, 45 minutes, or until vegetables are tender and sauce is thick.

HERB CRESCENT ROLLS

Make ahead, then keep warm to the side of the grill.

Bake at 375° for 15 minutes.
Makes 16 rolls.

- 2 packages (8 ounces each) refrigerated crescent rolls
- ¼ cup (½ stick) butter or margarine, melted
- ¼ cup chopped parsley
- 2 teaspoons leaf basil, crumbled

1. Open refrigerated rolls, following label directions; separate into triangles. Brush with melted butter or margarine; sprinkle with a mixture of parsley and basil.
2. Roll up each triangle from the wide end and shape into crescents on a large cookie sheet; brush with remaining butter.
3. Bake in moderate oven (375°) 15 minutes, or until golden brown. Transfer to a napkin-lined basket.

QUICK CHEESE BISCUITS

Chunks of Cheddar cheese bake in the center of each biscuit.

Bake at 400° for 10 minutes.
Makes 20 biscuits.

- 2 packages (8 ounces each) refrigerated flaky biscuits
  Cheddar cheese
  Milk
  Poppy seeds

1. Open refrigerated biscuits, following label directions; separate each into 10 biscuits; cut a large "X" in the center of each biscuit.
2. Cut twenty ½-inch cubes of cheese from a block of Cheddar; insert a cheese cube in center of each biscuit. Brush tops of biscuits with milk and sprinkle with poppy seeds. Arrange on cookie sheet.
3. Bake in hot oven (400°) 10 minutes, or until biscuits are golden and cheese is melted; cool on cookie sheet on wire rack 10 minutes. Transfer to napkin-lined basket and keep warm at side of grill.

QUICK BREAD ITALIANO

Minutes in the kitchen and out comes this fragrant loaf.

Bake at 350° for 30 minutes.
Makes 1 small loaf.

- 2 packages (8 ounces each) refrigerated buttermilk biscuits
- 1 egg white
- 2 tablespoons bottled Italian salad dressing
  Sesame seeds

1. Open refrigerated biscuits, follow-ing label directions; separate each into 10 biscuits.
2. Arrange biscuits around edge of a small cookie sheet; press together and shape ends to form a round loaf.
3. Beat egg white and Italian dressing together in a cup. Brush generously over loaf; sprinkle with sesame seeds.
4. Bake in moderate oven (350°) 30 minutes, or until loaf is golden. Cool on cookie sheet on wire rack 10 minutes; loosen with a spatula.

GRILLED CORN

Serve this barbecue favorite with pools of melted butter.

Grill for 15 minutes.
Makes 4 servings.

- 8 ears corn, unshucked
  Butter or margarine
  Salt and pepper

1. Build a medium fire, or set gas or electric grill to medium, following manufacturer's directions.
2. Remove silks but not shucks from corn; soak in water while grill heats.
3. Grill, turning often, 15 minutes, or until kernels are tender.
4. While corn grills, melt better or margarine on grill in a metal saucepan with a flameproof handle. Serve corn with melted butter, salt and pepper.

Suggested Variations:
CHEESE CORN ON THE COB: Add grated Parmesan cheese to the melted butter or margarine.

GARLIC CORN ON THE COB: Add 1 clove garlic, halved, to butter or margarine when melting it; remove before serving.

SKILLET BISCUITS

Bake them in your favorite iron skillet, then serve them in the same pan.

Bake at 400° for 10 minutes.
Makes 10 biscuits.

- 1 package (8 ounces) refrigerated buttermilk biscuits
- 2 tablespoons butter or margarine
- 1 medium-size onion, chopped (½ cup)
- ½ teaspoon leaf sage, crumbled
  Salt and pepper

1. Open biscuits, following label directions; separate into 10 biscuits.
2. Heat butter or margarine in an 8-inch skillet; sauté onion until soft in butter; add sage to skillet; season with salt and pepper.
3. Dip biscuits into onion mixture to coat. Arrange biscuits, onion-side up, in skillet.
4. Bake in hot oven (400°) 10 minutes, or until biscuits are golden.

ANCHOVY-STUFFED TOMATOES

There's always room on the grill for a special vegetable dish.

Grill for 20 minutes.
Makes 6 servings.

- 6 large firm tomatoes
  Salt and pepper
- 1 can (about 7 ounces) tuna, drained and flaked
- 2 cups Italian-flavor dry bread crumbs
- 1 can (2 ounces) anchovy fillets, drained and chopped
- ¼ cup chopped parsley
- 2 tablespoons olive or vegetable oil
- 2 tablespoons grated Parmesan cheese

1. Cut a ½-inch slice from top of tomatoes; scoop out insides with a spoon and reserve for soups or sauces. Season tomato shells with salt and pepper; turn upside down on paper towels and drain 10 minutes.
2. Combine tuna, bread crumbs, anchovies and parsley in a medium-size bowl; divide mixture among tomato shells.
3. Arrange tomatoes in a heavy metal baking pan; drizzle with oil and sprinkle with grated Parmesan; cover with heavy-duty aluminum foil.
4. Place covered pan to back of grill and cook 20 minutes, or until tomatoes are tender. Serve hot or at room temperature.

PEPERONATA

Garden-fresh tomatoes, peppers and onions make a delectable vegetable dish.

Grill for 30 minutes.
Makes 6 servings.

- 3 tablespoons butter or margarine
- 3 tablespoons olive or vegetable oil
- 2 large onions, sliced
- 2 cloves garlic, minced
- 2 large red peppers, halved, seeded and cubed
- 2 large green peppers, halved, seeded and cubed
- 3 large tomatoes, chopped
- 2 teaspoons salt
- 1½ teaspoons mixed Italian herbs, crumbled
- ¼ teaspoon freshly ground pepper

1. Heat butter or margarine and oil in a large metal skillet with a flameproof handle on barbecue grill or on kitchen range. Sauté onions and garlic until soft in skillet.
2. Add peppers and tomatoes; sauté 3 minutes; add salt, Italian herbs and ground pepper. Cook, stirring often, at back of grill or on low heat, 30 minutes, or until tomato juices have boiled away and flavors are blended. Serve with grilled steak or chops, if you wish. ∎

SALADS & DRESSINGS

(Continued from page 94.)

SCANDINAVIAN SALAD

Pickles give this rosy salad its tangy taste.

Makes 6 servings.

- 3 medium-size boiling potatoes (1 pound)
- 1 can (16 ounces) whole red beets, drained and quartered
- 1 cup diced dill pickles
- 1 medium-size onion, finely chopped (½ cup)
- ½ cup dairy sour cream
- ½ cup mayonnaise or salad dressing
- ½ teaspoon sugar
- 2 tablespoons dill pickle liquid
  Salt and pepper
  Chilled lettuce leaves
  Dill pickles

1. Cook potatoes in salted boiling water in a large saucepan 25 minutes, or just until tender. Drain, reserving water for soups and sauces.
2. Return potatoes to saucepan and toss over low heat 5 minutes, or until potatoes are fluffy-dry; set aside to dry.
3. Combine beets, diced pickles, onion, sour cream, mayonnaise or salad dressing and sugar in a large glass or ceramic bowl. Peel cooled potatoes and cut into ¾-inch-thick chunks. Add potatoes and pickle liquid to beet mixture; toss just until combined. Season salad to taste with salt and pepper. Cover with plastic wrap and refrigerate at least 2 hours to blend flavors.
4. At serving time, line a shallow bowl with lettuce leaves. Toss potato salad again; add more pickle liquid, if necessary, to moisten salad. Mound salad in center of bowl and garnish with pickles, cut into fan shapes, if you wish.

MAKE-AHEAD SALAD

Salads like this one give you more time to concentrate on barbecuing.

Makes 6 servings.

- 1 medium-size head iceberg lettuce
- 1 large green pepper, halved, seeded and chopped
- 1 cup chopped celery
- 1 package (10 ounces) frozen peas
- 1 small onion, minced (¼ cup)
- 9 hard-cooked eggs, sliced
- 1 cup shredded Cheddar cheese (4 ounces)
  Dreamy Dressing (recipe follows)

1. Core, rinse and thoroughly drain lettuce; break into bite-sized pieces and arrange on bottom of 13x9x2-inch baking dish or a large salad bowl.
2. Sprinkle green pepper, celery, peas and onion over lettuce; layer egg slices

on top of vegetables. Sprinkle with half of cheese; spread DREAMY DRESSING over top and sprinkle with remaining cheese. Cover with plastic wrap and refrigerate at least 3 hours. Or make salad the day before and refrigerate overnight. Garnish with toasted almond slices and chopped pimiento, if you wish.

DREAMY DRESSING: Makes 1¾ cups. Place ¼ cup milk in container of electric blender; add 1½ cups cream-style cottage cheese, ¼ cup lemon juice, 1 tablespoon sugar and ½ teaspoon leaf tarragon. Cover and process on high speed, scraping down sides of container with rubber spatula, if necessary, 1 minute, or until smooth. Refrigerate until ready to spoon over salad.
CHEF'S TIP: To separate frozen peas more easily, rap package against counter or table edge before opening package.

SAVORY POTATO SCALLOP

Here is a casserole designed for meat and potato lovers.

Grill for 1 hour, 10 minutes.
Makes 6 servings.

- 2 pounds ground beef
- 2 teaspoons salt
- 2 teaspoons paprika
- ¼ teaspoon seasoned pepper
- ¼ teaspoon poultry seasoning
- 2 envelopes (about 1 ounce each) onion sauce mix
- 2 cups water
- 1 bag (1 pound) frozen mixed vegetables, partially thawed
- 4 large potatoes, thinly sliced

1. Build a medium fire in a covered grill, or set gas or electric grill to medium, following manufacturer's directions.
2. Combine ground beef, salt, paprika, pepper and poultry seasoning in a medium-size bowl; mix lightly, just until blended. Shape into a large patty in a large metal skillet with flameproof handle.
3. Brown on grill, 4 inches from heat, 5 minutes on each side; break into chunks. Sprinkle onion sauce mix over; stir in water. Heat, stirring constantly, just to boiling; stir in mixed vegetables.
4. Spoon one-third of mixture into a 12-cup metal casserole; top with half of the potatoes. Repeat layers, then spoon remaining meat mixture on top; cover grill.
5. Simmer on grill, 6 inches from heat, 1 hour, or until potatoes are tender when pierced with a two-tined fork. Serve with a salad of crisp greens and marinated artichoke hearts, if you wish.

CUCUMBER-LETTUCE SALAD

Delicious with barbecued chicken or fish.

Makes 6 servings.

- 1 medium-size head iceberg lettuce
- ⅓ cup water
- 1 teaspoon mixed pickling spices
- 1 teaspoon salt
- 1 teaspoon sugar
- ¼ teaspoon pepper
- ⅓ cup cider vinegar
- 2 large cucumbers, peeled and thinly sliced
- ¼ cup vegetable oil
- 1 tablespoon chopped parsley Radishes

1. Core, rinse and thoroughly drain lettuce; refrigerate in plastic bag or large lettuce crisper.
2. Combine water, pickling spices, salt, sugar, pepper and vinegar in a small saucepan; bring to boiling and simmer 2 minutes; strain and cool.
3. Place cucumber slices in a large glass or ceramic bowl. Stir oil and parsley into cooled vinegar mixture; pour over cucumbers. Cover bowl with plastic wrap. Refrigerate 1 hour, stirring occasionally.
4. Tear lettuce into bite-sized pieces; add to cucumbers; toss lightly.

BASIC FRENCH DRESSING

Be sure to serve this classic dressing at your salad bar.

Makes 1 cup.

- ¾ cup vegetable or peanut oil
- ¼ cup cider or wine vinegar OR: ¼ cup lemon juice
- 1 tablespoon minced onion
- ¾ teaspoon salt
- ⅛ teaspoon pepper
- ½ teaspoon Worcestershire sauce
- ½ teaspoon dry mustard
- ½ teaspoon sugar
- ½ teaspoon paprika
- 1 clove garlic, halved

1. Combine oil, vinegar or lemon juice, onion, salt, pepper, Worcestershire sauce, mustard, sugar, paprika and garlic in a jar with a screw top.
2. Shake to blend well; refrigerate at least 2 hours; remove garlic. Shake before serving.

Suggested Variations:

POPPY SEED DRESSING—Add ⅓ cup honey and 1 tablespoon poppy seed.

BLUE CHEESE DRESSING—Add ¼ cup crumbled blue cheese.

PARMESAN DRESSING—Add ¼ cup grated Parmesan cheese.

HERB DRESSING—Add 1 tablespoon minced parsley and 1 teaspoon crushed leaf basil, dill, oregano or tarragon.

TANGY SAUSAGE SALAD

Hot German-style potato salad mixes together quickly if you cook the potatoes ahead of time.

Grill for 15 minutes.
Makes 6 servings.

- 9 medium-size potatoes, pared and diced (about 3 pounds)
- 1 small onion, chopped (¼ cup).
- 1 cup thinly sliced celery
- ½ cup thinly sliced dill pickle
- 1 package (12 ounces) cocktail franks, sliced
- 3 tablespoons butter or margarine
- 3 tablespoons prepared mustard
- 3 tablespoons brown sugar
- 3 tablespoons cider vinegar
- 3 tablespoons water
- 1 teaspoon salt

1. Cook potatoes in boiling salted water in a medium-size saucepan, just until tender; drain. Stir in onion, celery and pickle.
2. Build a medium fire, or set gas or electric grill to medium, following manufacturer's directions
3. Sauté cocktail franks lightly in butter or margarine in large metal skillet with flameproof handle; stir in mustard, brown sugar, vinegar, water and salt; heat just to boiling.
4. Pour over potato mixture in a wooden salad bowl; toss lightly. Serve hot with pumpernickel bread and buttered zucchini.

SPRINGTIME POTATO SALAD

The tiny new potatoes of spring team with dillweed and sour cream.

Makes 6 servings.

- 12 tiny new potatoes
- 2 tablespoons vegetable oil
- 2 tablespoons lemon juice
- 2 teaspoons salt
- ¼ teaspoon pepper
- 2 tablespoons chopped fresh dill OR: 2 teaspoons dried dillweed
- 1 large cucumber, pared, quartered, seeded and chopped
- ¾ cup dairy sour cream Iceberg lettuce

1. Cook potatoes 15 minutes, or just until tender, in boiling salted water in a large saucepan; drain. Peel potatoes and return to saucepan; toss over very low heat 5 minutes to dry. Place in a large glass bowl.
2. Combine oil, lemon juice, salt, pepper and dill in a jar with a screw top; cover and shake well; pour over potatoes and toss to coat. Cover bowl with plastic wrap and chill at least 3 hours.
3. Just before serving, toss potatoes with cucumbers and sour cream. Line a salad bowl with iceberg lettuce; fill with salad; garnish with fresh dill.

COOKOUT BEAN BAKE

The perfect choice to prepare ahead and bring to the picnic grounds to bubble to perfection at the side of the grill.

Grill for 1 hour.
Makes 6 servings.

- 3 cans (about 1 pound each) oven-baked beans
- ⅓ cup light molasses
- 3 tablespoons prepared mustard
- 2 tablespoons cider vinegar
- 1 teaspoon instant minced onion
- 1 package (1 pound) frankfurters, cut in half
- 1½ cups biscuit mix
- ½ cup water
- 2 tablespoons vegetable oil
- ⅓ cup cornmeal

1. Build a low fire, or set gas or electric grill to slow, following manufacturer's directions.
2. Empty beans into an 8-cup shallow metal casserole; stir in molasses, mustard, vinegar and onion; arrange frankfurters down middle; cover.
3. Cook on grill, 8 inches from heat, 40 minutes, or until bubbly-hot.
4. Prepare biscuit mix with water, following label directions; drop onto hot casserole; brush with oil; sprinkle with cornmeal. Cover dish.
5. Cook on grill 20 minutes longer, or until biscuits are done.

SWISS POTATO SALAD

White wine dressing layers with potato slices and Spanish onion to make a salad with a difference. Serve with grilled chicken

Makes 8 servings.

- 8 large Idaho potatoes
- ¾ cup dry white wine
- ⅓ cup vegetable oil
- ⅓ cup lemon juice
- 2 envelopes or teaspoons instant chicken broth
- 2 teaspoons salt
- ¼ teaspoon freshly ground pepper
- 1 Spanish onion, thinly sliced Leaf lettuce

1. Cook potatoes 30 minutes, or just until tender in boiling salted water in a large kettle or saucepan; drain. Peel potatoes and cut into thin slices.
2. Combine wine, oil, lemon juice, instant chicken broth, salt and pepper in a 2-cup measure; mix well.
3. Spread a layer of potato slices in a 13x9x2-inch glass dish; spoon part of the dressing over; top with some of the onion slices. Continue layering until potatoes, dressing and onion slices are all used. Cover with plastic wrap; allow to stand at room temperature 3 hours.
4. Just before serving: Line a salad bowl with leaf lettuce; arrange salad in bowl; garnish with finely chopped parsley and hard-cooked egg slices. ■

INDEX & CREDITS

cook's guide

Page 69: Salad seasoning for oil and vinegar dressing in ROAST TURKEY SEVILLE is Spice Islands.

Page 78: Lemon-lime carbonated beverage in RIBS AND ORANGE KABOBS is 7-UP®.

Page 105: Salad seasoning for oil and vinegar dressing in PEKING PORK is Spice Islands.

buyer's guide

Pages 1 and 72: Copper sauté pan, Williams-Sonoma, P.O. Box 3792, San Francisco, California 94119; napkin and napkin ring by Vera.

Page 8: Tulip wine glass by Bulgarian and round white chop platter, The Perfect Pan, 4040 Goldfinch Street, San Diego, California 92103.

Page 10: Raclette Pan, The Perfect Pan, 4040 Goldfinch Street, San Diego, California 92103.

Page 14: Tumblers by Toscany and French Pyrex® pitcher, The Perfect Pan, 4040 Goldfinch Street, San Diego, California 92103.

Page 16: Oval casserole in basket, wine glass and white soup bowl, Williams-Sonoma, P.O. Box 3792, San Francisco, California 94119.

Page 18: Salad plates, dinner plates, mugs, bowl, platter and flatware by Heller, The Perfect Pan, 4040 Goldfinch Street, San Diego, California, 92103.

Pages 30, 31, 32: For more information on what you want and need to know about buying, storing and preparing meat, the MEAT BOARD MEAT BOOK is an illustrated 166 page book by Barbara Bloch, with introduction by Julia Child. Deluxe hard-cover @ $9.95 or quality paperback @ $4.95. Add 75¢ for postage and handling. Send check or money order payable to "Meat Board Meat Book", Dept. FC, 485 Madison Avenue, Third Floor, New York, New York 10022. Be sure to include your name, address and zip.

Page 33: Crestline American Made Hibachis #2704 by Crestline Industries, Corp., Tillman St., Raritan, New Jersey 08869.

Page 34: Smoke 'N' Pit #2100 series, Smoke 'N' Pit Corp., P.O. Box BC, Byran, Texas 77801.

Page 35: Canister with classic round seal, large salt and pepper and 2-quart pitcher by Tupperware, Orlando, Florida.

Page 36: Individual stackable dishes and covered 4-cup measure by Tupperware.

Page 37: Grab-it and Covers by Corning Ware and 2-quart utility covered casserole and 3-quart utility dish, Baker-in-a-Basket by Pyrex®, Corning, New York; Swinger II #4405 Deluxe Smoker Grill by Meco, Metals Engineering Corp., P.O. Box 3005, Greeneville, Tennessee 37743.

Page 38-39: Farberware Open-Hearth broiler and rotisserie by Farberware, Bronx, New York; plastic steak marinater by Tupperware; Woodland 1½-quart oval casserole in Woodland by Pyrex®.

Page 40: Big Boy Deluxe Convertible #1808 by Kelley Manufacturing, P.O. Box 1317, Houston, Texas 77001; Grill-ette by Jenn-air, Jenn-air Corp., 3035 Shadeland Ave., Indianapolis, Indiana 46226. 24" Hooded Grill with Warming Oven #6124 by Structo, Division of King-Seeley Thermos Co., Freeport, Illinois 61032.

Page 42: Jacuzzi Gas Grill by Jacuzzi Brothers, Inc., 11511 New Benton Highway, Little Rock, Arkansas 72203.

Page 43: Weber Charcoal Kettle #800 by Weber-Stephen Products Co., 100 N. Hickory Ave., Arlington Heights, Illinois 60004; Electric Smoker by Smoker Products, Highway 175 East, Mabank, Texas 75147.

Page 44: Buddy-L-#6685 Smoker Wagon by Neosho Products, Co., P.O. Box 622, Neosho, Missouri 64850; Charmglow Gas Barbecue #3200 by Charmglow Products, Inc., a division of Beatrice Foods, Co., Bristol, Wisconsin.

Page 49: Champagne glasses and candle holders, by Toscany; wine glasses by Rumanian; ice bucket by Kosta Boda; cutting board hand crafted by Prometha Designs; glass tea pot and glass warmer by Jena Glass, Germany; glass plates by Astia, The Perfect Pan, 4040 Goldfinch Street, San Diego, California 92103.

Page 50: Crochet twine placemats from Philippines; linen-polyester napkins from Ireland; hand-made European silk flowers; Bohemian crystal vase by Boda; earthenware plates in Recostone from West Germany; Navy/white print, coffee server, ½-litre pitcher, cups, napkin rings in hand-decorated English China by Calico all available at Bazaar Del Mundo, Old Town State Park, San Diego, California. Mailing address: 2754 Calhoun Street, San Diego, California 92110.

Page 59: Wine decanters for sale *only* at Simi Winery, Healdsbury, California.

Page 60: Blue Anchor Ripenright Fruit Bowl with scientifically designed vents to help fruits ripen to eating perfection is available in three sizes:

Model 102 12" pear shape $15.95
Model 201 10" peach shape   10.00
Model 301 10" pear shape   10.00
   (Price includes delivery)

Order directly from Blue Anchor, Inc., P.O. Box 15498, Sacramento, California 95813; white shallow baker, wine glasses, wine decanter and stock pot, Williams-Sonoma, P.O. Box 3792, San Francisco, California 94119.

Page 62: Oval fish platter, salad basket, relish basket, picnic basket, wine glasses, Williams-Sonoma, P.O. Box 3792, San Francisco, California 94119.

Page 83: Glass sauté pan by Sial, glass sauté pan by Siama, glass lasagna dish by Heller, napkin by Vera, The Perfect Pan, 4040 Goldfinch Street, San Diego, California, 92103.

Page 84: Glass plates by Astia, The Perfect Pan, 4040 Goldfinch Street, San Diego, California 92103.

Page 86: Large glass salad bowl from Bazaar Del Mundo, Old Town State Park, San Diego, California. Mailing address: 2754 Calhoun Street, San Diego, California 92110.

Page 95: Cake dome and stand by Riekes Crisa, The Perfect Pan, 4040 Goldfinch Street, San Diego, California 92103.

Page 96: Assorted wine glasses and tumblers, The Perfect Pan, 4040 Goldfinch Street, San Diego, California 92103.

All other items in the photographs are privately owned and not for sale.

acknowledgements

The editors gratefully acknowledge the help of **Toni Griffin,** teacher of haute cuisine and Northern Italian cooking in San Diego, who acted as our West Coast contributing editor; **Al Reese** and **Ed Tidwell** of the San Diego Convention and Visitors Bureau; **Caryl Saunders** and Western Iceberg Lettuce; **Ronald E. Hull** and The Imperial Valley Vegetable Growers Association; **Pat Vandon** and Simi Winery in Healdsburg, California; **Bill Marvin** and

Slinkey's El Monte in Sausalito, California; **Marge Rice** of the San Diego Evening Tribune; **Joseph Marino** of Moceri Produce, Inc., 5255 Lovelock Street, San Diego, California 92110, (714) 299-0640; **Ron Kiefer** owner of K-Mar Market (also known as Ron Kiefer's) now located at 4025 Goldfinch St., San Diego, California 92103, (714) 295-5353, featuring USDA aged prime beef, fresh milk-fed veal, poultry, fish and farm-fresh produce; American Lamb Council and **Bill Broscovak;** National Live Stock and Meat Board and **Mark Thomas;** Vacation Village, Mission Bay, San Diego, California; United States Forestry Service at Baker Beach, Golden Gate National Recreation Area, San Francisco, California; Seafood Marketing Authority of Maryland; National Safety Council; Lone Star Historical Drama Association of Galveston, Texas; Lodge Food Service, University of Montana, Missoula, Montana; Office of Commerce and Industry, Louisiana Department of Commerce; American Egg Board; California Frozen Végetable Council; Charcoal Barbecue Institute; Florida Orange Juice; Florida Vegetables; Green Giant Company; Knox Unflavored Gelatin; National Casing Sausages; National Peanut Council; Pickle Packers Institute; Self-Rising Flour Corn Meal Program; Shrimp Association of America; Sunkist; Tabasco; T-fal; U.S. Trout Farmers Association and Wheat-Flour Institute. Line drawings by **Adolph Brotman.**

index

Coconut Sipper, 99
Coffee Italiano, 98
Coffee Praline Ice Cream, 99
Coho Salmon, 68
Cold Cassoulet Salad, 93
Colorado Burgers, 24
Colorado Dogs, 20
Coney Island Hot Dogs, 109
Connecticut Burgers, 108
Connecticut Dogs, 20
Cooked Salad Dressing, 92
Cookout Bean Bake, 122
Cool as a Cucumber Mold, 90
Corn
   Grilled, 120
   on the Cob, Cheese, 120
   on the Cob, Garlic, 120
Corn Bread, 119
Corn Paprikash, 118
Corned Beef, Barbecued, 107
Corned Beef, Glazed, 105
Cornish Hens, Gingered, 66
Country-Style Ribs, 106
Creamy Dressing, 92
Creamy Italian Dressing, 94
Cress-Tomato Platter, 91
Crown Roast of Hot Dogs, 20
Crown Roast of Lamb, 12
Crumb-Coated Steak, 55
Crumbs, Buttered Bread, 65
Crumb Topping, 55
Crystal Clear Iced Tea, 100
Cucumber-Lettuce Salad, 122
Cucumbers in Sour Cream, 91
Currant Glazed Chicken, 68
Curried Swordfish, 64
Curry Bread, 117
Curry Vinaigrette, 94
Dakota Ribs, 103
Dartmouth Punch, 100
Delaware Burgers, 108
Delaware Dogs, 20
Deviled Chicken Legs, 63
Dill-Cheddar Bread, 118
Dilled Lamb Chops, 51
Dip, Soy, 113
Dip, Zippy Horseradish, 113
Dipping Steak, 112
Double Strawberry Dessert, 100
Dreamy Dressing, 121
Dressing, Basic French, 122
Dressing, Creamy Italian, 94
Drink, Grape-Pineapple, 101
Duchesse Potatoes, 51
Duck, Chinese, 68

East-West Stir-Fry Steak, 55
Fabulous Fried Onion Rings, 117
Far Eastern Barbecue, 55
Farm-Style Potato Salad, 89
Fast Food Burgers, 108
Fiesta Casserole, 77
Fillet of Beef, Grilled, 106
Fish, Baker Beach Grilled, 63
Fisherman's Soup, 64
Florentine Grilled Steak, 57
Florida Burgers, 108
Florida Dogs, 24

Frankfurters, Turkey, 20
Franks, German Skillet, 25
Franks, Mexican, 111
Freezer Steaks, 112
French Fried Potatoes, 119
French Grilled Salmon, 64
French Potato Salad, 90
Frontier Lamb Riblets, 103
Fruit
   Basket, Mission Bay, 94
   Cup, Santa Clara, 101
   Soup, Chilled, 100
Fruit Fizz, 100

g&h

Garlic Bread, 117
Garlic-Grilled Pork Chops, 112
Garlic Corn on the Cob, 120
Georgia Burgers, 108
Georgia Dogs, 24
Georgia Peach Nog, 100
German Potato Salad, 93
German Skillet Franks, 25
Glaze
   Basic Burger, 114
   Brown Sugar, 97
   Lemon-Pineapple, 114
   Plum Chutney, 114
   Barbecue Chutney, 115
Glazed Corned Beef, 105
Gingered Cornish Hens, 66
Ginger Sauce, 114
Gorgonzola Salad, 90
Gourmet Beef Tenderloin, 113
Gourmet Grilled Steaks, 54
Grape-Pineapple Drink, 101
Green Onion Butter, 57
Green Pepper Jam, 29
Grill-Roasted Potatoes, 102
Grilled Clam Bake, 64
Grilled Corn, 120
Grilled Fillet of Beef, 106
Grilled Halibut Steaks, 67
Grilled Lamb Chops, 53
Grilled London Broil, 113
Grilled Onion and Mushrooms, 117
Grilled Rock Lobster Tails, 68
Grilled Salmon Steaks, 67
Grilled Swordfish, 64
Grilled Thighs and Drumsticks, 69
Grilled Trout, 65
Halibut Steaks, Grilled, 106
Ham
   California Glazed, 107
   Maryland Glazed, 12
   Steak, Beer-Basted, 52
Hamburgers for a Crowd, 110
Hawaiian Burgers, 108
Hawaiian Dogs, 24
Herb Crescent Rolls, 120
Herb Dressing, 122
Herb 'N' Lemon Steak, 113
Herb Vinaigrette, 119
Herbed Burgers, 110
Herbed Club Rolls, 117
Hibachi Shrimp, 67
Hobo Supper, 111
Home-Dilled Pickle Sticks, 28
Homemade Chili Sauce, 28

Horseradish Butter, 57
Horseradish Dip, Zippy, 113
Horseradish Sauce, 97
Horseradish Sauce, Spicy, 115
Hot Bacon Dressing, 92
Hot Dog Onions, 119
Hunting Hills Chicken, 65

i&j

Ice Cream, Coffee Praline, 99
Iceberg Orientale, 88
Idaho Burgers, 24
Idaho Dogs, 24
Illinois Burgers, 24
Illinois Dogs, 25
Imperial Salad Bowl, 94
Indiana Burgers, 108
Indiana Dogs, 24
Instant Banana Whip, 101
Iowa Burgers, 24
Iowa Dogs, 24
Italian Barbecued Chicken, 66
Italian Dressing, 90
Italian Sausage Dogs, 20
Jam, Green Pepper, 29
Jay's Barbecue for a Crowd, 104
Jumbo Jims, 110

k&l

Kabobs
   Antipasto, 79
   Bavarian, 80
   Cheese, Toasted, 78
   Kielbasa, 76
   Lemony, 77
   Moroccan Lamb, 78
   Mustard Chicken, 75
   Mustard Sausage, 77
   Polynesian, 78
   Prawn, 76
   Spanish Lamb, 76
   Vegetable, 77
Kabobs Italiano, 78
Kalua Pork, 104
Kansas Burgers, 24
Kansas Dogs, 108
Kentucky Burgers, 24
Kentucky Dogs, 20
Key West Ribs, 102
Kielbasa Kabobs, 76
Kun Koki Burgers, 111
La Mesa Pepper Cups, 117
Lamb
   Chops, Dilled, 51
   Chops, Grilled, 53
   Crown Roast of, 12
   Kabobs, Moroccan, 78
   Kabobs, Spanish, 76
   Leg of, Barbecued, 102
Lamb, Butterfly, 106
Lamb in Sour Cream, 107
Lamb Cumberland, 102
Lamb Steak Au Poivre, 52
Leg, Butterfly Pork, 107
Leg of Lamb, Barbecued, 102
Lemon-Butter Baste, 97
Lemon-Herb Marinade, 97

salad bar

Barbecues are a great way to entertain a crowd. The only problem comes when the crowd is hungry and eager to eat and the food needs more time on the grill. How to keep guests' appetites appeased, yet not ruined for the main event? Do what more and more restaurants are doing—plan to use a salad bar for the first course.

Let guests serve themselves the salad course, matching and mixing with happy abandon from a salad bar with a tantalizing display of chilled greens, beans, olives, pickles, fruits and vegetables, with an assortment of dressings on the side.

It takes a little advance planning—and a good helping of imagination—to do the salad bar at home, but there can be nothing better as an ice-breaker, as guests hover over the pickled herring, the bean sprouts and assorted cheeses while watching the meat sizzle on the barbecue.

In the planning stages it's essential to prepare lists of serving dishes and utensils to be used, food choices and a fairly precise time schedule. If you're planning a theme to your party, ethnic cookbooks at your elbow can be thought-starters. Your local library can provide books on foreign celebrations as well as cookbooks crammed with menu ideas. Even if you're not much of an artist, a diagram of approximate positioning of the foods on the table will be invaluable. Since you're going to be chilling a lot of items, you will want to check refrigerator space as well as sources for extra ice. Cold things must be kept very cold for both appetite appeal and safety, particularly in the case of meat, fish and egg-base dishes. Good containers to hold the ice are aluminum foil roasting pans, plastic dishpans, even a baby's bathtub would work fine. Outdoors, a wheelbarrow or child's small wading pool could be pressed into service, providing a conversation piece as well as good display space. Bowls, such as those to hold shredded or chunk western iceberg lettuce, should be nested into the ice so that they won't tip or skid. For the dieter, provide some wedges of iceberg lettuce, and for the tower-builder, cut some thick lettuce rafts to serve as a sturdy foundation.

Other greens to offer for special tang could be young, tender leaves of spinach, shredded green or red cabbage, sprigs of watercress. Most of the preparation can be done ahead of time, with the carefully rinsed and drained greens chilling in plastic bags. (Wedges and rafts chill better on trays covered with a damp towel). Add-ons to the basic greens can range from tomato slices and avocado crescents to chicken strips, pickled meats and vegetables, fried noodles or cubes of fresh fruit. Variety and amount would, of course, vary in proportion to the size of the group and the theme of the party.

At the front end of the salad bar provide plates of a generous size—china, plastic or glass, not paper. Plates and eating utensils should be cold, but not chilled, particularly if it is a casual, sit-anywhere party. Napkins should be good-sized and plentiful. At the other end of the table provide a cluster of dressings, both clear and creamy. For the spartan salad eater, oil and vinegar or lemon juice should certainly be included, but the basic French dressing can then take many forms. The creamy dressings can start from a base of mayonnaise, boiled dressing, sour cream, cottage cheese or yogurt, depending on your whim and your talents. (See salad dressing recipes, page 87.)

Whatever the dressing, it is a courtesy and a convenience to your guests to make the serving vessel a pitcher or small wine carafe for easy, spill-proof pouring. Identify the dressings with labels so that guests needn't guess, sniff or taste to discover their favorites.

Rolls, assorted breads (mix light and dark, soft and crunchy), crackers and bread sticks all have a place at a salad bar, with butter cut into convenient pats.

While you're planning the salad bar, check and make a list of all possible serving bowls. Mixing bowls, soup bowls, salad bowls, sauce dishes are obvious choices, but don't miss counting freezer containers, ramekins or camouflaged cottage cheese containers. If you still feel you're short of your needs, a stroll through your local variety store will fill you with dozens of ideas—small plastic flower pots, a child's beach pail, or deep dish aluminum pie pans.

And while the choice of serving dishes is enormous, the selection of foods to put in them is limitless. We've supplied lists of suggestions, but your own experience or knowledge of your guests will lead you to dozens of discoveries of your own.

You can offer a big smörgåsbord variety or decide on a theme like fruit, cheese and nuts or vegetables and seafood. Or choose an ethnic approach and develop an Italian theme around antipasto salad. For antipasto salad, consider salami strips, cheese strips, marinated artichokes, marinated beans, fresh or pickled mushrooms, giardinira vegetables, pepperoncini, calamari vinaigrette, sliced zucchini and caponata (pre-pared eggplant).

For an Oriental theme, consider bean sprouts, water chestnuts, fried noodles, sliced celery, chicken strips, shrimp, cold cooked rice, pineapple, green pepper, ginger, chutney and toasted almonds with a soy sauce base dressing.

For a Mexican theme, offer makings for a taco salad to be assembled as follows: corn chips, shredded lettuce, hot taco-flavored ground beef, chopped tomato, chilies and onion, sour cream and shredded cheese.

Think hot, too. By providing a hot vinegary dressing, you allow the gourmet to prepare his own wilted lettuce salad, made more tempting with a toss of bacon crumbles. A chilled raft of iceberg lettuce, or buttery slices of California avocado, heaped high with steaming hot chili, topped with shredded cheese and a sprinkle of chopped onions, is an unusual and remarkably delicious salad. Cater to all the taste buds with sour, sweet and salty choices. Give a nod to the natural food enthusiast with alfalfa sprouts or sunflower seeds, and heap high the cottage cheese for the dieter.

If there's one thing for sure about a salad bar, it allows everyone to have exactly what he wants on his plate, and it allows you to join the group around the table, socializing rather than fretting in the kitchen. With a salad bar, the barbecue chef is given the time to grill all the food to a turn, without pressure from starving guests.

SUGGESTIONS FOR SALAD BAR: Fruit—fresh, frozen, canned or dried; served separately or in combination: orange sections; grapefruit sections; apple wedges; banana slices; peach slices; fruit cocktail, drained; pear slices; nectarine slices; papaya slices; pineapple cubes; figs; grapes; cherries, pitted; plum slices; persimmons; melon balls; berries (strawberries, blueberries, raspberries, blackberries); dates, pitted; prunes, pitted; raisins.

Vegetables—fresh, frozen, canned or dried; served separately or in combination: asparagus spears; avocado, diced, sliced, rings, crescents or guacamole; green beans, marinated; cooked dried beans and garbanzos; lima beans, marinated; 3-bean salad; bean sprouts; alfalfa sprouts; cooked potato or potato salad; carrots, shredded, sliced, sticks or cooked whole baby; cauliflower, raw or cooked; corn; celery, sliced; celery root, shredded; cucumber, slices or sticks; green onion, sliced; onions, chopped white, yellow or red; fresh onion rings; fried onion rings; chives, chopped; mushrooms, fresh or pickled; Brussels sprouts, raw or

(Continued on page 93.)